AMERICAN HISTORY AND CULTURE	JAZZ AND RELATED MUSIC & DANCE
U.S. involvement in World War I, 1917–18	*Ragtime, Piano Rag Music, L'Histoire du Soldat,*
Black Sox baseball scandal, 1918	Stravinsky, 1918

1920

AMERICAN HISTORY AND CULTURE	JAZZ AND RELATED MUSIC & DANCE
Nineteenth Amendment gives women right to vote, 1920	Dixieland emerges beyond boundaries of New Orleans
First regularly scheduled radio program, KDKA, Pittsburgh, 1920	Era of classic blues singers
Main Street, Sinclair Lewis novel, 1920	Hillbilly music develops in rural South
Prohibition, 1920–33	Modern gospel evolves
Ku Klux Klan membership reportedly at 5,000,000, early 1920s	Beginnings of big-band swing music
Harlem Renaissance, mid 1920s–30s	Charleston and other ballroom dance styles popular
Art deco popular, mid 1920s–30s	Mamie Smith records *Crazy Blues*, 1920
Teapot Dome Scandal, 1924	Race records introduced, 1920
Scopes Trial, 1925	Cotton Club opens in Harlem, 1922
The Great Gatsby, F. Scott Fitzgerald novel, 1925	Fletcher Henderson band premiers in New York, 1923
The Gold Rush, Charlie Chaplin film, 1925	Louis Armstrong plays for King Oliver's Creole Jazz Band, 1923
Sacco and Vanzetti executed, 1927	*Rhapsody in Blue*, George Gershwin, 1924
First nonstop transatlantic flight, by Charles A. Lindbergh, Jr., 1927	Bix Beiderbecke's record debut with the Wolverines, 1924
Strange Interlude, Eugene O'Neill play, 1928	Ma Rainey records for Paramount, 1924
St. Valentine's Day massacre, 1929	First Duke Ellington recording, 1925
Stock market crash, 1929	First recording by Louis Armstrong's Hot Five, 1925
The Sound and the Fury, William Faulkner novel, 1929	*Showboat*, Jerome Kern musical, 1927
A Farewell to Arms, Ernest Hemingway novel, 1929	*The Jazz Singer*, first talking movie, 1927
	Louis Armstrong records *Heebie Jeebies*, 1927

1930

AMERICAN HISTORY AND CULTURE	JAZZ AND RELATED MUSIC & DANCE
Over 13 million radios in U.S., 1930	Era of urban blues, centered in Chicago and Kansas City
American Gothic, Grant Wood painting, 1930	Country-and-Western music develops
Empire State Building completed, 1931	Lindy, jitterbug, rumba, and conga in vogue
Tobacco Road, Erskine Caldwell novel, 1932	Stride piano popular
Lindbergh kidnapping, 1932	Boogie-woogie develops
New Deal legislation introduced, 1933	Jazz center moves to New York
Fallingwater, Frank Lloyd Wright residence, 1936	Woodie Guthrie popularizes folk music
Amelia Earhart vanishes in flight over Pacific, 1937	Leadbelly's blues and folk songs popular
Of Mice and Men, John Steinbeck novel, 1937	Duke Ellington records *Creole Rhapsody*, 1931
"War of the Worlds," Orson Welles radio broadcast, 1938	Billie Holiday's record debut, with Benny Goodman, 1933
Our Town, Thornton Wilder play, 1938	*As Thousands Cheer*, Irving Berlin musical with Ethel Waters, 1934
Fair Labor Standards Act, 1938	Hammond organ invented, 1935
Nylon production begins, 1938	Electric guitar invented, 1935
Snow White and the Seven Dwarfs, Walt Disney film, 1938	*Porgy and Bess*, George Gershwin folk opera, 1935
Gone with the Wind, film adaptation of Margaret Mitchell's novel, 1939	Swing Era, 1935–46
The Wizard of Oz, film adaptation of Frank L. Baum's children's book, 1939	Count Basie at the Roseland Ballroom, 1936
World's Fair, New York, 1939–40	Benny Goodman's Carnegie Hall Concert, 1938
	Ella Fitzgerald records *A-tisket, A-tasket*, 1938
	Coleman Hawkins records *Body and Soul*, 1939

(continued at the back of the book)

ALL THAT JAZZ!

JACK WHEATON
University of San Diego

Ardsley House, Publishers, Inc.
New York

Address orders and editorial
correspondence to:
Ardsley House, Publishers, Inc.
320 Central Park West
New York, NY 10025

ISBN: 0-912675-92-6

Printed in the United States of America

10 9 8 7 6 5 4 3 2 1

In
Memory
of my
Mother

CONTENTS

/■/

SPECIAL TOPICS

/■/

LISTENING ASSIGNMENTS

/■/

GENERAL GUIDELINES

i   Find a quiet place.   ii   Close your eyes.   iii   Get comfortable.
iv   Focus your attention entirely on the music.
v   Listen several times with the following specific guidelines in mind.
It's better to listen once a day for five days than five times the same day. Let the music sink in.

1st time: General mood. What emotions are being presented (mad, sad, glad, scared, sensual, humorous, or inspirational)?

2nd time: Try to identify the instruments (percussion, string, brass, woodwind, keyboard) and vocal tone color (bright, clear, dark, raspy).

3rd time: Concentrate on the rhythm section. Focus on tempo (slow—fast), dynamics (loud—soft), style, and on how well each player supports the ensemble or soloist.

4th time: Concentrate on the soloist or singer. Focus on range (low, medium, high), dynamics, tone color, dramatic effects (sobs, moans, growls, etc.).

5th time: Focus on the overall effect and on your personal evaluation of the selection.

/■/

I wish to thank Lee Bash of Bellarmine College, Gilbert Bond of Emory University, and Horace J. Bond of University of Louisville for their careful reviews of the manuscript and their many useful suggestions for improvement.

Thanks to Shirley Tanzi and David Zuckerman for their drawings of many of jazz's greatest figures and to Jason Trotta for his sketches of musical instruments. I am grateful to Ethel Malvik and Dena Wallenstein for their thorough editorial work. Special thanks are due to Karen Bernath for book design and to Laura Jones, who typeset the book.

J. W.

PREFACE

/■/

Jazz, that exciting American phenomenon which defies easy definition, may be the most influential music developed in this century. The name evokes images of bands that "swing," of hornmen improvising solos, and of exciting syncopated rhythms. Yet there are styles of jazz that do not completely adhere to the features we most readily associate with jazz, such as improvisation, syncopation, and personalization. Perhaps, as an Afro-American music, jazz can more easily be defined as the musical coming together of two very different musical cultures, African and European. As such, it reflects the heritage of these cultures as well as the experiences and innovations of generations of Americans. Jazz is particularly important for a clear understanding of the black experience in America. Until the 1960s, the history of black Americans was captured almost exclusively in their music.

But first and foremost, jazz is fun: fun to listen to, fun to play. Jazz has brought the exciting dimension of spontaneity back to the art of musical performance. The shared responsibility and voluntary cooperation that go on in any jazz group is decidedly American in character. As Thelonious Monk, the great jazz pianist and composer, once said: "Jazz is freedom. Think about it!"

All That Jazz! purports to help nonmusicians understand and appreciate the excitement, originality, and historical significance of jazz. Through the study of this inspiring material, students should not only learn a great deal about America, about black Americans, and about contemporary art and music, but also a little about themselves. It is hoped that they will develop a life-long hobby of listening to and supporting jazz.

The text is divided into three parts. The first part provides some historical background on the development of Afro-American music, examining, in particular, contributions from Africa, from western Europe, and from the United States itself. The evolution of jazz is examined in relation to its development as a folk art, as a commercial art, and as a fine art.

Because it is as important to train listeners as it is to teach the history of jazz, the second part of the book is aimed at the development of listening skills. Why is rhythm so important to jazz? What essential rhythmic device does jazz use that classical music does not? What are blue notes and what role do they play in jazz? What is improvisation? What are the different approaches that can be taken when improvising? The listening skills that will develop as these and similar questions are answered should heighten the students' enjoyment of all types of music.

The third section of the book deals with the relationships between aesthetics, technological advances, and social changes in this country and how they have affected jazz. Computer technology has changed the ways in which music is composed, performed, recorded, and listened to. The present and future of jazz and the need for jazz as a universal art form is examined closely in the final chapter of the book as is the growing importance of jazz players and writers from outside the United States. Finally, the text shows why it is crucial for the United States to take immediate steps to subsidize and preserve jazz, and why jazz is considered an "endangered species" in today's music world.

The text is interspersed with many extra features—a New Orleans Parade, Jazz on Film, Jazz Festivals—that complement the material discussed. There are extensive lists of outstanding jazz musicians and groups—blues singers, big bands, bop musicians—in order to familiarize the student with some of the important names associated with jazz.

Each chapter contains listening assignments that guide the student to an understanding and appreciation of the era, the style, the performer, or the instrument under discussion. Many of these songs are chosen from the readily available Smithsonian Collection of Classic Jazz. A summary follows each chapter. In addition, there are questions for review and for discussion, topics for further research, suggestions for further reading and listening, and a listing of films and videos relevant to the chapter.

Other useful features to aid the student are margin definitions, available as needed, as well as an extensive glossary, numerous interesting (and informative) illustrations, and a detailed chronology of important events in jazz history juxtaposed with significant events in American history. The book also contains a bibliography, a discography, and a videography.

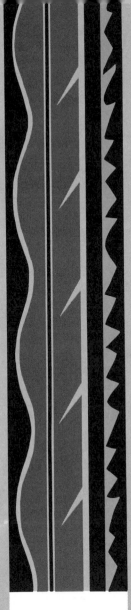

PART I

The
Development of
Afro-American
Music

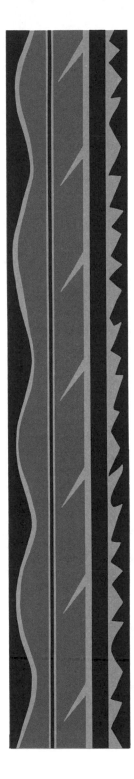

I
HISTORICAL BACKGROUND

/■/

Take a man from his home,
then strip him to the bone.
Bust up his family,
take away his rights.
Starve him and chain him
until there's no more fight.
Take away his language,
take away his clothes.
You've almost got it all,
heaven knows.
But you forgot to take
his music and his rhythm.
And some day your kids
will grow up
dancin' to em'.

—JW

———

JAZZ styles range from the early Dixieland of the 1920s, to such diverse movements as bop and cool, to today's high-tech fusion. These styles have a number of characteristics in common—for example, improvisation and syncopation—but perhaps more importantly, they share a common background. Jazz, in all its manifestations, grew out of the Afro-American music which preceded it, including spirituals, work songs, minstrelsy, and other forms. These styles, in turn, emerged from the collective experiences of Afro-Americans and the musical traditions of four continents: Africa, Europe, North America, and South America.

triangle trade: a pattern of colonial trade between New England, the West Indies, and west Africa, involving the importation of slaves to the New World

■/■ SLAVERY

Strange as it now seems, slavery was practiced by Africans even before the intrusion of Europeans, but their attitude toward slaves was different. In Africa, the slaves were considered members of the family with some rights, and it was doubtful that they would ever have been sold. If they displayed military or managerial ability, they could rise to prominent positions in the household. Some slaves even became generals or senior administrators in their adopted tribes.

Who were these slaves in Africa? Some were born into slavery; some were enslaved as a penalty for a crime, a compensation for a family dispute, or a retribution for a defaulted debt; some were kidnapped; and some were given by a subject people as tribute to a powerful ruler. But by far the greatest proportion were captives taken in wars.

The early impact of slavery in Africa and Europe was small. Initially, it was fashionable to have a black slave as a personal servant—sometimes called a *blackamoor*. As the demand for such human luxuries was limited, the first slaves were only a small part of a ship's cargo.

The economic basis of the slave trade began with the Spanish colonization of the West Indies when the demand for labor exceeded the availability of Indian slaves and other forms of forced labor. Black slaves were thought to be stronger and more aggressive than Indians and more able to cope with the work on plantations in the warmer regions. In 1510, royal orders were issued for fifty slaves to be sent from Spain to the island of Hispaniola (Haiti and the Dominican Republic). The first direct delivery took place in 1518. It was not until 1619 that the first slaves arrived in the mainland English colonies. It has been estimated that altogether between ten to fifteen million African slaves were imported to the New World.

The rise of the triangle trade dramatically increased the use of slaves in the New World. One form of the *triangle trade* consisted of

1. sending rum from New England to west Africa in exchange for
2. slaves sent to the Caribbean in exchange for
3. sugar cane or molasses for the return trip to New England.

Slave auction at Richmond. [Picture Collection, The Branch Libraries, The New York Public Library.]

jig: a lively, springy, irregular dance in triple meter

reel: a fast dance in which partners face each other in two lines

fiddle: a violin

middle passage: the trip across the Atlantic by slave ships from the west coast of Africa to the Caribbean

On the slave ship each slave was assigned a bunk space that was approximately 18 inches wide and 6 feet long. Slaves were stacked like cordwood. To help cut down on the death rate, they were occasionally brought on deck, hosed down, and forcibly exercised. Usually a fiddler was hired to play jigs and reels while crew members used whips and prodders to force blacks to dance. This is one of the reasons the violin, or *fiddle*, became a detested instrument to slaves. It was not unusual for one-half or more to die on the *middle passage* (the trip across the Atlantic from the west coast of Africa to a destination in the Caribbean). The number of survivors depended on the weather and accommodations on board. Occasionally, rampant infectious disease would wipe out an entire "cargo." Those who did survive the trip across the Atlantic were restored to health, *seasoned* (trained to be docile, cooperative, nonsurly, and helpful), and otherwise prepared for further travel. Stripped of their personal identities, tribal roots, families, customs, ways of life, and ways of dress, these ancestors of today's black Americans were somehow able to hold onto their religions and their music, bending both to fit their new environments.

Slave girl raffled along with a horse. [Picture Collection, The Branch Libraries, The New York Public Library.]

jujuism: a system of
west African tribal beliefs
that attributes magical
powers to an object or to
a ritual

Dahomey: former name
of the African country,
Benin

Ibo: a member of an
African tribal group in
Nigeria renowned for
trade and art

For hundreds, maybe thousands, of years, music and dance have been the primary art forms of the African. It's not surprising, therefore, that the slaves arriving from Africa and the West Indies into the New World continued this tradition. They brought their separate tribal heritages with them, but during the restoration and training period in the Caribbean slave pens—where the survivors of the various tribes were thrown into close proximity with each other on a daily basis—the widely different musical and religious traditions of blacks from various central and western African tribes began to blend. The *juju* (witchcraft)-practicing Arada and Yoruba tribes of Dahomey and Nigeria dominated this integration and sharply influenced the musical sounds of the Ibo, Senegalese, and Congolese.

Once the Africans had been prepared, they were sent to one of three places:

1. Another island in the Caribbean, where they would work the sugar plantations;
2. Brazil, where they would work Portuguese-owned cotton, sugarcane, and later, rubber plantations; or
3. The United States (through New Orleans), where they would work southern cotton plantations.

They carried with them to these destinations the musical traditions of their own tribes as well as those of tribes they had been exposed to while in "training" in the Caribbean, adapting these African elements to the musical instruments and traditions of their new homes. Thus were born three different Afro-American musical traditions.

■/■ THE CARIBBEAN

Most western European countries, particularly those near the Mediterranean, were part of the original Roman empire, which had relied heavily on slave labor. Portuguese and Spanish slave owners took the attitude that although they controlled the physical part of the slave, they did not control, nor did they wish to control or influence, the slave's mind—except for the necessary training in obedience and specific skills. They believed that they owned the right to the slave's labor and little else. It was illegal to be cruel to a slave, and the law allowed slaves under Portuguese and Spanish masters to have one day off a week. On that day, any labor done by the slave had to be paid for. Many slaves taken to the Caribbean or to Brazil eventually purchased their own freedom in that way.

Negroes Sunday Market at Antigua by W. E. Bestall, engraved by Gaetano Testoline, 1806. [Picture Collection, The Branch Libraries, The New York Public Library.]

voodoo: a West Indian religion involving supernatural ceremonies, derived from African cult worship and elements of Catholicism

channeler: a person through whom spirits of the dead are supposedly able to contact the living

macumba: a cult of African origin prevalent in southern and central Brazil

In the Caribbean under Spanish and Portuguese masters, therefore, the slaves never completely forgot their native religions or tribal rhythms. The Arada and Yoruba tribes, with their gods and music, had the strongest influence on the spread of African spirit worship throughout the Caribbean, Brazil, and New Orleans. There is detailed documentation available about the continuation of African cult ceremonies in the Caribbean, where they became known as *vaudou* or *vodun*, or, later, *voodoo*.

Music, song, and dance are an integral part of these sacred supernatural ceremonies, which were basically the same in the Caribbean and Brazil. Certain rhythms are played on drums, gourds, rattles, and other percussion instruments. These rhythms must be played by master drummers. The slightest difference in tempo, style, or volume can cause the spirits to stay away. The drums often become the "voice" of the summoned demon as well. Those chosen for their trance abilities (we call them *channelers* in today's society) open themselves up for possession by these spirits by dancing or singing to the rhythms.

Once the trance subject is possessed, others witnessing the ceremony pay homage to the spirit by presenting flowers and gifts to the trance medium. In return, the spirit often gives advice on love, marriage, and family and financial problems. In the French movie *Black Orpheus*, which was set in Brazil, there is a scene in which Orpheus, seeking information about Euridice, seeks out a trance medium and, through the *macumba* ceremony, hears the voice of his beloved.

Trinidad is another source of Yoruba secret-society cult music, much of which is dedicated to the Yoruba god of thunder, *Shango*. Originally, drums were used within these ceremonies. When they were banned, the Trinidad blacks resorted to using large, hollow bamboo sticks called *tambos*. However, they were easily used as war clubs, and sometimes, after too much rum during carnival periods, the drummers would start beating on each other. The U.S. Navy, using Trinidad as a base prior to and during World War II, outlawed tambos. On the Virgin Islands, where the U.S. Navy also outlawed the use of tambos, the innovative islanders were forced to find a substitute. They took the empty steel oil drums that were plentiful on the island, cut off the bottoms, hammered out the tops so that they would play different pitches when struck by a mallet, and created the steel band, the unique sound we all associate today with *calypso* music.

In Jamaica, the Obiah cult gets its name from the Ewe word *obia*, which means "charm." On the exotic isle of Carriacou in the lush Grenadines of the Caribbean, a local dance, strongly Ashanti in origin, includes words from the Ibo, Mandingo, Arada, and Congo tribes. Another example of African cultural influence in the Caribbean is a ceremonial healing song entitled "Cariba Dambella Bother Me." Dambella is the name of the Benin snake god.

Haiti is the site of the most successful religious amalgamation. Dambella is often depicted as St. Patrick, the Christian saint who

Steel band. [British West Indian Airways.]

La Rumba,
danced by
Ted Shawn and
Ernestina Day.
[Picture Collection,
The Branch Libraries,
The New York Public
Library.]

allegedly drove the snakes out of Ireland. Ogun, the African jumu-god of iron and war, is often found on the voodoo altars represented by the Biblical warrior angel Michael—dressed in full armor.

The voodoo music of Haiti claims to have the power to attract spirits that possess selected trance dancers through the use of specific repetitive, hypnotic rhythms. Like the original dances from Africa, these repetitive and complex rhythms seem to have a strong effect on some of the participants as well. Wild-eyed, many of them either move around in a trance-like state or leap violently in the air.

LISTENING ASSIGNMENT

"Haitian Fight Song," Charles Mingus. *Smithsonian Collection of Classic Jazz*, side G, #8 ▪ This song contains elements of calypso, jazz, gospel, blues, and funk. How does Mingus create the aggressive excitement and raw energy of this recording?

---

reggae: a Jamaican popular-music style blending calypso, blues, and rock 'n' roll

high life: a musical style involving African rhythms and American blues, pop, and rock

rumba: a Cuban dance with complex rhythms

bolero: a lively Spanish dance in triple meter; the Cuban form is in a slow duple meter

mambo: a fast ballroom dance of Caribbean origin

cha cha: a fast ballroom dance, similar to the mambo, with a quick three-step movement

soncubano: a song-and-dance form of African origin—prevalent in Panama and on the Caribbean coast of Columbia

danzón: a Puerto Rican dance of African origin

guarcha: a Cuban dance rhythm of African origin

conga: a Cuban dance performed in a single line, consisting of three steps forward, followed by a kick

candomble: a cult of African origin found in the Bahia state of Brazil

call-and-response: group repetition of, or response to, a soloist's (or another group's) verse or refrain

polyrhythm: the combination of two or more simultaneous rhythmic patterns

polymeter: the combi-

> **LISTENING ASSIGNMENT**
>
> "Juan Mil Ciento," Irakere. *Irakere*, Columbia • This explosive eleven-piece Cuban group brings together African influences, Cuban influences, jazz, and rock, and spits them out with fiery abandon. The rhythm is Cuban mambo. Which solo instruments do you hear? Which instruments give the piece a "rock" quality?

The slaves that remained in the Caribbean to work the sugarcane fields, therefore, blended their religious and musical traditions with local styles and produced calypso (later *reggae*), and *high life*. The island of Cuba, in particular, managed to preserve many original African musical styles and introduced the first wave of Latin jazz through the rhythm and dance forms of the *rumba*, *bolero*, *mambo*, *cha cha*, *soncubano*, *danzón*, *guarcha*, and *conga*.

■/■ BRAZIL

Brazil has the second-largest black population in the world (Nigeria has the largest). Bahia, a Brazilian state, is a Yoruba religious stronghold. Belief in *candomble* has become so widespread in this part of Brazil that this religion is practiced, in various degrees, by both black and white Brazilians, often combined with elements of Catholicism. Bahia has preserved more traditional African elements in their cult music than has any other area in Latin America or the Caribbean.

The macumban singing style, which originated with the African Yoruba tribe, incorporates the ancient call-and-response technique as well as the other common African musical devices of repetition, polyrhythm, polymeter, and falsetto. The basic singing style is virtually the same as that heard today in western Nigeria.

> **LISTENING ASSIGNMENT**
>
> "Europa," Gato Barbieri (by Carlos Santana). *Caliente!*, A & M 75021-3247 • This is one of the most exotic, sensual, and moving recordings to come out of Brazil. Note the passion with which Barbieri plays, and the balance between the lyrical melody and the soft rhythms underneath. This rhythm is too slow to be a samba or a bossa nova. It is a *bolero*, a soft, slow dance beat. What emotions are emphasized in this recording?

nation of contrasting time signatures, for example $\frac{4}{4}$ simultaneously with $\frac{3}{4}$; also called *cross-rhythm*

falsetto: an unnaturally or artificially high male voice

samba: a rhythmic Brazilian ballroom dance of African origin

bossa nova: a jazz-influenced music and dance style of Brazil

The slaves that remained in Brazil to work the cotton, sugarcane, and rubber fields blended their musical traditions with local styles and produced the *samba* and *bossa nova* ("new dance" or "new touch") music and dance forms.

Recently, Paul Simon, the well-known pop-rock composer, recorded an album in which he featured drummers and singers from Bahia. The album is fittingly called *The Rhythm of the Saints*.

LISTENING ASSIGNMENT

"The Rhythm of the Saints," Paul Simon. *The Rhythm of the Saints*, Warner Brothers (CD) 2-26098 ▪ Recorded in Bahia, Brazil, this is a good example of African influences on the music of Latin America. Notice how Paul Simon combines these African influences with his soft rock vocal style. What creates the excitement in this work?

Brazilian dance by Nem Brito.
[Photofest.]

A slave-pen at New Orleans, before an auction. [Picture Collection, The Branch Libraries, The New York Public Library.]

■/■ THE UNITED STATES

In Catholic New Orleans, a combination of social elements provided a unique atmosphere for the development of jazz. The slaves often found commonalities between elements of their juju religion and Catholic religious practices, which enabled the Africans to identify with Catholicism more easily. These similarities included sacred statues (idols), medals (charms), the call-and-response patterns of the masses, and the similar use of ornamentation, pomp, and ceremony, special feast days, clerical dress, and regal titles.

Slaves sent to the parts of the South where the Protestant form of Christianity was practiced found it more difficult to identify with the church. Even here, however, they found some connection with their native religions. The Christian doctrine of baptism (particularly by full immersion in a lake or stream) had its counterpart in the water-initiation ceremonies of some African tribes. The familiarity of this custom was one of the attractions that Christianity offered to slaves who sought Christian conversion and baptism. And even today, in the Protestant black churches of America, there is ample evidence of spirit possession (after rhythmic singing, dancing, and clapping), where certain individuals (usually women) are suddenly possessed by the spirit. This type of acceptable Christian religious experience (within certain fundamentalist Protestant churches) offers a parallel with the African custom of willing possession by a god (or demon). On the whole, however, the Protestants seemed more determined to obliterate all vestiges of the slaves' African heritage.

Of all the western European countries involved in the slave trade, the British were the least experienced in or culturally conditioned to the institution of slavery. The British found it bizarre and immoral. Ironically, *because* of this lack of familiarity and acceptance of the practice of slavery, English-speaking Americans could justify slavery only by believing that blacks were inferior—morally tainted or mentally or emotionally unstable. This, in turn, led to a conviction on the part of most white Christian slave owners that slaves needed to be changed mentally as well as physically—brainwashed into believing that western European traditions, religion, and culture were superior to their own.

Slaves on a South Carolina plantation dancing to African music, about 1800. [Abby Aldrich Rockefeller Folk Art Collection, The Williamsburg Museum.]

makin' juba: a lively dance, accompanied by rhythmic hand-clapping and body-slapping, developed by plantation slaves

tap dancing: a dance in which rhythm is audibly tapped out by the dancer's feet

work song: a folk song sung by workers or prisoners, often with a rhythm to match that of their work

spiritual: a religious song emphasizing Old Testament bondage themes

shout: a syncopated solo song that revived the African custom of worshiping by singing and dancing

minstrelsy: a popular 19th-century entertainment originally involving white singers, dancers, and comedians performing in blackface

gospel: a religious vocal style that developed after the Civil War, emphasizing the New Testament and personal salvation

ragtime: a syncopated, late 19th-century piano style, based on the musical forms of the rondo, the minuet, and the march

blues: a secular vocal style, characterized by the frequent use of flatted (blue) notes, originated by blacks in the late 19th century

jazz: a 20th-century improvisatory style combining African, American, and western European influences

This attitude extended to African music. The use of drums by African slaves was prohibited because plantation owners were afraid that slaves would signal each other and organize a rebellion. African slaves substituted bones, spoons, and even body slapping in rhythm (called *makin' juba*) for the loss of their drums. This loss eventually helped to create a form of American entertainment later called *tap dancing*.

In spite of the repressive racial attitudes, therefore, American slaves were able to hold on to, modify, and re-create their native African music even though African religious cults were stamped out. However, instead of the calypso music that developed in the Caribbean, blacks in the United States produced work songs, spirituals, shouts, minstrelsy, gospel songs, ragtime, blues, and jazz, which includes Dixieland, boogie-woogie, swing, bop, avant-garde, funk, soul, fusion, and the many other jazz styles that the rest of the world sees as our most original and important contribution to world culture. Each of these Afro-American musical forms will be dealt with in detail in later chapters, along with a particular examination of the role of New Orleans in the development of American jazz.

The rich heritage of American religious and folk music encouraged rapid modification of original African musical styles. African slaves quickly latched onto the new (to them) musical expressions and styles, taking what they liked and making it into something original, something of their own.

It's amazing to realize how much of our culture today has been influenced by the African tradition since, in most instances, everything African was supposedly taken away from the blacks brought to this country. Increasingly, anthropologists, sociologists, historians, and musicologists are examining African traditions more closely and with greater respect. It is increasingly suspect to call a group of people *primitive* when, in many instances, they had learned to make peace with their environment and live in balance with nature (and to a certain extent) their fellow man for hundreds and possibly thousands of years.

■/■ MERGER

It was only much later, beginning in the 1940s, that these three separate styles and traditions—of the Caribbean, Brazil, and the United States—began to merge, the first interaction resulting in the introduction of Cuban dance rhythms into American jazz.

Dixieland: an instrumental jazz style born out of New Orleans marching bands

boogie-woogie: a popular jazz piano style before World War II which evolved from the blues; also called "barrel house" after the New Orleans saloons in which it was born.

swing: *n. or adj.* a four-beat jazz style popular in the 1930s and early '40s, often performed by big bands, having a smoother beat and more flowing phrasing than Dixieland

bop: a post-World War II jazz style that features highly complex solos, dissonant chords, and extreme tempos

avant-garde: unorthodox and experimental music

funk: a musical style that combines rhythm-and-blues and gospel

soul: an emotional, personalized form of rhythm-and-blues

fusion: a blend of blues, bop, rock, ethnic music, electronics, and other musical influences; heavily dependent on synthesizer use

musicologist: a scientist or scholar who studies music history, theory, and/or the physical nature of sounds

hard bop: an aggressive "hot" jazz style popular in the 1960s and early '70s, characterized by driving rhythm sections and tenor-sax soloists

By the end of World War II, two distinct Afro-American dance styles existed in this country. One was American jazz; the other was Cuban.

In 1947, Dizzy Gillespie introduced the brilliant Cuban-born conga drummer Chano Pozo to the jazz scene in a New York City Town Hall concert. That event was the beginning of the Afro-Cuban jazz style in the United States. Chano Pozo, whose grandparents were African, came to Dizzy from the Lucumí religious sect of Cuba, a neo-Yoruba cult whose roots stemmed from western Nigeria and whose songs can be understood even today by Yoruba-speaking Africans.

As a result of the excitement caused by the introduction of this new jazz style, Max Roach, the well-known bop drummer, left the United States for a short period of time to study native rhythms in Tahiti. Art Blakey, the hard-bop combo leader and premiere jazz drummer, left to study drumming with some of the master drummers in west Africa. After returning to this country, both Max and Art recorded albums reflecting their experiences and new ideas. These albums were "Holiday for Skins" (Roach) and "The African Beat" (Blakey). A similar search for the cultural roots of Afro-American music was undertaken in the 1970s and '80s by several well-known rock 'n' roll drummers.

Cuban dances and Cuban bands had become very popular in the United States by the late 1950s. Bands like Perez Prado's, Machito's, and Luis Arcaraz's reflected the mambo craze in the United States at this time.

The second wave of Latin jazz styles to come to the United States came from Brazil in the 1960s. Brazil's exciting samba, bossa nova, and other dance and rhythm forms are now a part of modern jazz styles. This second wave of rhythms that has so strongly influenced modern jazz began with the early recordings of Stan Getz, Charlie Byrd, and Astrud Gilberto. Later, the wonderful, sensuous melodies and rhythms of Luiz Bonfa and Antonio Carlos Jobim offered a welcome respite from the aggressive, blaring, and overstated sounds of American pop music during this period.

LISTENING ASSIGNMENT

"Night in Tunisia," Bud Powell Trio (by Dizzy Gillespie). *Smithsonian Collection of Classic Jazz*, side F, #5 ▪ Dizzy Gillespie went to Cuba early in his career, brought back many of the standard Cuban rhythms, and introduced them into jazz. Note how they interact with standard jazz rhythms.

A slave auction in New Amsterdam, 1643. [Picture Collection, The Branch Libraries, The New York Public Library.]

SUMMARY

Attitudes towards slaves have varied in different societies. Slaves in Africa, most of whom were war captives, had some rights and were considered members of the family. Portuguese and Spanish slave owners tried to control only the slaves' labor, not their minds, and outlawed excessive cruelty to slaves.

The experience of African slaves in the New World was quite different. Spanish colonists in the West Indies began importing slaves in large numbers when the demand for labor exceeded the availability of Indian slaves and other forms of forced labor. Blacks were thought to be stronger than Indians and to be better able to cope with the heavy work demand in a hot climate. The *triangle trade*, an economic exchange involving New England, Africa, and the Caribbean, facilitated the spread of slavery in the New World. The captured Africans were stacked so tightly in their bunks on the slave ships that frequently half of them died of disease before they reached the Caribbean. Those Africans who survived the *middle passage*, the journey from Africa to the Caribbean, were restored to health and *seasoned*, that is, trained to be docile and cooperative. They either remained in the Caribbean or were sent to Brazil or the United States. The slaves' tribal traditions merged with those of their new homes and three different Afro-American musical traditions were born.

African spirit worship spread throughout the Caribbean, where it merged with Christianity. Ritual dances retained their African voodoo character. The ensuing blend of African religious and musical traditions with local Caribbean styles produced *calypso* and *high life* music.

A similar blending occurred in Brazil, which preserved many traditional African elements, such as the singing style, *candomble*, and produced new dance forms, such as the *samba* and *bossa nova*.

Slaves in the United States found connections between their native religions and Christianity, and despite slave owners' efforts to obliterate all traces of the African heritage, elements of their religions merged with the Christianity they practiced. African music, as modified by American slaves and their environment, evolved into a variety of styles, ranging from work songs to spirituals.

It wasn't until the 1940s, as Latin jazz styles became popular in the United States, that the three musical traditions which developed separately in the Caribbean, Brazil, and the United States began to interact and to merge.

■ Questions on Chapter 1

A. *In your own words* write one or two sentences describing each of the terms listed in Questions 1–8.

1. triangle trade _____

_____

2. middle passage _____

_____

3. jujuism _____

_____

4. voodoo _____

_____

5. calypso _____

_____

6. reggae _____

_____

7. call-and-response _____

_____

8. polyrhythm _____

_____

In Questions 9–12 fill in the blanks.

9. A _____ is a lively, springy, irregular dance in triple meter.

10. Another word for a violin is a _____.

11. A _____ is a person through whom spirits of the dead are supposedly able to contact the living.

12. A _____ is an unnaturally or artificially high male voice.

B.
13. How did the *triangle trade* increase the number of slaves brought to America?

14. Describe the influence of African spirit worship on the religious practices of blacks of the Caribbean.

15. In what ways did the religious practices of blacks in Brazil develop in a manner similar to those of the Caribbean?

16. In what ways did African religious and musical traditions survive to influence the culture of slaves in the United States?

17. What environmental and societal conditions helped to produce the three different regional variations of Afro-American music?

18. In what ways did Catholicism provide a more suitable background for the development of jazz than Protestantism?

19. How did English and Spanish/Portuguese slave owners differ in their attitudes towards African traditions? How did this affect slave life in the United States, the Caribbean, and Brazil?

■ Topics for Further Research

A. What beliefs and rituals were included in the African spirit worship of the Arada and Yoruba tribes, and how did they change or remain the same in the Caribbean and Brazil?

B. Describe the history of slavery in the Caribbean. How did it differ from that in the United States?

■ Further Reading

Haley, Alex. *Roots*. New York: Doubleday & Co., 1976.

Kaufman, Frederick and John P. Guckin. *The African Roots of Jazz*. Sherman Oaks, Calif.: Alfred Publishing Co., 1979. (Chapter 1)

Southern, Eileen. *The Music of Black Americans: A History*, 2nd ed. New York: W. W. Norton & Co., 1983. (Chapters 1–2)

■ Further Listening

Evolution of the Blues, Jon Hendricks. Columbia.

Olantunji! Drums of Passion, Olantunji. Columbia, CK-8210.

Out of Africa. Ryko Records, RCD-20059.

Roots (soundtrack), Quincy Jones. A & M Records.

■ Films and Videos

Black Orpheus (1959). Score by Luiz Bonfa and Antonio Carlos Jobim.

Olantunji and His Drums of Passion (video). In concert with the Grateful Dead.

Paul Simon: Graceland, The African Concert (video). In Zimbabwe with Miriam Makeba and Hugh Masakela.

Roots (1977). Popular miniseries based on Alex Haley's novel.

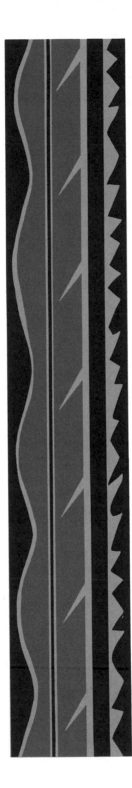

2
CONTRIBUTIONS FROM AFRICA

/■/

It all goes back, mon,
to de roots
of Africa.
All de rhythm
and all de dance
from Africa.
Listen to de drums,
they'll tell you so.
Listen to de singers,
they're in the know.
I think we all have
the same mother—
Africa.

—JW

■/■ AFRICA TODAY

The continent of Africa is over three times the size of the United States. With a population of over 300 million people and supporting two thousand tribal groups, each with their own dialect or language, Africa today offers the most diverse ecological and cultural mix on any continent. It includes at the present time, fifty-three nations, most of which claimed national sovereignty in the twentieth century. Regional and

mariachi band: a small band dressed in native costumes, playing traditional Mexican dance music

tribal loyalties, with their customs and traditions, go back thousands of years, complicating the process of modern nationalism.

Africa has the world's largest gold and diamond deposits, and is a primary source for titanium, which is used in steel production. Uranium and large oil deposits offer huge energy potential. The rich resources of Africa, many of them vital to modern technology, made the continent a battleground in the struggles between the older colonial powers and the emerging new nations, and between socialism and capitalism. Although Africa has, for the most part, cast off the yoke of colonialism, it has yet to unite and form itself into a powerful political union.

Africa therefore finds itself with the problem of preparing for the twenty-first century while still encumbered with nineteenth-century political, social, and economic problems. Many of its new nations are torn between trying to save old traditions, customs, and art forms while still finding a way of entering modern society.

■/■ AFRICAN MUSIC

Showing a strong Anglo-American rock influence, much of the popular music in Africa today is called *juju* or *high life*. This music features a vocal-calypso style in combination with traditional African rhythms and American blues styles. High life is associated with good times and merry-making. Today, high life has been affected by many social and environmental factors. High-life bands in metropolitan areas perform at weddings, in ballrooms, hotels, nightclubs, and cafes. Village musicians perform at similar functions, but to a lesser extent. Akin to the colorful *mariachi bands* of Mexico, early village bands helped to popularize high life by taking their music to the streets. Today high-life street bands can be heard in cities and villages all across west Africa.

Since the calypso music of the West Indies had its roots in west Africa and has remained pure, it has been easily assimilated back into west Africa. Of the foreign music presently played in Ghana and Nigeria, for instance, calypso is unquestionably the most prevalent. Jazz is becoming popular in Africa today partially as an outgrowth of the Africans' love of exuberance, improvisation, and percussion.

LISTENING ASSIGNMENT

"Synchro System," King Sunny Ade and His African Beats. *Synchro System*, Mango (CD) 162-539737-2 ■ Listen for rock, blues, jazz, and African influences.

Ghana Nightclub. [Photofest.]

■/■ TRIBAL ROOTS

The tribal African way of life was communal, based on strong and loving family relations that shaded into general compassion for the tribe or the community. All activities, from hunting and harvesting to leisure pursuits, were communal. Generosity and forgiveness were encouraged, malice and revenge abhorred. Tribal Africans were renowned for their sense of humor and, at the same time, their dislike of melancholy and sadness.

Music has always been more of a communal, group activity in tribal Africa than it is in the western world. African music was so functional, so a part of daily life, that many African tribes do not even have a separate word in their language for *music*. They have words for musical forms—

African ceremony in the motion picture, *White Hunter*. [Photofest.]

words like *song* or *tune*, but the idea of "music" by itself has never been abstracted from the things to which it belongs.

The traditional tribal music of central and west Africa has always included work songs, instructional songs, social-commentary songs, gossip-and-satire songs, and general songs for entertainment. Boat songs were popular when the main mode of transportation in this part of the world was the boat. Music was an integral part of all daily activities, including preparing meals, putting children to bed, and recording the origins, background, and major events in a tribe's identity.

Music played a dominant role in all the functions in African tribal societies. Kings were crowned, babies were born, men worked, couples married, victories were won, defeats were accepted, crops were harvested, and people died, all to the accompaniment of the appropriate musical sound.

In most instances, the climate and general geography of the region were not friendly to the development of architecture, written documents,

griot: a storyteller/poet/musician who entertains and keeps an oral history of a west African tribe or village

statues, or paintings. Music and dance, therefore, became the primary forms of artistic expression and entertainment.

Until recently, there was no written musical notation for African music. *Rote learning* (watching, listening, and then imitating) was the only way one could learn African tribal music.

Recent scientific studies on the hemispheres of the human brain have suggested that rote learning, once considered primitive and outdated, is really one of the best ways to learn certain skills, particularly skills that involve rhythm and movement. Today there are many contemporary rock musicians (Paul McCartney, Vangelis, and Bob Dylan, among others) who do not read music. Many of the early jazz musicians were musically illiterate. Only when the development of the swing era forced the smaller jazz units to expand and become big bands did the skill of reading music become important in jazz.

Music and religious worship are more closely bound together in Africa than they are in most other cultures. An African religious service cannot take place without music. (Yoruba and Dahomean ceremonial music summons the spirits: If there are no drums, there are no spirits, and so there can be no ritual.)

Music is the main message in an African religious ceremony. Music is not simply a prelude to a sermon, as it is in western European Christianity. One tribal legend claims that it was through the drum that God gave man the gift of speech. In other words, music—and most particularly rhythm—preceded the gift of human speech.

In Ghana, the Ashanti considered their master drummer close to God and therefore treated him with great reverence, dignity, and respect. Tribal societies witnessed the constant rhythms and cycles of nature and held them in great respect. Rhythm, nature, and God were often synonymous.

In Egbaland, Nigeria, and indeed throughout other areas of Africa, the livelihood and the status of the traditional musician were generally dependent upon the good will of their chief or king. The musician was a highly respected member of the king's court. His services had to be readily available for any given occasion upon the request of the king or chief.

Several factors affected the prestige of the musician in Africa: seniority, the type of instrument played, and the variations in the many different tribal-cultural values. In some tribes, the musician, or *griot*, had the right to mock anybody and could use insulting language without any tribal disciplinary action being taken against him. His role was similar to that of the European court jester, except that it was far more important.

If the reward for their clever songs and rhythmic limericks, for example, was not forthcoming or was considered insufficient, the griots often switched to outspoken and embarrassing or revealing lyrics in their spontaneously created songs. As a result, they were greatly feared and usually amassed considerable wealth in their lifetimes.

Music, when used to celebrate major holidays, tribal victories, and so on, was continuous and often went on for days, with musicians, dancers, and singers alike performing in shifts and resting in between. The closest the United States has ever come to a major African-style musical celebration was the now legendary Woodstock rock festival in upstate New York in 1969.

Native languages were rhythmic and tonal; for instance, in the Yoruba language, the word *aqua* has five distinctly different meanings, depending on the rhythmic and tonal inflection used when pronouncing the word. Africans often communicated with each other by using their "talking" drums, which could imitate the rhythm of speech and the vocal inflection used when speaking the actual words and could be clearly understood over long distances.

Music was an essential part of tribal poetry, religion, humor, gossip, and even legal hearings. In some tribes, courts of law allowed music as a vehicle for arguments between the prosecuting attorney and the defense.

According to the observations of early explorers, African instrumentalists enjoyed a higher status than did singers. Most important tribal rulers maintained court orchestras, and the orchestra leader was definitely a tribal VIP. The orchestra leader was always the master drummer, and was second in importance only to the chief of the tribe. The largest drum was reserved for the most important person in the tribe. This drum was played only on important ceremonial occasions, and only by the tribal chief or the master drummer.

Women participated as singers and dancers, but the instrumentalists were all men, who were taught by elders of the tribe—with each succeeding generation handing down the musical traditions to the next generation. The role of the young musician in the tribe was very important because the identity and history of the tribe was carried from one generation to the next through music and poetry.

The principal and essential traits of African tribal music, then—its melodic, harmonic, and rhythmic characteristics—are all linked to the making of a "speaking instrument," and its highest expression was in the act of worship. For instance, the Dogon of Mali believed that music, and more precisely, the drum, was the vehicle through which the word of God was brought to man. Music, dance, and drumming were the means of prayer and the deepest forms of religious expression for the African. In contrast, the western European generally sees the highest form of religious piety or devotion in the act of silent prayer. Even today, when we see on television a group of Africans returning from a funeral, we are

Women posing with a tom tom. Women were not allowed to play a ceremonial drum. [Picture Collection, The Branch Libraries, The New York Public Library.]

generally puzzled by the fact that they are singing and dancing. These African traditions of making music the primary vehicle for expressing deep religious convictions were brought to the New World and modified through cultural interaction into such practices as the marching bands at funerals in New Orleans and the intense emotion found in traditional spirituals and contemporary gospel music.

A musical performance in tribal Africa was a multisensory experience and could not be separated into single events. As important as the music and the musicians were the costumes, the dancing, and the audience participation.

Tribal Africans did not think of music as "accompanying" the dance. To the African, dancing and music were two parts of a whole. This tradition survived in Afro-American music until the late 1940s, when bop emerged as the first jazz style to disengage itself from dancing.

LISTENING ASSIGNMENT

"Diamonds on the Soles of Her Shoes," Paul Simon. *Graceland*, Warner Brothers CD 2-25477 ▪ Which tribal African elements do you hear in the voices accompanying Paul Simon? How is this style different from standard rock music?

Watusi dancers of the Belgian Congo. [Photofest.]

■/■ SURVIVALS IN JAZZ

rap: a popular music
style characterized by
spontaneous, rhyming
lyrics, strong rhythms,
and the virtual absence
of melody or harmony

verse-chorus form: the
alternation of a familiar,
fixed chorus with an
original verse

rhythm-and-blues: a
popular-music style with
strong repetitive rhythms
and simple melodies,
often using blue notes

call-and-response form:
group repetition of, or
response to, a soloist's
(or another group's)
verse or refrain

After more than 350 years of contact with European and American cultures, the musical characteristics of African tribal music are still alive. They're found in ragtime, blues, swing, rock, rap, funk, gospel, soul, and all other forms of Afro-American music.

What are these elements of African tribal music that have survived?

Verse-Chorus Form. Africans liked to alternate fixed refrains with original verses in their songs. Vocal and instrumental soloists were free to express themselves spontaneously so long as they kept returning to a familiar chorus.

This musical form—the juxtaposition of the new and the familiar—is typical of many of the forms used in today's music, particularly rhythm-and-blues, gospel, soul, funk, and jazz. The establishment of a familiar melody at the beginning of the chorus is juxtaposed with creative improvised verses.

Call-and-Response Form. This is by far the most common form of tribal African music surviving today. A very graphic example of this technique was illustrated by folk-singer Harry Belafonte several years ago in his "Banana Boat Song," which opens with Harry singing "day-oh," quickly echoed by a chorus of voices.

In Africa, there are four types of *call-and-response* patterns:

1. Exact group repetition of the soloist's verse.
2. Group repetition of the soloist's refrain.
3. The soloist singing the first half, and the group—the refrain.
4. Group versus group.

Examples of all four variations of call-and-response can be found in spirituals, gospel songs, work songs, early instrumental jazz, and some types of the blues.

In the typical black church, there is usually a regular interchange between the preacher and some members of the congregation. Whenever the preacher says something important, members of the congregation react by saying "amen."

Solo Breaks.   In this typical African musical technique, the many-layered rhythms accompanying a singer or instrumental soloist stop suddenly, drawing attention to the soloist. These breaks in the rhythmic accompaniment are usually short—but they do allow the singer or solo instrumentalist an opportunity to be heard alone by the listener with no other distractions.

Solo breaks are used in jazz to interrupt the monotony of the steady rhythms and to dramatize whatever the singer or solo instrumentalist is performing. Solo breaks usually occur at the beginning or at the end of a solo section.

Bass Ostinatos.   Repetitive bass patterns, so typical of today's rock music, are African in origin. In this technique, the lowest-pitched instrument repeats a short, rhythmic melody again and again while other instruments add chords, melodies, and complementary rhythm patterns above it. This gradual addition of voices creates an ever-changing musical kaleidoscope of interesting patterns for the listener.

Riffs.   *Riffs* differ from bass ostinatos in that they are shorter, more melodic, and occur in higher-pitched instruments. They are similar to the ever-present "amen" used to spark the delivery of a black preacher by members of his congregation.

Riffs are usually three to nine notes in length, varying in rhythmic length from two beats (one-half of a $\frac{4}{4}$ measure) to two measures (eight beats in $\frac{4}{4}$ time). A good example of the multiple use of riffs in a big band to create excitement is the last part of Count Basie's classic big-band recording of "One o'Clock Jump."

B. B. King often uses riffs behind his blues solos. During the swing era, arrangers created excitement in their arrangements by stacking riffs on top of one another as they approached the ending, creating an ever-

solo break: a technique in which rhythmic accompaniment stops suddenly and briefly in order to draw attention to the soloist

ostinato: a short, repeated musical idea, usually in the bass range

riff: a short, repeated phrase used as an accompaniment for a soloist

$\frac{4}{4}$ **time:** a time signature denoting four beats to the measure, or a form of *duple* meter

B. B. King. [Photofest.]

improvisation: spontaneous composition

polyrhythm: the combination of two or more simultaneous rhythmic patterns

layered rhythm: polyrhythms that are often added one at a time

Latin music: the music of Latin America, particularly Cuba and Brazil

jazz-rock: a style that combines elements of jazz and rock

increasing amount of rhythmic tension and anticipation. Riffs are used a lot in Latin and jazz-rock music, as well.

Improvised Solos. Improvisation is the heart and soul of African tribal music. In African musical traditions, no effort is made to repeat a traditional tune or melody exactly. Singers and instrumentalists feel free to personalize songs so long as the original melody can still be recognized. Later in the tune, even the original melody is often discarded for the excitement of spontaneous composition, called *improvisation*.

Improvisation is essential to jazz. The combination of the spontaneous (the improvised) with the preconceived (the arranged) gives jazz its uniqueness, excitement, and drive.

Polyrhythms. *Polyrhythm* is the combination of two or more basic rhythmic patterns at the same time. *Layered rhythm* is another term for polyrhythm, although this term often implies more than two simultaneous rhythms, which are usually added one at a time. The use of polyrhythms or layered rhythm is common in jazz, with some styles of jazz using this technique more than others. Dixieland, Latin, jazz-rock, and fusion frequently use layered rhythms.

Polyrhythm occurs in the children's song, *Row, Row, Row Your Boat*, for example. When sung as a round, the slow "row, row, row" is sung simultaneously with "merrily, merrily, merrily," a much faster pattern of notes.

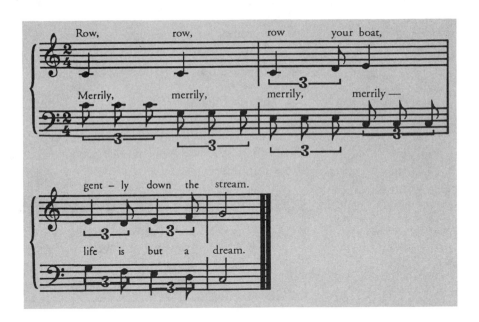

**cross-rhythm/poly-
meter:** the combination
of contrasting time sig-
natures, for example, $\frac{4}{4}$
simultaneously with $\frac{3}{4}$

meter: the grouping of
accented and unaccented
beats

Cross-Rhythms. Another characteristic of African rhythm, called *cross-rhythms* or *polymeter*, occurs when several differently constructed meters, or underlying patterns of accented and unaccented beats, are played or sung simultaneously.

For example, if we were to take *Row, Row, Row Your Boat* and change the meter of the "merrily, merrily" section, the result might look off balance, like this:

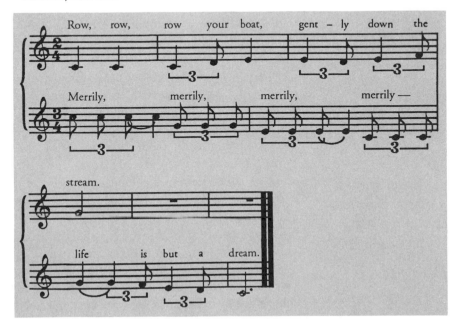

interval: the difference in pitch between two tones

octave: in western European music, an interval of twelve half steps

scale: a succession of tones ascending or descending according to fixed intervals

blue note: a flatted note common in blues and jazz, created by lowering the third, fifth, or seventh note of the major scale one half step

major scale: a scale with the sequence of intervals: whole step, whole, half, whole, whole, whole, half

whole step: an interval of two half steps

half step: the smallest defined interval in music

lowered note: a note that has been moved down one half step

dissonance: a combination of tones that together produce a harsh or discordant sound

This example is an analogy only—it is unlikely that you would see such a combination of time signatures written into the music by the composer. More often, the players create cross-rhythms spontaneously as they improvise.

The combination of different meters creates a churning, forward-driving effect that can be very exciting. Because they are used to create drama and anticipation, cross-rhythms are seldom used for long periods of time within a song. They usually occur towards the end or the climax of a musical selection.

LISTENING ASSIGNMENT

"Akiwowo," Olantunji. *Olantunji! Drums of Passion*, Columbia CK-8210 ▪ Listen for the layered rhythms. How many separate rhythms can you count? Notice how the head drummer uses cross-rhythms to create excitement. Identify as many instruments as you can.

Blue Notes. The fact that the piano and organ eventually became the dominant instruments in western European music forced the compression of the number of possible consecutive musical intervals available within an octave to twelve—for example,

$$C, C^\sharp, D, D^\sharp, E, F, F^\sharp, G, G^\sharp, A, A^\sharp, B$$

African tribal music was under no such constraint; its many scales often had more than twelve consecutive intervals to the octave. Some had less, but with different "sounding" intervals. Many of the Afro-Americans' favorite tribal intervals are not found in European scales, so they had to invent or adjust the European scale to fit their needs. One of the techniques they employed was the use of *blue notes*.

In Afro-American music, the major scale is adjusted to accommodate blue notes. The major scale (do-re-*mi* / *fa*-sol-la-*ti* / *do*) is made up mostly of whole steps, with half steps occurring between *mi* and *fa* and between *ti* and *do*. Blue notes are created by lowering the *third* (*mi*), the *fifth* (*sol*), and the *seventh* (*ti*) notes one-half step each. These three lowered notes become the "blue" notes of the scale. In doing this, the order of half steps and whole steps have been rearranged creating a new and "bluesy" sound. Today we commonly call this major scale with the lowered third, fifth, and seventh notes the "blues" scale. It has become one of the most commonly used scales in contemporary music.

To create the harmonic tension desired by the blues musician, the normal scale tones are kept in the chords beneath the melody. The resulting dissonance created between the blues notes in the melody and the normal scale tones approximates the Afro-American's search for lost tribal scale tones. This dissonance creates tension, and is the heart and soul of the "blues" sound.

Glissando. A *glissando* is the technique of sliding up or down to the next melodic note, creating a continuous sound. African singers and instrumentalists favored the use of the glissando. This technique has been taken over by jazz musicians and blues singers. Today, we often hear it in television commercials featuring rock guitarists who slide wildly in and out of blue notes.

Audience Participation. In African tribal tradition, there was no separation between performers and audience. Everybody got into the act and participated in one way or another, by dancing, tapping a foot, singing, shouting, yelling, or hitting a percussion instrument. In the western world today, we can approximate this coming together of audience and performer in black churches, pep rallies, and jazz and rock concerts. Hand clapping by those not actively playing, singing, or dancing was expected in Africa. Sometimes the hand clapping became highly syncopated and complex. Black slaves introduced complex hand clapping on America's plantations in the game, makin' juba. This led, later, to the drum solo and the solo tap dancer. Modern jazz singers today, like Bobby McFerrin, have recalled this earlier technique and integrated it into their performances.

Syncopation. *Syncopation*, defined as a "displaced accent," occurs when the normal accent on the downbeat is replaced by an accent that falls on the upbeat. Syncopation is an essential characteristic of jazz. In western European musical traditions, rhythmic accents, for the most part, fall on downbeats. Syncopation is a vital part of Afro-American music, from work songs, spirituals, gospel, and blues to the current craze in American popular music called *rap*.

Nondevelopmental Music. The Greco-Roman/Judeo-Christian foundations of western European civilization placed great emphasis upon logic and linear thinking. Music has to "evolve," "go somewhere," "mean something." Most music created in this cultural context has a beginning and a developmental section (which usually evolves toward some sort of musical climax), followed by an obvious and complete ending.

African culture viewed life—and music—differently. Within their cultural context, life was seen as cyclical, rather than evolutionary. Intuition and spontaneity were valued over logical deduction and devel-

board fade: the gradual fading out of a musical piece by the recording engineer

opment. Unlike the music and art of western Europe, African tribal music was under no philosophical imperative to evolve, to build to a climax, and mean something. Music wasn't forced to prove anything—it simply had to be exciting, pleasant, and satisfying to both the listener and performer. African drummers, soloists, and singers kept on doing what they were doing until they or their audience were bored. When that happened, they changed to something new and different. Endings were often vague or nonexistent; the implication was that the music would resume where it left off at a later time.

The open-endedness of African tribal music has had a particular appeal to rock musicians. Many pop and rock recordings end with a "board fade," rather than an obvious and complete ending, suggesting the music is continuous and unending.

Repetition.   There is more repetition in African tribal music than there is in most styles of western European music. There are usually subtle changes in the repetitive phrases, but the Africans stay with the phrase until they have wrung every drop of interest out of it. To western ears, the music sometimes sounds monotonous. However, close observation will reveal a myriad of subtle changes with each repetition. Bob Marley, a well-known Jamaican reggae singer, was supposed to have said: "It don't make no matter how many time you sing it. You sing it 'til it gets sour to your mouth."

Emotional Intensity.   One of the single greatest differences between western European vocal styles and African vocal styles is the degree of emotional intensity. There are no limits to the amount of emotional intensity in African or Afro-American vocal styles. Singers cry, moan, wail, bark, sob, growl, yell. Anything that adds to and does not detract from the meaning of the music is permissible.

In the African tradition, a "fine" tone does not count; the criteria for choosing singers are different. The ability to express emotion freely in musical form is valued over a singer's tone. The sound of the voice is often based on the situation and its demands. The voice may be harsh or soft, piercing or tender, depending on the time, the place, and the situation. For instance, a clear voice is used to sing of the bride newly brought into the community; a hushed voice is used to sing of something one would prefer to keep quiet; a mocking voice is used for humor or satire.

To develop a "beautiful voice," in the European sense, is not the main goal of the African singer. The goal is to "live" the actions of everyday life by means of the voice. A "fine voice" does not count for much in African vocal traditions because the criteria for choosing a singer are social, not musical. The singer may be the witch doctor, an elder, or a young mother. If the last, her songs may consist of cooing to an infant, warning off a threatening neighbor, or celebrating a husband's prowess as a lover. Sometimes she may join with other women in sharing humorous and gossip songs while doing the laundry down by the river.

Buzz Tones. Africans have traditionally liked *buzz tones*, anything that produces "raspy" sounds. This is one tonal characteristic that is common to both singers and instrumentalists. Singers would often deliberately distort their vocal tones in order to produce this tone, which we sometimes call a *whiskey voice*. Today, we hear it in the vocal styles of singers like Louis Armstrong, Ray Charles, Janis Joplin, B. B. King, Joe Cocker, and James Brown. The "gravel-voice" effect is African in origin, as are similar tones occasionally played on trumpets, saxophones, clarinets, and even guitars.

The commonly used African instrument called the *kalimba*, or hand piano, is often modified to produce the buzz-tone by attaching bits of metal to the prongs that are plucked by the fingers. In the West, early black pianists often put thumbtacks into the key-hammers on old upright pianos to approximate the same sound. These sounds are considered "down and dirty" in our culture, but they are a common sound in Africa.

Falsettos. The high-pitched male *falsetto* voice is considered "macho" in African, Polynesian, and other tribal cultures. In our western European culture, the high-pitched male voice is considered effeminate, due largely to the former practice of castrating promising young boy sopranos before puberty to preserve their soprano voice into adulthood. This unfortunate practice began somewhere around the 15th century in Europe and ended sometime during the early part of the 19th century. Even the great Austrian composer, Franz Joseph Haydn, almost had this operation performed on him when he was a young boy. As a result, the male falsetto voice in Europe became associated with artificially induced femininity. Today, however, we hear male blues, jazz, and rock singers using their extreme high falsetto registers in a very "masculine" way, as in the African tradition.

Festivals. The two- or three-day music festival is an African tradition. In tribal Africa, holidays often witnessed dancing, drumming, and singing continuously for as long as two to three days at a time. Musicians took turns playing, and singers and dancers rested only when tired, returning later to resume their activities.

In our western world today, the best example of this kind of multisensory experience is found in the Mardi Gras and Carnival parades in New Orleans, Brazil, and the Caribbean.

Congolese dancers and drummers. [Photofest.]

double entendre: a double meaning

Charleston: a vigorous rhythmic ballroom dance, popular in America in the 1920s, with origins in Africa

cakewalk: a dance with a strutting or marching step

jitterbug: a strenuously acrobatic dance performed to boogie-woogie and swing music

lindy: an energetic jitterbug dance, with African influences

Double-Entendre Lyrics. Africans always admired the clever use of words when making up a song. This tradition is preserved today in annual calypso contests held in the Caribbean. Competitors are given a subject to sing about just before they perform. The singer who makes up the cleverest lyrics is the winner.

Later, in the United States, *double-entendre* lyrics became an important survival and communications technique used by slaves in the south prior to the Civil War. Double-entendre lyrics found in spirituals, work songs, shouts, and later, the blues, allowed blacks to communicate controversial thoughts and opinions without arousing the suspicions or animosity of their masters or, later, the white power structure in the South.

Dance Forms. Popular dances such as the *Charleston,* the *cakewalk,* the *jitterbug,* the *lindy,* and the *twist* are direct derivations of African

twist: a couples dance with African influences, composed of strong rhythmic turns and twists of the body

jazz ballet: jazz music for dancers, in which both the players and dancers can improvise

dances. In one of these popular dances of the 1920s, the Charleston, the hand-crossing and uncrossing movements at the kneecaps are virtually unaltered from the African juba dance. Lerone Bennett talks about films shot in African villages showing perfect examples of what we now call the Charleston.* The swaying motion of the *twist* of the 1960s dates back to Africa. In 1913, two black Americans wrote the lyrics for a Broadway show song "Ballin' the Jack." The lyrics of this song actually instruct the audience on how to do what was originally an African dance.

First, you put your two knees close up tight.
Then you sway 'em to the left; then you sway 'em to the right.
Step around the floor kind of nice and light.
Then you twis' around and twis' around with all your might.
Stretch your lovin' arms straight out in space.
Then you do the Eagle Rock with style and grace.
Swing your foot way 'round, then bring it back.
Now that's what I call "ballin' the Jack!"

The 1930s witnessed the African influence on popular American dance again. Another popular dance, called the *lindy*, introduced the common African practice of dance partners breaking or separating from each other temporarily. Pure African dance movements became integrated into jazz and modern dance through the vehicle of primitive dance—later called *jazz ballet*.

Before the Mayflower, 6th ed.

SUMMARY

With two thousand tribal groups and rich natural resources, Africa is both home to a diverse ecological and cultural mix, as well as a battleground for political and social movements, not the least of which is the conflict between old traditions and modern society.

High-life, a musical style popular in Africa today, combines American rock and blues influences with traditional African rhythms. Music in Africa has traditionally been a communal activity with a dominant role in important social events such as marriages, births and deaths, religious festivals, crop harvests, and military victories. All elements of a tribal musical performance—the music, costumes, dancing, audience participation—are equally important and unseparable.

Many traditions of African tribal music are essential characteristics of modern American popular music. African techniques that influenced the development of Afro-American music include *polyrhythms*, *cross-rhythms*, and *syncopation. Blue notes*, lowered notes that don't fit into European scales, were another important contribution, as were *buzz tones*— deliberately distorted and raspy vocal or instrumental tones. In addition, many popular dance forms, such as the Charleston and jitterbug, are derived from African dances. These and other contributions from African musical tradition played a crucial role in shaping popular music as it developed in the United States.

■ Questions on Chapter 2

A. *In your own words* write one or two sentences describing each of the terms listed in Questions 1–22.

1. makin juba _____

   _____

2. tap dancing _____

   _____

3. work song _____

   _____

4. spiritual _____

   _____

5. minstrelsy _____

   _____

6. ragtime _____

   _____

7. blues _____

   _____

8. bop _____

   _____

9. rap _____

   _____

10. verse-chorus form _____

    _____

11. call-and-response form _____

    _____

12. solo break _____

    _____

13. ostinato _____

    _____

14. riff _____

_____

15. blue note _____

_____

16. lowered note _____

_____

17. dissonance _____

_____

18. glissando _____

_____

19. board fade _____

_____

20. buzz tone _____

_____

21. double-entendre lyrics _____

_____

22. Charleston _____

_____

In Questions 23–31 fill in the blanks.

23. _____ is a vocal style that emphasized the New Testament and personal salvation and that developed after the Cival War.

24. _____ is an instrumental jazz style that had its roots in New Orleans marching bands.

25. A popular jazz piano style that evolved from the blues before World War II was _____.

26. _____ is a musical style that combines rhythm-and-blues with gospel.

27. A scholar who studies music history, theory, and/or the physical nature of sounds is called a _____.

28. _____ is unrehearsed, spontaneously created, and spontaneously played music.

29. Polyrhythms that are added one at a time are called _____.

30. A raspy singing voice is sometimes called a _____.

31. _____ is a strenuously acrobatic dance performed to boogie-woogie and swing music.

B. 32. Contrast the uses of music in African tribal cultures and the uses of music in our society today.

33. What role did music play in African religious ceremonies?

34. Why was the *griot* an important figure in African tribal societies?

35. Define and discuss *syncopation, improvisation*, and *personalization*.

36. Describe, in your own words, five additional characteristics of African tribal music that were translated to jazz and other American musical forms. Identify examples of each characteristic from music with which you are familiar.

37. Discuss the statement:
> *African music is more emotional than western European music.*

Do you agree or disagree with the statement? Why?

■ Topics for Further Research

A. Research the cultural and political history of a west African nation, such as Ghana or Nigeria, paying particular attention to musical traditions and the impact of the American slave trade.

B. How does the nation chosen balance tribal tradition with twentieth-century political and social realities?

■ Further Reading

Kaufman, Frederick and John P. Guckin. *The African Roots of Jazz.* Sherman Oaks, Calif.: Alfred Publishing Co., 1979. (Chapters 2–7)

Nettl, Bruno, et. al. *Folk and Traditional Music of the Western Continents*, 3rd ed. Englewood Cliffs, N.J.: Prentice-Hall, 1990. (Chapter 7)

■ Further Listening

Graceland, Paul Simon. Warner Brothers, 2-25447.

Synchro System, King Sunny Ade and His African Beats. Mango, 162-539737-2.

■ Films and Videos

Accapella (video). Directed by Spike Lee.

Jazz Parades (video). Narrated by Alan Lomax.

Malcolm X (1992). Directed by Spike Lee.

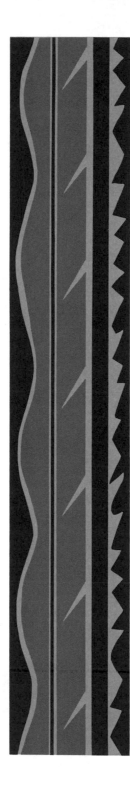

3
CONTRIBUTIONS FROM WESTERN EUROPE

/■/

A goodly song we here have writ
For singing in four parts—to wit,
The Tenor, Cantus, Alto, Bass
A courtly text do interlace
And prettily together fit,
In sweetest concord sounding it.
To lift up hearts in glad content.
'Twas Amphion did the song invent.

—HANS SACHS*

■/■ GEOGRAPHY AND CULTURE

Geography and climate must be considered when studying the history of any civilization or society. For instance, the colder climate, with its cycle of four seasons, undoubtedly had an effect upon the development of European culture and art. Survival in climates with short growing seasons and long, cold winters demands long-range organization and planning.

Central and western Africa, for the most part, have two seasons: the dry season and the rainy season. The rainy season is short and the growing season lasts most of the year, so little planning is needed to

---

*Sixteenth century: "The Singers." Trans. by Christiane Cooper.

prepare for the future. Survival in the jungle, however, depends upon spontaneity. A quick response to sudden danger is needed.

The climatic differences between Europe and Africa, therefore, have contributed to the differences in their approaches to life and art. The weather cycle of most of Europe forced the primitive inhabitants of that region to think ahead and to plan—to develop logical, linear, and sequential thinking skills. These survival techniques were eventually embedded in their religion, philosophy, and art forms. Logic, planning, and meaning became important. In music this resulted in distinct differences between beginnings, middles, and endings.

Reading, a linear skill, became an important part of learning in Europe. Architecture, books, painting, and sculpture all thrived in the colder and dryer European climatic environment. The high-art music of western civilization (classical music and opera) requires planning and preconception in both its creation and performance. In contrast, the high art of African tribal civilization required spontaneity and flexibility, with very little preplanning—either in conception or performance.

The electronic-cybernetic world culture that is developing today demands both linear and spontaneous creative skills. We live today in one of the most exciting periods in history, a period when the differences between East and West are disappearing and creative and cultural interaction are becoming necessities for survival.

Usually, major social changes occur in the arts before they occur in everyday life. Jazz is just one of the many arts moving toward this synthesis between Eastern and Western thought. To date, aside from jazz, the most successful cultural integration in the arts has occurred in modern dance and comedy. Both demand a balance between the preconceived and the spontaneous.

Popular television shows, like "In Living Color" and "Saturday Night Live," have standardized formats that balance the preconceived and the spontaneous. Talk-show hosts, like Johnny Carson and Phil Donahue, have attracted large audiences by balancing their formats. Guests who are liable to say or do spontaneous, outrageous things have always been popular on these types of television shows.

LISTENING ASSIGNMENT

"Django," The Modern Jazz Quartet. *Smithsonian Collection of Classic Jazz*, side A, #1 ▪ Notice the classical approach used at the beginning and ending of this piece to give it a "European" quality.

folk music: music handed down within a culture, often by oral tradition

rhythm: the pattern of long and short notes and accented and unaccented beats, encompassing both tempo and meter

time signature: a symbol, such as $\frac{4}{4}$ or $\frac{3}{4}$, used in written music to describe the grouping of beats per measure

measure: the unit of music contained between two bar lines

phrase: a short unit of song—the musical equivalent of a sentence

period: a musical passage within a composition, complete in itself—the musical equivalent of a paragraph

form: the internal structure of a musical composition

Spontaneity and predictability are also balanced today by most top artists in rock and pop concerts. Even modern-day sports games offer the excitement of predictability and spontaneity in a loosely combined format.

It was inevitable that the improvised skills of jazz and the conventional styles of European classical music would combine with American popular and folk music. There had to be a blending of these three diverse traditions into one style for America to lay claim to an original music of its own.

■/■ RHYTHM

Syncopated rhythms have been suspect in Europe ever since Saint Augustine wrote the *City of God* in the fifth century. Saint Augustine outlined the agony of the European man who felt that he had to suppress his natural base instincts or be consumed by them. To Saint Augustine, moderation or compromise was not possible.

Our natural instincts are closely tied to the rhythms and drives of our bodies. According to Saint Augustine, syncopated rhythms activate unconscious body movements like clapping and foot tapping, thus leading to the surrender of the conscious mind's control over the body's drives. Supposedly, this eventually weakens the mind's ability to suppress the body's baser instincts. As a result of Saint Augustine's influence on the medieval mind, syncopated rhythms were eventually driven out of all formal European music and did not begin to reappear until the end of the nineteenth century. What this did to European music was to force it to emphasize melody, form, and harmony over rhythm and to emphasize the preconceived over the spontaneous in performance. The situation, of course, was the reverse in Africa, where rhythm was *the* most important ingredient of music.

European traditions, however, did introduce some necessary rhythmic innovations to American jazz. The use of time signatures and the division of written music into measures, phrases, and periods were important European contributions. In fact, the whole tradition of putting music into written form was a European innovation.

■/■ FORM

Form was only loosely defined in African music. The internal structure of a musical composition could vary widely from performance to performance. If this African "looseness" regarding form was transferred to traditional theater, then no two performances of *Hamlet* would ever be the same because the actors could choose, in the course of the play, to

fugue: a polyphonic type of composition used in baroque music

prelude: a piece of music used as an introduction to a fugue

baroque: the style in music, art, and architecture, characterized by ornament and dramatic effect, that was at its height in Europe from approximately 1600 to 1750

melody: a succession of single notes producing a distinct musical idea

sonata: a solo form common to western European classical music, usually three or four movements (sections) in length

concerto: an instrumental solo accompanied by a symphony orchestra

symphony: a classical music work for orchestra in three or four movements

opera: a play set to music, in which the dialogue is sung to the accompaniment of an orchestra

harmony: the combination of tones into chords and chord progressions

nonharmonic music: music that lacks functional harmony

chord: a combination of two or more notes sounded simultaneously

chord progression: a series of chords that relate to each other

ad-lib or leave out lines or to change the action around a bit—just so long as they started and ended together. What a *Hamlet* that would be!

The European concept of "form" in music resembled the European concept of "lines" in architecture. Composers carefully measured the stresses and balances of their musical phrases against each other, keeping in mind the symmetry of the whole composition.

In a cathedral such as Notre Dame in Paris, you can see the visual expression of the European's need for order and balance. To the European mind, symmetry, logic, and balance were necessary for artistic satisfaction. Musical forms like the fugue and prelude, used by Bach and Handel during the baroque period (1600–1750), were comparable to the basic architectural principles used to build the great cathedrals.

The European concept of "musical form" is one of the most important contributions to Afro-American music. Form imposes logic and symmetry without destroying spontaneity. Form also controls and balances content, allowing the preconceived and the spontaneous to complement, not compete, with each other. Form also introduces order, which is particularly important in lengthy works.

■/■ MELODY

Jazz musicians are strongly influenced by the creative concepts of melody writing developed in Europe. The melodies of sonatas, concertos, symphonies, and operas are probably the most important European contribution to world music. Jazz is indebted to Europe for refining and developing practical and aesthetic concepts regarding melody.

■/■ HARMONY

The complex harmonic system developed in Europe is another important contribution to world music in general and to jazz in particular. African tribal music is *nonharmonic*; that is, it relies on the excitement of syncopated layered rhythms and continuous melodic improvisation, rather than on chords and chord progressions. The concept of vertical organization of two or more notes into units called *chords* is a western European phenomenon not common to African tribal music. Neither are the often complicated chord progressions found in western European classical music.

The strong emphasis on rhythm is what gives jazz its emotion; chords and chord progressions are what make it logical and interesting. Jazz balances emotion with logic by adding the European dimension of harmony to the African dimension of rhythm.

SOPRANO SAX   C-MELODY SAX   ALTO SAX   TENOR SAX

From an ad for saxophones, 1931.
[Picture Collection, The Branch Libraries, The New York Public Library.]

heavy metal: a heavily amplified, aggressively played rock style

saxophone: a wind instrument consisting of a conical brass tube, keys, and a single-reed mouthpiece

clarinet: a single-reed wind instrument with finger holes and keys

flute: a wind instrument that produces sound as air is blown across a hole

reed instrument: an instrument that has a cane reed attached to a mouthpiece, which passes the vibration caused by a stream of air into the tube of the instrument

soprano, alto, tenor, baritone, and bass sax: members of the saxophone family, in order of descending pitch

Today, the monotonous mumblings of the fringe heavy-metal rock groups show what music is like when it is based almost entirely on raw, primitive emotion. On the other hand, the bewildering world of highly stylized twentieth-century classical composition—with its emphasis on everything *but* emotion—is equally disturbing. Jazz balances these two extreme musical points of view.

■/■ INSTRUMENTS

One of the most important western European contributions to jazz was its musical instruments, and of these, among the most important was the saxophone.

Saxophone. The saxophone was invented in the nineteenth century by a Belgian named Adolphe Sax, largely because Napoleon liked marching bands (they inspired his troops) and the clarinet and flute were impractical wind instruments for a marching band. The last of the reed-instrument family to develop (it was not commonly used until after 1920), the saxophone has become one of the most popular instruments in jazz. The saxophone family includes the soprano, the alto, the tenor, the baritone, and the bass. In jazz, the alto and tenor sax are the most popular instruments.

piano: a musical instrument in which felt-covered hammers, operated from a keyboard, strike metal strings

dynamic range: the range of sounds, from the softest to the loudest

keyboard instrument: an instrument, such as the synthesizer, piano, or organ, operated by pressing the keys on a keyboard

pipe organ: a keyboard instrument in which compressed air entering pipes creates sound

clavichord: a keyboard instrument in which depressing a key causes a metal blade (a *tangent*) to strike a string

virginal: a rectangular harpsichord popular in the 16th and 17th centuries

spinet: a small harpsichord or a small upright piano

harpsichord: the precursor to the piano; a keyboard instrument in which strings are plucked by leather or quill parts attached to keys

guitar: a stringed instrument with a long fretted neck, a flat body, and typically, six strings which are plucked or strummed

violin: the soprano instrument of the string family, held horizontally against the shoulder or collarbone and bowed

banjo: a plucked string instrument

marimba: an instrument made of strips of

Spinet. [Picture Collection, The Branch Libraries, The New York Public Library.]

Piano.   The piano was invented in 1709 by an Italian named Bartolommeo Cristofori. The piano was developed to offer a wider *dynamic* ("soft-to-loud") *range* of expression. Previous keyboard instruments, with the exception of the pipe organ, were very limited dynamically. The original name of the piano was *piano e forte* ("soft and strong"). The piano allowed a much wider range of musical expressiveness than its predecessors, the clavichord, virginal, spinet, and harpsichord. By the early 1800s, the piano had become the premier European instrument. Throughout the history of Afro-American music, the piano has held center stage.

Guitar, Violin, and Banjo.   Both the guitar and the violin (in a much more primitive form) originated in Africa, as did the banjo, marimba, and the xylophone. Long before the improved European versions, Africa had also developed its own string, woodwind, brass, and percussion instruments. Western Europe, however, with its talent for technology, science, and manufacturing, soon managed to improve on all of these musical instruments.

wood that are amplified underneath with tubes and that are struck with sticks

xylophone: a high-pitched, bright-sounding instrument made of graduated wooden bars which are struck with mallets

string instruments: a family of instruments having strings stretched across a frame that are bowed or plucked

woodwind instruments: a family of instruments in which sound is produced by a current of air passing over a reed or an open aperture

brass instruments: a family of wind instruments usually made of brass, and played by the buzzing of lips through a brass mouthpiece

percussion instruments: a family of instruments played by striking with the hands or a stick or other object

Jazz benefited from its access to European instruments which, except for percussion instruments, are capable of a much wider range of musical expression.

Brass Instruments. The brass instruments used in jazz today—the trumpet, cornet, flügelhorn, trombone, and occasionally, the tuba and French horn—were all developed in Europe. So called because they are made out of brass, usually coated with a gold or silver lacquer finish, brass instruments were familiar to Africans long before they were improved upon by Europeans. African trumpets, however, were used only for special occasions, such as signaling the arrival of the chief of the tribe.

The soprano-alto voices in the brass family are the cornet, trumpet, and flügelhorn. They all sound in the same register, but have slightly different tonal qualities. The cornet, a cousin of the trumpet, has a more mellow sound and looks smaller. The trumpet, because of its more brilliant tone, began to succeed the cornet in popularity in jazz of the 1930s, eventually replacing the cornet altogether, except in traditional New Orleans groups. Because of the carrying power of both instruments, they always carried the lead or melody in the early New Orleans marching bands and Dixieland ensembles. The flügelhorn, possessing a rich and mellow sound, did not become a commonly used jazz instrument until the 1960s.

Tenor banjos.   **Tuba.**   **French Horn.**

[Picture Collection, The Branch Libraries, The New York Public Library.]

trumpet: a powerful soprano brass instrument consisting of a cup-shaped mouthpiece, a curved tube, and a flaring open end

cornet: a soprano brass instrument

flügelhorn: a mellow-sounding alto brass instrument

trombone: a tenor brass instrument with a slide

tuba: the bass instrument of the brass family

French horn: an alto instrument of the brass family

register: the tonal range of an instrument or voice from its lowest note to its highest

tonal quality: the character of sound peculiar to a specific instrument

tenor range: the range of notes comprising the next-to-lowest part of four-part harmony; a high-pitched male voice range

slide: the U-shaped section of a trombone that can be pushed in or out to change the length of the air column and alter the pitch

pitch: the degree to which an instrument, voice, or sound is high or low

contrapuntal line: the secondary of two or more combined melodies

lead line: the main melody

sousaphone: a type of brass tuba

string bass/bass viol: the largest and lowest

The trombone is lower in pitch than the cornet or trumpet. It sounds in the tenor range. Because of its slide, the trombone can quickly and easily adjust pitch and can blend more easily with voices than can the cornet or trumpet. In jazz, the tenor trombone is favored. This instrument is part of the Dixieland ensemble front line, usually playing a *contrapuntal line* (second melody) against the trumpet's *lead line* (main melody).

The bass voice in the brass choir is the tuba, sometimes called the *sousaphone*. It was used as the bass-line instrument in early New Orleans bands. By the mid-1920s the brass bass had been replaced by the more flexible string bass, or bass viol, which is also less fatiguing to play.

Saxophone and trombone in a vaudeville act, about 1927. [Picture Collection, The Branch Libraries, The New York Public Library.]

pitched instrument of the string family

cymbals: brass or bronze disks played by striking with a mallet or against one another to produce a sharp, ringing sound

conga: a tall conical drum played with the hands

bongos: a pair of small tuned drums played with the fingers

cowbell: an Afro-Cuban percussion instrument, sometimes called *cencerro* or *campana*

claves: cherry-wood sticks struck together for rhythmic accompaniment in Afro-Latin music

maracas: a pair of gourd-shaped rattles filled with seeds or pebbles and used as a rhythm instrument

tambourine: a small open drum with metal jingles

tambourim: a variant of the tambourine, without metal jingles

timbales: two con-joined open metal drums, similar to bongos, but wider in diameter and played with drumsticks

high-hat cymbals: a pair of cymbals mounted on a rod so that the push of a pedal can drop the upper onto the lower

foot-pedal: a drum-set device that allows a drummer to operate the bass drum with his foot

samba whistle: a whistle used to signal dance-step changes in a samba march

Percussion Instruments. Almost all of the percussion instruments commonly used in the West today are of African origin. The jazz drummer's cymbals originated in Africa, but Turkey perfected the process that produces the sound of the modern cymbal. Even today, most good cymbals are made in Turkey.

Latin percussion instruments—the conga, bongos, cowbell, claves, tambourim (a variant of the tambourine), maracas, and timbales—are all African in origin and have undergone few changes. Only the high-hat cymbal, foot-pedal, and the samba whistle are American in origin. The idea of having one drummer assume several tasks is American and grew out of a jazz tradition developed early on in the New Orleans marching (brass) bands.

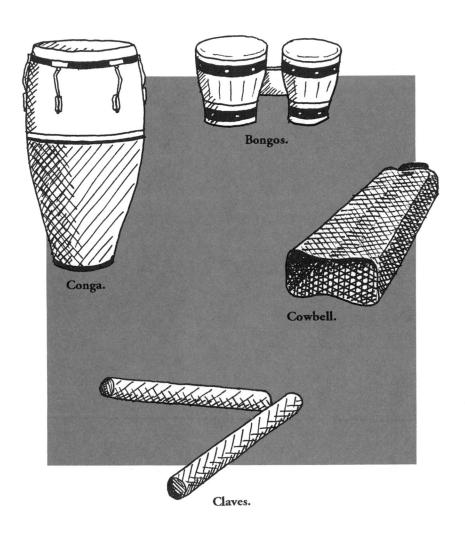

Bongos.

Conga.

Cowbell.

Claves.

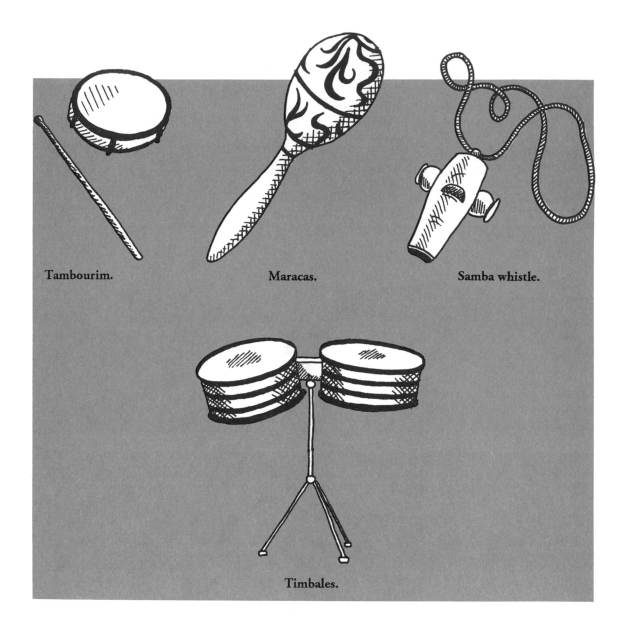

Tambourim.

Maracas.

Samba whistle.

Timbales.

■/■ THE IMPORTANCE OF MUSICAL LITERACY

The emphasis on being able to read music is European in origin. Many of the early jazz musicians could not read music, but certainly could play very well by ear. However, many black musicians in New Orleans were classically trained to read music, and they taught other jazz musicians to read music as well. This opened up the rich musical heritage of western European music to black musicians and had a strong influence on the development of early instrumental jazz. Exposure to western European music in turn broadened the compositional and improvisational skills of the early black musician and was one of the reasons jazz was able to evolve from a folk art to a fine art.

Music manuscript from Bologna, 1487.
[Picture Collection, The Branch Libraries, The New York Public Library.]

swing era: a period of American music in the 1930s and '40s dominated by big-band swing music

big band: a jazz ensemble of ten or more pieces, usually made up of saxophones, trumpets, trombones, and a rhythm section (piano, bass, drums, and guitar)

jam session: an informal or impromptu gathering and performance of jazz musicians which encourages experimentation with new sounds and new styles

The swing era of the 1930s and '40s, with its emphasis on big bands, forced the few jazz musicians who could not read music to learn how. Twenty or more musicians could not play the complex arrangements written for these larger ensembles without the ability to read music. Other advantages of being musically literate included the ability to learn new music quickly. It allowed larger ensembles to play together without weeks of rehearsal. Furthermore, it enabled bands to travel and perform anywhere in the world, confident that local musicians would be able to read the written arrangements and follow the verbal stylistic instructions. The only disadvantage of musical literacy was a de-emphasis on personalization of the music and on spontaneity. Fortunately, by the 1940s, jazz styles had pretty well balanced the two skills of reading and improvising.

■/■ FORMAL CONCERTS

The European tradition of formal concerts was eventually adopted by the jazz world. This move forced jazz musicians and composer-arrangers to play and write for more critical and attentive audiences. Intellectual and aesthetic concepts were stimulated in the process, and jazz moved into the arena of fine art.

In 1924, The Paul Whiteman Orchestra premiered George Gershwin's heavily jazz-influenced *Rhapsody in Blue* in Aeolian Hall in New York City to rave reviews. Carnegie Hall allowed jazz through its doors in 1928 with W. C. Handy's concert and ten years later with the wildly successful Benny Goodman Carnegie Hall Concert. Duke Ellington continued the tradition from the 1940s through the 1960s with annual concerts of serious jazz.

Norman Granz's "Jazz at the Philharmonic," one of the first successful touring jazz concerts, began in the late 1940s. The Granz concept of

> **LISTENING ASSIGNMENT**
>
> "The Birth of 'Rhapsody in Blue': Paul Whiteman's Historic Aeolian Hall Concert of 1924." Musical Heritage Society, MHC 229531X, cassette #2, side 4 ▪ This is a reconstruction of the original concert, with the original orchestration. Although it lacks improvisation, it contains a lot of influences from early jazz. Would you classify this as a classical work with jazz influences or as a jazz piece presented in a classical format?

allowing the audience to witness an authentic *jam session* conducted by the top jazz players of the day helped to solidify the concept of jazz being presented in a formal concert format.

Audiences want to be intellectually challenged as well as emotionally stimulated by the music of today. The move towards a concert setting helped jazz to focus and refine its style and to appeal to a broader audience.

SUMMARY

An emphasis on logical, linear, and sequential thinking developed in Europe in response to a seasonal climate that required advance planning. European art and music, consequently, stress structure and forethought, in contrast to the African emphasis on spontaneity and flexibility.

Despite a de-emphasis on rhythm and a religious distrust of syncopation, which was too closely tied to the body's "base" natural instincts, the European tradition did contribute written rhythmic innovations to American jazz—time signatures and the division of written music into measures and phrases. The European concept of form emphasized symmetry and balance in a composition, allowing the preconceived and the spontaneous, which coexist in Afro-American music, to complement each other, rather than compete. The European tradition also contributed aesthetic concepts regarding melody and a complex harmonic system based on chords and chord progressions. Important jazz and pop instruments, such as the saxophone and piano, were also developed in Europe, although most commonly used percussion instruments are African in origin. The importance today of musical literacy and the rich heritage of written European music available to the American musician are both passed down from the European tradition, as is the use of formal concerts, which eventually encouraged jazz musicians and composers to perform for more critical audiences.

Obviously, western European contributions to jazz are as important as are the African contributions. It's impossible to have "jazz" without both musical traditions. In the brief period of jazz's history, any attempt to separate these two traditions has failed.

Jazz brings a balance to twentieth-century music. This balance between the preconceived and the spontaneous is now an expected part of any concert—not only jazz concerts, but also pop, rock, and even some of today's classical music concerts.

Jazz is neither African nor European; it is American. The contribution of American political concepts and culture were vital to the birth and development of what would eventually become a widely respected and enjoyed international art form. Being "born in the U.S.A." was necessary for the evolution and development of jazz.

A. *In your own words* write one or two sentences describing each of the terms listed in Questions 1–10.

1. folk music _____

_____

2. baroque _____

_____

3. rhythm _____

_____

4. melody _____

_____

5. concerto _____

_____

6. symphony _____

_____

7. opera _____

_____

8. register _____

_____

9. contrapuntal line _____

_____

10. jam session _____

_____

In Questions 11–20 fill in the blanks.

11. _____ is the phrase structure that holds a musical piece together.

12. A _____ is a combination of two or more notes sounded simultaneously.

13. _____ is a heavily amplified, aggressively played rock style.

14. The saxophone, clarinet, and flute are examples of _____ instruments.

15. The piano, organ, and synthesizer are examples of _____ instruments.

16. The violin, guitar, and banjo are examples of _____ instruments.

17. A _____ is made of strips of wood that are struck with sticks and are amplified with tubes underneath.

18. In _____ instruments the sound is produced by a current of air that passes over a reed or an open aperture.

19. _____ instruments are played by striking with the hands or a stick or other object.

20. A rhythm instrument consisting of a pair of gourd-shaped rattles that are filled with seeds or pebbles is called _____ .

B. 21. How did geography and climate play a role in the development of western European music and art?

22. Why was the Church opposed to syncopated rhythms?

23. What are the most important contributions of western European music to jazz?

24. Which European musical instruments are most prominently featured in instrumental jazz?

25. Which commonly used jazz instruments are African in origin?

26. Why did musical literacy become important to jazz as bands grew larger?

27. Discuss the statement,

   Spontaneity is more important in jazz than in western European classical music.

   Do you agree or disagree with the statement? Why?

■ Topics for Further Research

A. Discuss musical forms of the baroque period. What did these forms have in common with each other and with the artistic ideals of the period?

B. Describe the evolution of the piano from earlier keyboard instruments, such as the clavichord, virginal, spinet, and harpsichord.

■ Further Reading

Grout, Donald J. and Claude Palisca. *A History of Western Music*, 4th ed. New York: W. W. Norton & Co., 1988. (Chapters 1–12)

Nettl, Bruno, et. al. *Folk and Traditional Music of the Western Continents*, 3rd ed. Englewood Cliffs, N.J.: Prentice-Hall, 1990. (Chapters 3–6)

■ Further Listening

Carmen, Bizet.

Emperor Piano Concerto, The, Beethoven.

Four Seasons, The, Vivaldi.

Symphony No. 5, Shostakovich. The Leningrad Symphony.

■ Films and Videos

Amadeus (1984). The life and music of Mozart.

Impromptu (1991). Chopin and Liszt featured.

Music Teacher, The (1988). Belgian.

4
BORN IN THE
U.S.A.

/■/

Take a sound
from an African rain forest.
Mix it with the sobs and wails of slaves.
Throw in a little military-band music,
a few familiar Christian hymns,
a sea chantey, and a work song or two—
and you have a new sound,
something never heard before
anywhere in the world.
Add some technological things,
like phonographs and radios,
railroads, mass production,
Hollywood, installment buying,
mass advertising, and eternal optimism,
and you have the American dream.
Its theme song is jazz!

—JW

———

JAZZ was born in the United States. Its cultural roots are in Africa and Europe, but it was conceived in America, and it was the political and cultural experiences within the United States itself that shaped European and African music into jazz.

minstrel show: a popular 19th-century entertainment originally involving white singers, dancers, and comedians performing in blackface. After the Civil War, black minstrelsy flourished.

coon songs/Ethiopian songs: late 19th- and early 20th-century songs by white minstrels about blacks that reinforced racial stereotypes

jubilee: an all-black pre-Civil War plantation show

Early settlers in America brought with them a ragbag of mostly western European traditions out of which this country called America grew. But the skills necessary to explore, settle, and conquer a continent demanded a practicality that often warred with these cultural and historical traditions. As a result, Americans became pragmatists and futurists, willing to try anything once and willing to discard anything from the past that didn't adapt well to their new environment.

As has been stated, the most important event in the history of Afro-American music was the coming together of two divergent musical styles and traditions. These two musical traditions not only took widely different approaches to the art of making music, but had different mindsets regarding their concepts of "reality."

Jazz might have been the first art form to bring two widely different cultural traditions together, but it will not be the last. The same thing is happening in dance, fashion, literature, and cinema. As science increasingly shrinks the size of the world, art cannot help but move in the direction of integrating widely divergent styles and concepts.

▪/▪ THE MINSTREL SHOW

The *minstrel show* was a distinctly American entertainment. This form of entertainment began in northern cities in the 1820s with all white performers, who were gradually replaced by black entertainers from the 1840s on. The popularity of the minstrel show reached a zenith between 1850 and 1870. It's no accident that minstrel shows became popular at a time when racial tensions were increasing. The portrayal in most of the songs and skits of the black slave leading a humorous, childlike, and carefree life was designed to relieve some of the growing guilt and anxiety over the slave issue that would soon divide the nation.

White men dubbed their faces black, sang "coon" songs and "Ethiopian" songs, and, in general, made a travesty of the black experience in the South. The *coon song*, an outgrowth of white minstrelsy, often portrayed the black American as a childish, oversexed buffoon, thus helping to reinforce racial stereotypes that later generations of black artists had to work to overcome. These "coon" songs were very popular and made a lot of money for the sheet-music industry in the late 1800s and early 1900s.

The idea for the minstrel show originated with a northern white musician who had visited a southern plantation and witnessed an all-black show called a *jubilee*. Jubilees were performed at holidays and on special occasions by slaves for their masters, usually on the lawn in front of the "Big House." For the jubilee, slaves dressed in their master's

A vaudeville "coon" act, 1905.

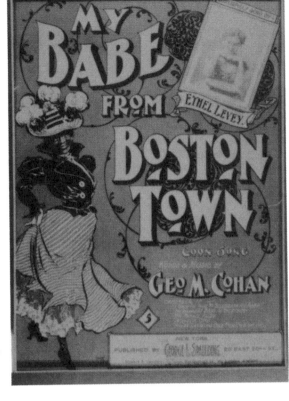

The sheet-music cover for
George M. Cohan's song
is labeled "coon song."

[Picture Collection, The Branch Libraries, The New York Public Library.]

makin' juba: a lively dance, accompanied by rhythmic hand-clapping and body-slapping, developed by plantation slaves

vaudeville: one of the most popular entertainment forms in America from about 1900 to 1930—consisting of animal acts, jugglers, singers, mimes, and other individual and group performances

and mistress's old clothes and mimicked them in song and dance. Special rewards—usually in the form of sweets—were given for the best performances.

Makin' juba was a form of self-entertainment slaves enjoyed during the brief rest periods in their daily routines. Several slaves (usually males) would form a circle, facing each other in pairs. To the cadence of a four-beat rhythm, they would tap their feet on beats one and three and clap their hands on beats two and four. One at a time, each slave would improvise a rhythmic solo by slapping his hands on his body, or on any handy utensil. This eventually developed into tap dancing.

At the time of the jubilee, talented and energetic young male slaves were encouraged to strut in competition. The winner would get a cake as a prize. These "cakewalk" steps were later incorporated into vaudeville dance routines.

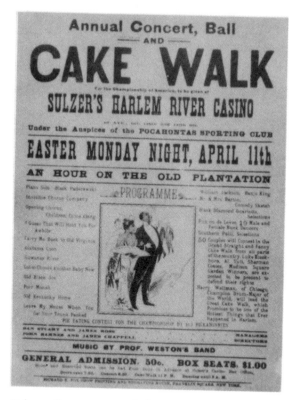

Cake walk—poster and sheet-music cover. [Picture Collection, The Branch Libraries, The New York Public Library.]

Jim Crow: a caricature of the male plantation slave

Zip Coon: a late-nineteenth-century caricature of the urban black male

comic sallies: sketches that poke fun at society or specific individuals

variety show: a vaudeville show consisting of individual performances of songs, dances, and skits

Africans have a long tradition of mimicry, and so they took to this new type of entertainment like ducks to water. Their skits were entertaining and unusual. No wonder some enterprising northerner saw the value in re-creating these skits for northern audiences. As mentioned earlier, the skits and songs also captured the lighthearted, childlike nature of the slave without focusing on the darker moments and the hopelessness of the situation. Eileen Southern, in her book *The Music of Black Americans*, comments:

Two basic types of slave impersonations were developed: one in caricature of the plantation slave with his ragged clothes and thick dialect; the other portraying the city slave, the dandy dressed in the latest fashion, who boasted of his exploits among the ladies. The former was referred to as Jim Crow and the latter as Zip Coon.*

Comic sallies, solos, variety shows, parodies, sketches, and dances were all included in these early all-white minstrel shows. The minstrel

*pp. 88–90.

show was the first musical format to display the amazing creativity, humor, and originality of the black man to white audiences—through white actors. Although the minstrel show was, on the whole, an insult to the dignity of black Americans, it served, nevertheless, to demonstrate their originality and talent.

The Africans' love for music and their seemingly "natural" sense of rhythm led to the establishment of many all-black orchestras on southern plantations before the Civil War. The fact that playing in the orchestra meant that you could avoid backbreaking labor and get better food and accommodations encouraged many young black slaves to develop their musical skills.

After the Civil War, all-black minstrel groups toured in lively shows performed in large tents or theaters. When one of these groups arrived in town, the members would quickly form a parade and, dressed in their flashiest clothes, march down the town's main street while their brass band *ragged a march* (syncopated a traditional military tune). These early bands were precursors of early instrumental jazz, later called *Dixieland.* The minstrel show itself was the forerunner of the all-black New York Broadway musical revues that began in the 1920s.

Jim Crow, as depicted in an American lithograph from about 1830. [Picture Collection, The Branch Libraries, The New York Public Library.]

A scene from the motion picture, *Minstrel Man.* [Photofest.]

Stephen Foster, one of the first widely popular American song-writers, wrote for minstrel groups such as Christy's Minstrels, in the 1840s to 1860s. Although he lacked formal musical training, he had a natural gift for composing poignant and timeless melodies. His knowledge of black singing came from black church services and minstrel shows. His charm came from the simplicity and directness of his music. His sentimental songs about the South (although he grew up in Cincinnati) helped to keep the post-Civil War minstrel show a popular form of American entertainment.

The first important black composer in the Afro-American tradition, James Bland, wrote music for black minstrel shows in the late 1800s. Many of his songs were later published by the growing sheet-music industry in New York and have become a permanent part of our pop-

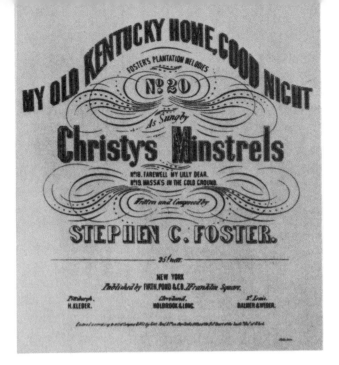

A copy of the sheet music of Foster's *My Old Kentucky Home*. [Picture Collection, The Branch Libraries, The New York Public Library.]

tune repertoire. Among his more familiar songs are *In the Evening by the Moonlight*, *Oh, Dem Golden Slippers*, and *Carry Me Back to Old Virginny*. Eileen Southern says this about James Bland:

> At the height of his fame, James Bland (1854–1911) was advertised as "The World's Greatest Minstrel Man" and "The Idol of the Music Halls." His songs were sung by all the minstrels, black and white—by college students, and by the American people in their homes and on the streets.*

■/■ RELIGIOUS MUSIC

Many immigrants were fleeing religious persecution in Europe when they came to the American colonies in the seventeenth and eighteenth centuries. For this reason, religious music—particularly hymns, carols, spirituals, and gospel songs—has always been an important part of our nation's musical heritage. The simple structure of the early Protestant hymns was the foundation for most black spirituals, gospel songs, and, later, the blues.

---

* The Music of Black Americans: A History, 2nd ed., p. 234.

One of the first styles of music the black slave was exposed to in the New World was religious music. Slave owners reluctantly admitted that black people were human and, consequently, had souls that needed to be saved, according to Christian doctrine. White plantation owners therefore usually offered some sort of primitive spiritual training to black slaves. In most instances, religious gatherings were the only social events permitted to blacks on the plantations. Black church services were often the only opportunity for blacks in the pre-Civil War South to gather together in large groups.

The balconies in many white churches were designated *Colored*, and blacks were sometimes allowed to attend. Later, free itinerant black preachers were allowed to minister to the spiritual needs of plantation slaves. These black preachers controlled the emotional pace of their services in much the same way that interlocutors in minstrel shows and masters of ceremony in vaudeville revues controlled the pace, energy, and emotion in these early forms of entertainment. In 1801, Richard Allen, minister of the African Methodist Episcopal Church, published a hymnal designed specifically for his all-black congregation. This was an important event in the history of both black music and the black Christian church in America.

The participation of blacks in the revival movement, called the "Second Awakening" (1780–1830), exposed many white worshippers for the first time to black music, style of worship, and dance. Foreign visitors to the United States marveled at the emotional intensity, stamina, and rhythmic inventiveness of this new style of worship. The diary of one white eyewitness to these events records this impression of white and black worshippers at one of these camp meetings:

> Their shouts and singing were so very boisterous that the singing of the white congregation was often completely drowned in the echoes and reverberations of the colored people's tumultuous strains.*

The black spiritual was partially shaped by the setting of these evangelical religious camp meetings, where thousands of blacks and whites, sitting in separate sections, assembled under the stars and, amid the blaze of campfires, listened to fiery preachers tell them about the glories of heaven and the fiery pits of hell.

Spirituals. Unfortunately, most of the slaves sent to the United States were restricted in their singing, but white masters were reluctant

---

*Fredrika Bremer, *The Homes of the New World*, vol. 1 (New York: Harper & Bros., 1853), pp. 306–17.

to stop a slave from humming or softly singing a spiritual or hymn.

Slaves expressed feelings of frustration, humiliation, rage, and impotence through their music. The lyrics of Negro spirituals generally dealt with a better life to be found somewhere—if not now, then in the next life.

Some of the slower spirituals featured lyrics that expressed only despair and hopelessness. Perhaps the best known of these is *Lay This Body Down*. Some other slow spirituals included *Go Down, Moses*; *Deep River*; *I Want To Go Home*; *Nobody Knows de Trouble I've Had*; *Sweet Little Jesus Boy*; *When My Trials Are Over*; and *I Never Heard Nobody Pray*.

The deeply moving spirituals that developed in the black community between the early 1600s and the Civil War contain some of the world's most beautiful melodies. European composers soon discovered this vast wealth of new music and used its original melodies as themes for their symphonies, concertos, ballets, and operas.

Antonin Dvorak, the world-renowned Czech composer, visited America in the late 1800s, came in contact with spirituals, and incorporated several of them in his *New World* symphony. The slow movement of this symphony is based upon the popular negro spiritual *Goin' Home*.

Not all spirituals were slow and serious, however. There were lively spirituals, as well. These lively spirituals, always an important part of the pre-Civil War black church service, were usually very syncopated. Rhythmically, Africans maintained their prediliction for syncopation by clapping hands on the second and fourth beats of the measure and singing or playing behind the beat, thus creating rhythmic tension. A partial list of some of the more familiar lively black spirituals from this period would include *Michael, Row the Boat Ashore*; *All God's Chillun' Got Shoes*; *Down by the Riverside*; *When the Saints Go Marchin' In*; and *Dry Bones*.

Black spirituals, in fact, fell into a number of categories. Some were meant to be sung only during religious services, whereas others were

---

LISTENING ASSIGNMENT

"Soon and Very Soon," Andrae Crouch. *Big Town*, Atlantic (CD) 82185-2 ▪ At the very end of this modern-gospel selection, Andrae Crouch tries to re-create the authentic spiritual sound as it was sung on the pre-Civil War plantations. Notice the leader and chorus, the steady rhythm, the freely improvised sounds of the leader, and the use of the small drum or tambourine.

An early spiritual, *No More Peck o' Corn for Me.*

designed to be sung while "sittin' around." Some were intended to be used only in conjunction with the *shout*, a syncopated circle dance (usually led by someone with a tambourine) in which the original African custom of worshiping by singing and dancing was revived. The names given to these lively spirituals were *shout spirituals*, *ring spirituals*, or *running spirituals*. Some of the more popular of the southern black-church shouting spirituals were *Oh, We'll Walk Around the Fountain*; *The Bells Done Ring*; *Pray All the Members*; *Go Ring That Bell*; and *I Can't Stay Behind*.

Many spirituals were thinly disguised songs of protest. The lyrics often dealt with Old Testament stories about Israel's bondage, first in Egypt and then in Babylonia. A "promised land" and the emergence of a powerful leader who would one day set the slaves free were often the focal points of the lyrics.

The day-to-day suffering of the slaves was eased by the promise of a better tomorrow. Spirituals gave the black man hope, by allowing slaves to look forward to a brighter tomorrow, in heaven.

Spirituals were also used to signal from one plantation to another, particularly during the time when the underground railroad was engaged in smuggling slaves north to freedom.

Mastering the art of *double entendre* ("dual meaning"), Afro-Americans often communicated at two different levels through the lyrics of their early songs. One meaning was for the white owners and society in general; the second, more subtle, meaning was for the slaves themselves. Spirituals such as *Steal Away*; *Didn't My Lord Deliver Daniel?*; and *Children, We All Shall Be Free* were meant as incitements to escape from bondage, whereas *We'll Stand the Storm* and *We Shall Walk Through the Valley in Peace* were meant to comfort faltering spirits. "The River Jordan" was, on another level, the Ohio River, the dividing line between free and

gospel: a religious vocal
style that developed after
the Civil War, emphasiz-
ing the New Testament
and personal salvation. It
evolved into modern
gospel in the 1930s.

acoustic guitar: a guitar
that is not electrically
amplified or modified

slave states. Shoes (*All God's Children Got Shoes*) were symbols of "free" blacks. (Field hands were required to work barefoot to discourage them from running away.)

After the Civil War, freed blacks began to dislike spirituals because of their association with slavery. Since there are no recordings of early spirituals, one can only guess at the energy and emotion of the early performances, which were usually unaccompanied, or accompanied only by hand clapping. Many early spirituals were preserved in written form, but before the invention of the phonograph, there was no way to pre-serve Afro-American musical style. Fortunately, the invention of the phonograph allowed us to preserve later performances of spirituals.

The strongest and most lasting contributions to jazz made by black spirituals in the pre-Civil War period include:

1. The introduction of subtle syncopation (off-beat rhythms).
2. The use of spontaneous blue notes, which altered the origi-nal melody.
3. The personalizing of song material, using improvisation and tonal distortion.
4. The emotionalized interpretations, using shouts, moans, glissandos, growls, falsettos, buzz tones, whispers, and yells—thus intensifying the lyrics and song.
5. The use of the African call-and-response patterns.

The fact that the performances were improvised meant that no two per-formances were ever the same.

Early Gospel. After the Civil War, gospel songs succeeded black spirituals as the religious musical style in the black community. Early gospel music was generally sung by individuals, trios, or quartets. The accompaniment was usually acoustic guitar, piano, or banjo. The tam-bourine was sometimes added as a percussion instrument.

Freedom meant a complete change of life-style for blacks. No longer guided or controlled by the group ethics of communal living and the standards of the plantation, blacks now had to deal with the world as free men and women and had to become self-sufficient.

This change of life style was reflected in the lyrics of early gospel songs, which emphasized individual responsibility and personal salva-tion, rather than group sufferings and longings.

Technology had a hand in changing the lyrics, as well. Probably no technological development in the late nineteenth century so affected black Americans as did the railroad. For blacks, the railroad was a sym-

modern gospel: a popularized form of emotional spiritual music rooted in early gospel, often accompanied by Hammond organ, bass, drums, and saxophone

bol of freedom, and the lure of romantic, distant places called many a young black man to wander the South, often earning a living singing the new music called *gospel* in small black churches.

One of the few ways a black man could express his freedom was to travel, something that was harder for black women to do because they bore the major responsibility in caring for the family. Moreover, society of that time did not approve of "traveling" women. The importance of the railroad in the lives of black men revealed itself in the number of gospel songs that included phrases about "getting on board the gospel train," about the railroad car wheels "rumbling through the land," and about the train that's "bound for glory!"

By the turn of the century, black preachers—with the help of singers and musicians—had become experts at whipping their congregations into states of emotional frenzy. The interplay between preacher and congregation often built to a fever pitch. This was followed by a fiery musical number featuring one or more exciting gospel singers.

Modern Gospel. There were over four million ex-slaves in the South at the end of the Civil War. Many were to leave the South for the larger northeastern cities, seeking work, fellowship, and protection from overt racism. New Orleans and Harlem had the largest black communities in the early 1900s. St. Louis, Memphis, Detroit, and Chicago eventually developed large black communities.

The modern gospel song thus developed in an urban setting and was often first heard in huge temporary tents erected for revival meetings by touring evangelists or in stadiums, tabernacles, or theaters. Gospel songwriters often borrowed their melodies and musical forms from the popular songs of the day, just as the earlier spiritual had often borrowed liberally from the wealth of American folk music readily at hand.

Many small storefront churches also sprang up in these new black ghettos, however, and lively gospel music was always an important part of their religious services. Most of these churches had their own gospel choirs. The larger established Baptist and Methodist churches often maintained two or three choirs, one of which was almost always a gospel choir.

Modern gospel music was shaped by Thomas A. Dorsey, a black blues pianist who, after being saved, gave up playing and composing secular blues songs in the 1920s in order to devote the rest of his life to composing what he called "gospel songs." His best-known song is *Precious Lord*. In 1932, Dorsey and his partner, gospel singer Sallie Martin, held the first annual Gospel Singers Convention. He inspired hundreds of touring gospel singers, ensembles, and choirs. Recently, his life was the subject of a television documentary called "Say Amen, Somebody."

Mahalia Jackson. [Photofest.]

pop: a commercial style of rock; also, any popular music written for the mainstream public before the rock 'n' roll era

By the 1940s, the record industry was discovering that recordings made by some of the better-known gospel singers were frequently best sellers, particularly those made by Rosetta Tharpe, Clara Ward, and Mahalia Jackson.

Mahalia Jackson was one of the earliest gospel singers to become famous. Fortunately, there are many recordings of her magnificent and powerful interpretations of gospel songs.

There is such a load of emotional energy, innovation, and deep feeling in gospel music that it has fed the entire pop-song industry of America since the 1950s. The many contributions made by black gospel to pop, rock, and jazz are often overlooked. Most of the current pop vocal styles have gospel roots. Soul music is built squarely on the black-gospel tradition. Even today, new groups like Take Six are reenergizing the pop-music industry with their exciting recordings of classic spirituals and gospel songs as well as new original material.

folk music: music handed down within a culture, often by oral tradition

sea chantey: a sailor's work song

Many rhythm-and-blues stars of the 1970s and '80s also evolved from the black-church tradition. Aretha Franklin, Ray Charles, James Brown, Al Green, and other pop and rhythm-and-blues singers started their careers in gospel choirs. Some, like Al Green, went back to gospel. Others, like Andrae Crouch, stayed with gospel music.

Modern gospel songs have also invaded the night clubs, gambling casinos, jazz festivals, and even the concert halls of America.

■/■ FOLK MUSIC

America is a melting pot, representing the ethnic roots of practically every race and nation in the world. As a result, America has a rich legacy of folk music: sea chanteys from off our coasts, canoeing songs from our

Barn dance, Rhode Island, about 1907. [Picture Collection, The Branch Libraries, The New York Public Library.]

American couples dancing the polka, 1848. [Picture Collection, The Branch Libraries, The New York Public Library.]

ballad: a slow and sentimental narrative folk song

barn dance: a social gathering, originally held in a barn, featuring square dancees and other forms of country music

Jew's harp: a small instrument whose frame is held in the teeth while a metal piece is plucked, producing a twanging tone

harmonica: a small wind instrument containing a set of metal reeds over which a player exhales or inhales to produce the tones

square dance: a dance involving four couples arranged in a square

novelty song: a humorous song in-

rivers, and ballads from our tall forests and wilderness areas. Down South, off the coast of the Carolinas and on the plantations, Afro-American music of all kinds flourished. In New Orleans, of course, one could hear Spanish, French, English, and Afro-American songs. On farms throughout the East and Midwest, fiddlers played at barn dances. Out West, the banjo, Jew's harp, or harmonica strummed or bowed, accompanying square dances, novelty songs, and cowboy songs.

The Irish brought their folk music to the land and sang lustily while laying steel for the transcontinental railroad that connected East and West. They were joined by powerful black steel drivers (like John Henry) who mixed their syncopated work songs with Irish *jigs* and Scottish *reels*. From the West came the sound of soft Spanish music, accompanied by a strumming guitar. In contrast were the exotic sounds of Chinese laborers as they put down steel for the transcontinental railroad.

The hora was danced vigorously at Jewish weddings, while German polkas *oom-pah-pah'd* into the night. Scottish ballads disappeared into the mountains of West Virginia, Tennessee, and Arkansas only to reemerge years later—with slightly new lyrics and melodies. The slaves did not overlook their heritage; they contributed to the pot while borrowing and adapting what they needed. According to Alan Lomax, author of *Folk Songs of North America*,

volving surprise lyrics

cowboy song: a work song of cowboys

jig: a lively, springy, irregular dance in triple meter

reel: a fast dance in which partners face each other in two lines

hora: a traditional Roumanian circle dance, now popular in Israel

polka: a lively couples dance in duple meter

litany: a solo line, often followed by a group response, resembling a form of prayer

field holler: a solo work song of post-Civil War rural black sharecroppers

intonation: something played or sung with a centered pitch

semicadence: a sequence of notes occurring midway through a verse or chorus

cadence: a sequence of notes that indicates the end of a verse or chorus

climax note: the highest note in the melody, usually occurring toward the end

Hearing the familiar strains of melodies brought over from "the old country" helped millions of blacks and whites adjust to their new, strange, and often even hostile environment.

Work Songs. Work songs were common in Africa, and slaves continued to use them after they were brought to the New World as a weapon against fatigue, boredom, loneliness, isolation, helplessness, and rage. The African structure in most of their work songs involved the use of a long *litany* (solo line) followed by a group response, usually comprising the second half of the tune. The litany lines are usually unrhymed, allowing the solo singer maximum freedom to improvise his rendition. Like most African poetry, these work songs achieve their striking aesthetic effect with startling imagery, balancing traditional formulations with fresh images, and with constant repetition.

Work songs were sung about the sea, the railroad, the levee, the fields, and other places where Americans labored. Singing in the fields helped to pass the time and helped to keep up the morale of the field hands.

The *field holler* was a solo song that was increasingly common after the Civil War when the lonely isolation of the black farmer, trying to work out a living on a few acres of leased land, was relieved by hollering, moaning, shouting, and singing. The field holler had a practical use as well. It was used to signal from one small plot of land to another, to check on a neighbor without hitching up a mule to a wagon and riding over to the next sharecropper's shack. The melody of most field hollers had little significance. The melody was little more than an intonation, though the usual two lines possessed a semicadence, followed by a cadence, as well as a climax note.

The field holler was the singer's soliloquy on the trivialities and frustrations of life as they directly affected him. Its verse was subjective, just as that of the blues, though probably not so poignant. Long, wavering one- or two-line calls, often using a high falsetto voice, were typical:

Mmmmmmmmmm! Boys, I've got a boy child in Texas. He ought to be 'bout grown.

(Line from an old field holler from the Texas Panhandle.)

After the Civil War, black men had to compete with white laborers for work. Often, the blacks ended up with the dirtiest and most dangerous jobs. Applying their indomitable spirits to adversity, black men made up work songs that became the foundation upon which the blues were built.

Now some people say a man's made out of mud,
But a poor man's made out of muscle and blood,
Muscle and blood, skin and bones,
A mind that's weak, and a back that's strong.

[Chorus]

You load sixteen tons, and what do you get?
Another day older and deeper in debt.
Saint Peter, don't you call me 'cause I can't go.
I owe my soul to the company store.

(Early American coal-mining work song.)

Many ex-slaves found themselves in trouble with the law. A form of semi-slavery was instituted in many parts of the South in the latter part of the nineteenth century in the form of chain gangs.

Many fine work and prison songs came out of the suffering and hardships of black Americans trying to make ends meet or, having lost to "Mr. Charlie," ending up in prison. There is an increasing interest on the part of musicologists in black prison and chain-gang songs.

Ol' Hannah (a pseudonym for the hot sun) is a classic prison work song that tells of a heat wave in 1904 which killed many prisoners in Texas. The use of poetic images without attribution is a general principle of African verse.

Go down, ol' Hannah. Well, well, well!
Doncha rise no mo'.
If you rise in the mornin',
Bring Judgment Day.

You ought come on this Brazos. Well, well, well!
Ninteen and four
You could find a dead man
On every turn row. [Where ploughs turn]

(*Ol' Hannah*)

Prison work songs represent the most cohesive body of labor music in the black experience. The Mississippi style of singing prison songs was usually characterized by the almost constant use of the buzz tone; overlapping of the lead singer with the chorus; and a rough, savage approach to the lyric. Although the sound was sloppy at times, its loose, deliberately relaxed approach, along with its highly syncopated and layered rhythmic structure clearly identified its African roots.

Ballads. English, Irish, and Scottish *ballads* (narrative songs) were included in minstrel shows and influenced the later development of the

▪ John Henry ▪

One of the most popular folk-song ballads is *John Henry*. John Henry was a 220-pound black railroad worker who became a folk hero to his people. Black men took solace in the fact that they generally had more strength and stamina than white men. The gradual erosion of physical work requiring these physical attributes damaged one of the foundations upon which this early black pride was built. Later, the world of professional athletics offered a new arena in which strong, well-coordinated black men could claim excellence in a predominately white world.

No one could work as long as could John Henry; the women would come out just to watch him work and hear him make the cold steel ring. Many versions of this story came into being: this tale of a proud, hardworking "hammer man" who refused to let a "new-fangled steam-driven spike-driving machine beat him down," but who eventually "hammered himself to death" in this epic struggle between man and machine.

▪1

John Henry was a little boy,
And he set on his father's knee,
Said, 'Before I'd let this drive me down,
Lawd, I'm goin' die wid dis hammer in my hand,
I'm goin' die wid dis hammer in my hand.'

▪2

John Henry said to his captain,
'Captain, w'en you go to town,
Won't you bring me back a nine-pound hammer?
I'm goin' drive dis steel on down.' (2)

▪3

Oh, w'en I want good whisky,
Oh, w'en I want good corn,
Baby, w'en I sing dat lonesome song,
Honey, down de road I am gone,
Honey, down de road I am gone.

▪4

John Henry had a little woman,
And de dress she wear was red,
And she went down de road and she never look back.
'I'm goin' weh my man fall dead.' (2)

The predecessor of the Virginia reel. [Picture Collection, The Branch Libraries, The New York Public Library.]

ballroom dance: any of a variety of social dances performed by couples in a ballroom, usually

black bottom: a dance characterized by emphatic, sinuous hip movements

blues. When a British ballad was interpreted by black singers, it was often almost unrecognizable—except for some of the original lyrics and isolated musical motifs. Southerners, in particular, were fond of sentimental ballads. The Civil War often saw men around the campfires at night, listening to the sounds of someone singing a sad ballad. A popular folk-song ballad told the story of a hard-working folk hero, John Henry. Later, other legendary ballads dealing with the black experience, like *Frankie and Johnny* and *The Saint James Infirmary* would show a stronger move toward the blues style, with the use of blue notes and syncopated phrases, until Leadbelly's *House of the Rising Sun* showed that the ballad and the blues had become synonymous.

Dances. Reels and jigs were familiar and favorite dances of the antibellum period in the South. The *reel* was more of a social dance, brought to the United States from Europe. The *jig* was a very lively solo dance. Its name originated from the French dance called the *gigue*. Happy songs and dances, like the Irish jig and the Virginia reel, were easily imitated by slaves.

Many popular American ballroom dance styles that began in the 1920s—like the Charleston and the black bottom—originated with blacks. The Charleston, the dance most closely associated with jazz, was

broadside: an early
form of sheet music

also the first widely popular social dance in America in which the partners danced independently of each other. This break from the traditional
form in which the man led the woman occurred during the Roaring
Twenties, an era of liberation for women.

■/■ TIN PAN ALLEY

American businessmen early on learned how to capitalize on America's
love of music. *Broadsides* could be purchased from street vendors in

**Twenty-eighth Street
off Fifth Avenue,
about 1916.** [Picture
Collection, The Branch
Libraries, The New York
Public Library.]

Tin Pan Alley: the early center of music publishing in America, 28th Street in New York City

colonial America. The songs printed on these sheets were usually political, satirical, or bawdy, and were early models for the sheet-music industry in America.

In the 1890s and early 1900s, the popular-music publishing industry was centered on Twenty-eighth Street in New York City. This was an ideal location for publishers thanks to nearby Union Square, which hosted a variety of music halls and theaters. Each publisher had a room or two and a piano on which aspiring songwriters could play their songs. The musical cacophony issuing from this street resembled the sound of a lot of tin pans being knocked together—hence its nick-name, "Tin Pan Alley."

Joseph W. Stern and Company, founded by two former salesmen, was one of the most important contributors to the music-publishing industry. This was the first publisher on Tin Pan Alley to have salesmen actively promote music to local shops and music distributors. The publishing company also initiated the practice of issuing orchestrations as well as piano scores of its publications. This decreased performers' reluctance to try new materials and dramatically increased sales of Stern's publications.

With the fierce competition that developed, quantity was valued over quality, as the Alley measured its success solely on the number of sheet-music copies sold. Creativity and innovation were sacrificed to audience whims and desires, as songwriters rushed to compose songs that would sell according to the latest craze. Despite its tradition of commercialism, three of the finest composers of the twentieth century came out of this background: Duke Ellington, George Gershwin, and Jerome Kern. Later, composing improvisers like Louis Armstrong, Billie Holiday, and even Miles Davis straddled the fence between fine art and commercial art.

SUMMARY

Although grounded in a mix of African and European traditions, jazz developed as an American music, guided by American culture and influenced by American musical forms.

The *minstrel show*, the first distinctly American entertainment, peaked at a time of increased racial tensions in the mid-1800s. White musicians painted their faces black, sang *coon songs*, and grossly caricatured the African-Americans they were mimicking.

Black minstrel groups toured after the Civil War, drawing music from such important composers as Stephen Foster and James Bland.

Religious music has always been important in American culture, and most slaves, although restricted from other social activities, were allowed religion. The deeply moving spirituals that slaves sang from the early 1600s to the Civil War expressed both despair and hope, humiliation and rage. Gospel music succeeded spirituals after the Civil War. Unlike their predecessors, gospel singers emphasized individual responsibility, salvation, and freedom, rather than group suffering. The modern gospel song developed in urban black communities in the early 1900s, with a lively, emotional energy found originally in church choirs and theaters, and later in recordings, jazz festivals, and concert halls as well.

The *folk music* of America includes *work songs*, *ballads*, and dances from a multitude of ethnic groups. The work song, a weapon against fatigue, boredom, and loneliness, included also *field hollers* and *prison songs*. Sentimental ballads were a favorite in the South and influenced the later development of the blues. Popular dances reflected a variety of influences, primarily European and African.

Finally, the concentration of American music publishers on Tin Pan Alley in the 1890s and early 1900s greatly influenced the popular-music industry as a commercial art.

These musical forms, which were "born in the U.S.A.," expressed experiences and emotions as varied as the singers and musicians themselves, and, together with the growing music-publishing industry, they laid the foundation for the popular music which was to follow.

■ Questions on Chapter 4

A. *In your own words* write one or two sentences describing each of the terms listed in Questions 1–13.

1. minstrel show _____
_____

2. coon song _____
_____

3. jubilee _____
_____

4. vaudeville _____
_____

5. Jim Crow _____
_____

6. Zip Coon _____
_____

7. Second Awakening _____
_____

8. underground railroad _____

_____

9. sea chantey _____

_____

10. field holler _____

_____

11. prison song _____

_____

12. Tin Pan Alley _____

_____

13. Virginia reel _____

_____

In Questions 14–17 fill in the blanks.

14. In a minstrel show, the man in the middle who banters with the end men is the
_____ .

15. _____ is a commercialized style of rock.

16. A _____ is a slow and sentimental narrative folk song.

17. A _____ was an early piece of sheet music.

B. 18. Why was the minstrel show important in the development of Afro-American music in the United States?

19. What important uses or functions did the pre-Civil War spiritual have for the slave?

20. In what ways did the religious music of the black community change and evolve after the Civil War?

21. What role did folk music (including work songs, ballads, and folk dances) play in the lives of black Americans and American immigrants?

22. What were early America's most important contributions to the development of Afro-American music?

23. Discuss the statement,
Minstrel shows were racist and insulting to blacks.
Do you agree or disagree with the statement? Why?

■ Topics for Further Research

A. Compare and contrast the music of Stephen Foster with that of James Bland.

B. Compare and contrast the folk music and traditions of the various immigrant groups of nineteenth-century America.

C. Compare and contrast the popular social dances of nineteenth-century America with the ballroom dances of the Roaring Twenties.

■ Further Reading

Lomax, Alan. *The Folk Songs of North America*. New York: Doubleday & Co., 1975.

Mellers, Wilfred. *Music in a New Found Land: Themes and Developments in the History of American Music*. New York: Oxford University Press, 1987. (Part I, Chapter 1, and Part II, Chapters 1–4)

Southern, Eileen. *The Music of Black Americans: A History*, 2nd ed. New York: W. W. Norton & Co., 1983. (Chapters 2–8)

■ Further Listening

Folk Songs of North America. Smithsonian/Folkways (vol. 1–10).

■ Films and Videos

Civil War, The (video).

Folk Music of Appalachia (video). Narrated by Alan Lomax.

Killer Angels (TV miniseries).

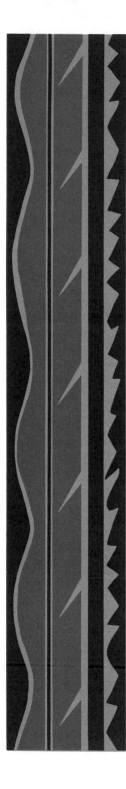

5
AFRO-AMERICAN MUSIC AS FOLK ART

/■/

The ghosts
of thousands of African tribal singers,
dancers, and drummers
hang over every blues singer's shoulder,
every ragtime pianist's fingers,
every Dixieland band's chorus,
and are encompassed and captured
in the sounds
of the passing brass band
in New Orleans as they swing their way
into the twenty-first century.

—JW

———

Most fine art goes through three stages: It begins as a folk art, becomes commercial, and finally, if it has any lasting value, matures and becomes fine art.

The improvisatory reality of folk-art Afro-American music (1870s–1920s) and the slick, highly stylized artistry of commercial music eventually met and propelled black folk music into the mainstream of American life.

folk art: functional art, passed down informally within its cultural context

ragtime: a syncopated, late 19th-century piano style based on the musical forms of the rondo, the minuet, and the march

rondo: a musical form with a short, catchy theme that alternates with contrasting material

minuet: a slow dance piece in triple meter

march: a musical piece with a measured, regular rhythm in duple time

cabaret: a restaurant or nightclub providing food, drink, and live entertainment

bordello: a house of prostitution

Folk art is a form of creative expression that originates within a tribal culture or modern urban subculture. Folk art tends to be functional, and the techniques for practicing it are taught by rote and handed down from generation to generation, usually within families or craft guilds.

Examples of folk art in contemporary North America include urban wall art (*graffiti*), Louisiana Cajun dance numbers, and urban black rap music. Native American folk art includes Zuni and Hopi Indian sand painting, Navajo blankets, Hopi dolls, and Eskimo decorated utensils carved from whalebone. Probably the most important European musical folk art is gypsy music.

There are no schools that teach folk art. It wasn't until the advent of the player piano, the 78-rpm record, the phonograph, and the radio that those outside the black community could learn how to play and write jazz. It was technology, therefore, that lifted jazz out of the black ghettos of America and into the living rooms of millions.

▪/▪ RAGTIME

The first widely popular Afro-American instrumental style was ragtime. Ragtime was the adaptation of Africanisms to the European keyboard musical forms of the *rondo*, *minuet*, and *march*. The military march was widely popular in America between the Civil War and World War I (witness the popularity of the John Philip Sousa Concert Band). Ragtime, in a sense, began by "ragging" familiar marches—by syncopating the rhythms, adding blue notes to the melody and often introducing daring harmonies. The term *ragtime* may be a shortened version of "ragged time," which would aptly describe the syncopated rhythms that are an integral part of this musical style.

An interesting contribution to the development of ragtime was the economic depression that occurred in America in the late 1800s. Many restaurants, cafes, cabarets, bordellos, and even dance halls had to cut down the size of their orchestras. In many instances, only the piano player was left. It suddenly became the pianist's job to sound like a four- or five-piece band. The left hand would simulate orchestral bass and banjo —in strict $\frac{2}{2}$ or $\frac{4}{4}$ time—to accompany a heavily syncopated melody with improvised embellishments in the right hand. This was no easy task, but in the process of trying to achieve it, America's first widely popular solo instrumental jazz style was born—ragtime.

In the South before the Civil War, the piano was considered a "white person's" instrument. Few blacks had access to a piano or were allowed to play on one. After the Civil War, pianos were being manufactured in

rag: a ragtime composition, syncopated and lively

counterpoint: the combining of two or more simultaneous melodies

America by the thousands. By the turn of the century, there were over two hundred piano manufacturers in the United States. Today, there are fewer than ten.

Competition, mass production, cheap labor, cheap transportation (the railroad), mass marketing (ads), and the real secret of America's success—the installment plan—allowed even the poorest black family to consider owning a piano. Many did. As a result, by the turn of the century, there were hundreds of talented black pianists adapting minuets, marches, and rondos into syncopated and lively tunes, eventually called *rags*.

Scott Joplin. Out of this crowd of new talent emerged one of America's greatest composers, Scott Joplin (1868–1917). Reared in Sedalia, Missouri, Joplin had the benefit of formal music instruction from a well-trained German music professor, who had immigrated to the United States at this time and settled in Sedalia. He became acquainted with Scott when he was a young boy and was able to discern the musical potential of this talented young man. As a result, Scott Joplin received years of valuable training in theory, counterpoint, orchestration, and composition; something few, if any, other black musicians of the period had achieved.

Scott Joplin dreamed of becoming the first black composer of classical music in America. He dreamed of writing opera, ballets, and symphonies. This dream was put on hold when Joplin chose to leave Sedalia in his late teens and seek his fortune as a ragtime pianist.

With the help of a New York music publisher named John Stark, Scott Joplin soon became the most popular composer of ragtime songs in the country. His *Maple Leaf Rag*, *The Entertainer*, *A Breeze from Alabama*, and *The Chrysanthemum* have all become classics. After settling in New York, he served as the producer of his own opera, *Treemonisha*, which was presented in 1915, in a nondescript hall in Harlem.

Unfortunately, his luck ran out. His royalties dwindled as a result of the gradual decline in the popularity of ragtime pieces. He discovered that his publisher had supposedly cheated him out of thousands of

---

LISTENING ASSIGNMENT

"Maple Leaf Rag," Scott Joplin. *Smithsonian Collection of Classic Jazz*, side A, #1 ▪ Listen to the left hand—note the constant movement between the bass note and the chord. Listen to the right hand—note the syncopated patterns and sudden dissonant chords and notes.

blues: a secular vocal style, characterized by the frequent use of flatted (blue) notes, originated by blacks in the late 19th century

dollars in royalties. No matter how hard he tried, he could not get the general public to accept him enthusiastically as a classical composer. America was not ready for a serious black composer. The final blow was a sudden and severe decline in his health. Joplin died of a degenerative brain disease after spending the last few years of his life confined to a New York mental institution.

Today, his rags have become widely famous again, largely through their use in the ragtime-era movie *The Sting*. His rags are familiar encore pieces for well-known concert pianists and have been recorded hundreds of times. Arrangements of his tunes for the world-renowned John Philip Sousa Concert Band helped to popularize jazz in Europe. Sousa's tours of Europe in the early 1900s were very successful, and the orchestrated arrangements of rags that his band played as encore selections became very popular.

■/■ THE BLUES

Paul Oliver, a British musicologist and expert on American blues, wrote in the introduction to his book *The Meaning of the Blues*:

> In the blues were reflected the effects of the economic stress on the depleted plantations and the unexpected prosperity of the urban centres where conditions of living still could not improve. In the blues were to be found the major catastrophes both personal and national, the triumphs and miseries that were shared by all, yet private to one, caused by poverty and migration, the violence and the bitterness, the tears and the happiness of all. In the blues an unsettled, unwanted people during these periods of social unrest found the security, the unity and the strength that it so desperately desired.*

At the same time that ragtime was commanding widespread popularity and gospel music was establishing itself as the successor of spirituals, a new secular vocal music was developing in the black communities of America that would later become the most popular musical style of the twentieth century. This style would be called the *blues*, a term which, as applied to Afro-American music, did not come into common usage until after 1900, even though songs of this type had been sung and passed on for many, many years.

No one knows exactly when the blues started. Most believe it began in earnest after the American Civil War. One of the first widely popular

---

*New York: Collier Books, 1960, p. 32.

eight-measure blues (most blues are twelve-measures in length) was a tune called *Frankie and Johnny.* Supposedly the pickets (guards) of the Union Army heard those of the Confederate Army singing this song just before the Battle of Vicksburg. After the war, some Northern soldier with a good musical memory took the melody back to New York, where it was published, and it soon became widely popular.

Some jazz musicologists believe that the blues is the most important of the Afro-American musical forms to develop in this country. The rich poetry of the lyrics, the inventiveness of the melodies, and the daring variations allowed in the harmonies have made the blues probably the most widely popular Afro-American musical form in the world. There isn't a style of music or an area of the world that has not been exposed to the blues.

The blues became a vehicle through which Afro-Americans could continue the African tribal practice of preserving all important events in an individual's life and in the community through music. The early blues of America is not only music, it is a social history of a subculture.

Rural, or "country," blues was the first widely popular blues style. From the end of the Civil War until the 1930s, rural-blues minstrels wandered the South, singing the blues in black rural dance halls called *juke joints,* in train stations, and just about anywhere else they could get someone to throw a few coins in their hats. Usually, they were self-accompanied by acoustic guitar and sometimes harmonica. Rural-blues singers were divided into two distinctly different regional styles: the Texas Panhandle and the Mississippi Delta.

The Texas Panhandle version of the rural-blues style featured singers with clear southwestern accents and high-pitched voices with a Texas twang. Their lyrics were often personal and dealt with male-female relationships, rejection, and loneliness. Fortunately, many of the more important singers of this style, like "Blind" Lemon Jefferson and his protege, Huddie "Leadbelly" Ledbetter, the most famous of all the rural-blues singers, were recorded. Their thick accents, wildly primitive accompaniment, and sad lyrics were the foundation for the later, more

---

LISTENING ASSIGNMENT

"Black Snake Moan," Blind Lemon Jefferson. *The Story of the Blues,* Columbia (CS) CGT-30008 ▪ This is a good example of the Texas Panhandle version of the rural-blues style. Listen to the "twang" in the high-pitched voice. Blind Lemon Jefferson accompanies himself on guitar. Notice how he switches from accompaniment to solo. What does the black snake represent and what is it moaning about?

"Blind" Lemon Jefferson. [Picture Collection, The Branch Libraries, The New York Public Library.]

sophisticated urban-blues style that developed after World War II.

The Mississippi Delta style was slower. The singers generally had deeper voices and sang with thick southern accents. W. C. Handy, known as the father of the blues, was the first serious black composer of the blues, and one of the first to write and publish blues songs. His *St. Louis Blues*, which was published in 1914, was not only one of the earliest important blues published, but the most famous blues of all time. Handy

---

LISTENING ASSIGNMENT

"Everybody's Down on Me," Lightnin' Hopkins. *Lightnin' Hopkins*, Smithsonian/Folkways 40019 ▪ This is an example of the Mississippi Delta rural-blues style. Notice the heavier accompaniment, the lower-pitched voice, and the thick southern accent.

---

decided to write blues after being inspired by a wandering black blues singer in a railroad station in 1903. Among his other well-known songs are *Beale St. Blues*, *A Good Man Is Hard to Find*, and *Memphis Blues*. Today, a large statue stands in the park by the Mississippi River in St. Louis, erected in honor of W. C. Handy, the composer who brought

LISTENING ASSIGNMENT

"St. Louis Blues," Bessie Smith and Louis Armstrong (by W. C. Handy). *Smithsonian Collection of Classic Jazz*, side A, #3 ▪ This may be the most popular blues ever written. What story is revealed in the song?

Huddie "Leadbelly" Ledbetter. [Picture Collection, The Branch Libraries, The New York Public Library.]

W. C. Handy. [Photofest.]

worldwide fame to the city. The great Mississippi Delta style rural-blues singers include Charlie Patton, John Hurt, and John Estes.

The rural-blues singers were more than entertainers. Because the subject of their songs ranged from current events to great legends and happenings in the black community, they helped preserve an important part of early black history, just as African musicians preserved their tribal history. Rural blues gave black Americans an identity, as well. Listening to the blues somehow made it easier for the listener to pick up his or her particular burden in life afterward and go on from there. The blues provided a catharsis and was a catalyst for anger, humiliation, frustration, and loneliness—the emotions that have the power to destroy. By singing about them, the singer got rid of them; by listening, the audience got rid of their blues, as well.

Blues faces reality unflinchingly, unlike most pop songs that escape into the unreal worlds of eternal love, happiness, and plenty. Blues lyrics say "This is the way it is; make peace with it." Pop song lyrics say, "I can't look at reality. I'll escape into fantasy."

Blues singers personalize their songs. Often a standard blues—like *St. Louis Blues*—becomes almost unrecognizable after it has been adapted to a particular singer's style. This continues the African tradition of personalizing each song and avoiding exact repetition of familiar melodies.

Eubie Blake. [Photofest.]

Other important blues and ragtime composers of this early period in jazz include Eubie Blake, Ben Turpin, James P. Johnson, Robert P. Johnson, and Joe Jordan.

■ Blues Singers ■

Rural **(1875–1920)**	**TEXAS PANHANDLE** Blind Lemon Jefferson, Robert P. Johnson, Huddie "Leadbelly" Ledbetter **MISSISSIPPI DELTA** John Estes, Lightnin' Hopkins, John Hurt
Classical **(1920–'40)**	Alberta Hunter, Ma Rainey, Bessie Smith, Ethel Waters
Urban **(1930s–'50s)**	"Big Bill" Broonzy, Jimmy Rushing, Big Joe Turner, Muddy Waters
Modern	Ray Charles, Jeannie Cheatham, Papa John Creach, Aretha Franklin, Etta James, B. B. King, Eddie "Cleanhead" Vinson, Dinah Washington, Joe Williams

■/■ JAZZ: ORIGINS AND MEANING

jazz: a 20th-century improvisatory style combining African, American, and western European influences

personalization: the use of recognizable elements of style that identify a performer

cool jazz: a jazz style of the 1950s, laid back and with subtle rhythm, unusual harmonies, and simple solo styles

free jazz: a free-form jazz style that disregards traditional structures

Third Stream jazz: a style that combines elements of classical music and jazz

The word *jazz* has been applied to many types of American popular music. It is a common name for most of the Afro-American musical styles to develop in the United States, and can be defined as a combination of improvisatory styles with western European form and harmony. Music labeled "jazz" includes several recognizable characteristics, which may or may not be found in every musical piece, but are widespread throughout most jazz forms: improvisation, syncopation, personalization, and the use of blue notes and the buzz tone. A number of popular American musical styles fall under the category of jazz. These include Dixieland, swing, bop, cool jazz, hard bop, free jazz, Third Stream, jazz-rock, and fusion.

The origins of the word are fuzzy, but it is a familiar term around the world to those who enjoy this type of music. Some of the theories behind the origins of the word "jazz" include the following:

1. When an itinerant black musician named Jazbo Brown, who was well known in Mississippi River Valley country, played in honky-tonk cafés, the patrons would shout, "More, Jazbo! More, Jaz, more!"
2. *Jazz* is a derivative of the French word *jasser*, which means "to chatter." The simultaneous improvisations of the early New Orleans jazz bands often sounded like people chattering.
3. Madams in the over two hundred brothels in the Storyville section of New Orleans would often proceed down the hall on busy nights, knocking on bedroom doors and urging the girls to "jazz it up" because customers were waiting.
4. *Jazz* is a corruption of the Elizabethan term *jass* which was used in brothels and carried some kind of sexual connotation.
5. In 1910, a black sign painter in Chicago produced a sign for the black musician Boisey James stating that "music will be furnished by the Jas. band." James, who played hot music and the blues, was nicknamed "Ol' Jas." Eventually, the music he played came to be called "Jas's music."

The word was originally spelled "jass," and the most popular theory is that the word was a derivative of *jasser*. There are several reasons for this. In 1918, a dixieland band from New Orleans, calling themselves a *jass band*, visited San Francisco. Early instrumental jazz often sounded like people chattering; the French derivative would be natural because the birthplace of instrumental jazz was New Orleans, and the French lan-

brass band: a marching band made up primarily of percussion, brass, and wind instruments

guage was commonly used by the Creoles in New Orleans. Whatever its derivation, an early definition of *jazz* can be found in a quote from an article by William Kingsley in the April 6, 1913, edition of the *New York Sun*: "Jazz is based on the savage musician's wonderful gift for progressive retarding and acceleration, guided by his sense of 'swing.'"

■/■ NEW ORLEANS

New Orleans, with its Spanish and French heritage, is one of the oldest cities in the United States, and its black community is one of the oldest and largest in the country. The cultural stability within this community helped to provide the foundation upon which much of what we call *jazz* today originated.

Brass Bands. The French tradition of having a community marching band play for all holiday and civic occasions is still a part of the New Orleans tradition. In addition, the African tradition of having a dignified, well-attended, and, if possible, expensive, funeral was also kept alive in New Orleans. Belonging to a secret society was one way to guarantee an elaborate send-off into the next world. According to Sister Johnson of New Orleans, "A woman's got to belong to at least seven secret societies if she 'spects to get buried with any style. . . . And the more lodges you belongs to, the more music you gits when you goes to meet your Maker."

The swinging brass band was the dominant feature of the typical New Orleans juju-oriented secret societies' funeral ceremonies. The brass bands were employed by the secret societies at funerals for the purpose of adding dignity to the occasion and tribute to the deceased. They marched behind the deceased at a very slow tempo, to such tunes as *Come Thee, Disconsolate* and *Nearer, My God, to Thee*. After the burial, a quiet recessional moved the funeral party away from the cemetery where, at a respectable distance, the band broke into a happy, up-tempo tune like *The Saints Go Marching In* or *Didn't He Ramble?*

The beat of the New Orleans marching band is a hybridization of the American military marching beat with the African impulse to displace beats and accent the normally weak beats. This process changed the plodding, walking march beat into a dancing beat.

The art of collective improvisation was born out of these early brass bands, which took military marches and "ragged" them, syncopating the rhythms, changing the harmonies, and swinging the accompaniment.

■ The Parade* ■

A New Orleans parade is as much a vigorous exercise in eurythmics, in dance, as it is an opportunity for drill-team swagger. The music compels the bystander to move and dance; there are no passive spectators at a New Orleans parade.

To envision a New Orleans parade on a day in any year from 1900 to the present, imagine a sunny forenoon in New Orleans, a holiday. On a side street, a band forms for a parade. The bandsmen are mostly black, and most are in their fifties or sixties.

Dressed in white shirts, dark ties and trousers, and black shoes, each wears a dark uniform cap, like a police officer's or bus driver's cap, with a name stitched across the brim in gold thread. The caps are old and worn. The men flutter valves and keys on their horns, blow fragments of jazz phrases through them to warm up, and adjust the tuning slides.

There are a couple of trombones, at least one clarinet, a couple of saxophones (soprano, alto, or tenor), and a bulky sousaphone (curled over the shoulder) to provide the *bass line* (the bottom notes). Then there are three or four trumpets (or cornets), possibly a baritone horn or mellophone, and at least two drummers.

The bass drummer has one small cymbal mounted on top of his drum that he will beat with a stiff bent wire when playing "hot" jazz. The other drummer has a snare drum that he carries by a sling over his shoulder.

Today's parade, an annual affair, is sponsored by a social-aid and pleasure club. The club members plan to parade up and down the streets of the district all afternoon, stopping at taverns and cafés along the way for rest and refreshment.

The club members are dressed neatly, in suits and fancy dresses decorated with bright sashes and emblems. Some of the women carry parasols trimmed with sequins, fringe, or feathers. One man holds a silky banner, embroidered with the club's name and the date of its founding. The grand marshal for the parade, who is also president of the club, wears a wide sash across his breast, with the club's name spelled out in florid type. The sash is embellished with sequins and glitter.

Club members line up, and the band falls into a loose formation ahead of them. The order or formation of a typical marching band often looks like this: Grand marshal out front. First

---

*Watch one of the jazz videos, *New Orleans: Til the Butcher Cuts Him Down* or *Jazz Parades*, which capture authentic New Orleans street parades.

row: trombone, trombone, sousaphone. Second row: clarinet, saxophone, (after 1930) saxophone. Third row: trumpet, trumpet, trumpet (replacing the cornet after 1930). Fourth row: snare drum, bass drum, cymbals (if there are three drummers).

As the parade forms, passersby stop to watch. Neighborhood children assemble in the streets. News of the soon-to-be celebration spreads quickly, and everyone is ready for the fun. With the order established among the marchers, the grand marshal nods to the band. Bandsmen cease their warming and tuning up. The leader signals the snare drummer, who strikes up a jazzed-up military cadence on his drum. The bass drummer joins in. All the marchers can hear the drums, and the parade starts with uncertainty. No one is exactly marching, but each parader tries to stroll in step with the cadence.

Children and the followers-for-fun group move loosely ahead of the band and the marchers along the sidewalks (called *barquettes* in New Orleans). This informal group is called the second line. The second liners will spill off the sidewalks when the parade warms up, capering and leaping in the air before the band and parodying the dignified posture of the grand marshal. If they get too out of hand, the grand marshal will warn them once or twice and then stop the band until they know who's boss.

The bandleader, who is usually one of the trumpet players, signals to the drummer, who then plays a "roll-off" signal. This warns the musicians to get ready to play. The drummer sets up the correct tempo for the next tune to be played by the band. Although the tempos vary little, it is important to try to find the right *slot*, or tempo, for each tune. The music will swing easier that way.

When the band begins to play the old marches, like *Panama*, *Rampart Street Blues*, or *When the Saints Go Marching In*, the dancing and cavorting in the second line is suddenly livelier. The sound of the band carries for several blocks, warning businesses, patrons, and others that they are on their way.

The parade gathers headway, and the marchers' joy is proportionate to the volume and intensity of the band's increasingly complex cross-rhythms. Through the first two strains of the song, the dancing and strutting are relatively restrained; but when the band winds up on the last strain, the bass drummer shifts from two beats per measure to four and the trumpets soar up into a series of chime-like high descending tones. Second liners now try to outdo themselves in elaborate dance steps, high-kicking struts, and ecstatic leaps.

The march ends suddenly, like a thunderclap. There is a beat or two of silence, and then the snare drum goes back to playing its military cadence as if nothing had disturbed it.

A contemporary Dixieland marching band in Denver.

Besides funerals and social-club parades, the street bands played for picnics, holiday celebrations, political campaigns, marriages, and civic events. And after the parades, the bands would go indoors at night and play in bars, brothels, cabarets, and dance halls. All of this activity kept early jazz musicians very busy.

Because the street bands fulfilled so many functions, both social and musical, their place in the community remained an important one through the first two decades of the twentieth century, even while dance bands were friendly rivals. Eventually, they became more of a tourist attraction, but a revival beginning in 1940 brought some elderly black musicians out of retirement and, in New Orleans today, there is a return to the tradition of the early street bands.

The opening of Preservation Hall in the quarter, where tourists and jazz fans can attend nightly jam sessions by the elderly, experienced New Orleans jazz musicians, added to the status and prestige of this early instrumental jazz style and helped to preserve its historical performance practices. A visitor to New Orleans today will still feel a sense of excitement and expectation, a feeling that at any moment a marching jazz band in bright new uniforms might step around the corner. You can almost hear its sound, a happy, joyous sound, like a locomotive whistle

Dixieland: an instrumental jazz style born out of New Orleans marching bands

Storyville: a black entertainment district in New Orleans, in whose streets, bordellos, and cabarets early jazz and blues developed in the late 19th and early 20th centuries

in the distance. This sound of a New Orleans marching band in the distance, about to round the corner, is the sound of American folk art at its finest.

Dixieland. Recently, Wynton Marsalis, New Orleans's dynamic new jazz superstar, said in an interview:

> The New Orleans style of music (Dixieland) is a classic example of democracy in action. Dixieland is collective improvisation, placing maximum emphasis on personal expression within a voluntary group format. The group encourages and nourishes individual development. That's America!
>
> (George Varga, *San Diego Union*, February 11, 1991.)

Dixieland music originated in the post-Civil War period in Storyville, a black entertainment center and red-light district in New Orleans. This musical style began as an insider folk art with roots in the music of New Orleans marching bands, military bands, and minstrel shows; and by the 1920s it had become a widely recognized and recorded jazz style. Dixieland jazz was the first important instrumental jazz style. Ragtime, its predecessor, was primarily a keyboard style. The first Dixieland bands developed, maintained, and perfected the arts of syncopation, collective improvisation, and personalization. Because the tradition of the marching band was common to both the black and the white communities of New Orleans, the first interaction between white and black musical styles began in that city. It wasn't long before the white bands were picking up on the new and exciting sounds from the black bands.

The first jazz recording ever, the 1917 song *Livery Stable Blues*, was made by the all-white Original Dixieland Jazz Band. It was an instant hit and caused a rush on the part of young record companies to find bands that could play this new music that they called *jazz*.

The early Dixieland bands often added "blue," or altered, notes to their melodies and borrowed freely from the melodies and rhythms of

---

LISTENING ASSIGNMENT

"Potato Head Blues," Louis Armstrong and His Hot Seven. *Smithsonian Collection of Classic Jazz*, side B, #1 ▪ This is considered to be one of the finest examples of 1920s Dixieland ever recorded. In addition to the classic solo by Armstrong, the listener is given a bonus by some impromptu scat singing by Armstrong. Listen for the balance in the arrangement, including the chorale at the end.

The Original Dixieland Jazz Band in London. From left to right: Billy Jones, Larry Shields, Nick La Rocca, Emile Christian, Tony Spargo. [Picture Collection, The Branch Libraries, The New York Public Library.]

street music: marches and religious music played in brass-band fashion

the itinerant rural-blues singers. Though their repertoire included rags, blues, and popular songs of the day, the bedrock of the New Orleans jazz repertoire remained street music—marches and religious music played in brass-band fashion. Besides influencing instrumental techniques and styles, brass bands broadened and enriched the repertoires of other musicians and groups; and the process was reciprocal.

When a tune like *High Society* became a local favorite, it was played by brass bands and also by solo pianists. When Jelly Roll Morton wanted to demonstrate his conception of "New Orleans style," he often chose to play *Panama*, the brass-band evergreen, and played a magnificent piano version of the jazz march. Piano rags were also played by bands and orchestras, and dance music was adapted to the march.

The typical early New Orleans Dixieland band was a scaled-down marching band, consisting of clarinet, cornet, trombone, piano, banjo, drums, and bass viol or sousaphone. Sometimes, as was the case with the great Joseph "King" Oliver's Creole Jazz Band, a second cornet (Louis Armstrong's) was used as well. The clarinet had the highest voice and

From left to right: Johnny Dodds, clarinet; "Baby" Dodds, drums; Honoré Dutrey, trombone; Louis Armstrong, trumpet; King Oliver, cornet; Lil Hardin, piano; Johnny St. Cyr, banjo (Chicago, 1923). Armstrong also played second cornet. [© Auction and Lance.]

obbligato: a high-pitched decorative part above the melody—usually played by the clarinet in a Dixieland ensemble

usually played harmony or an obbligato part against the melody, which was played by the cornet. The trombone usually played a countermelody, and the other instruments supplied the harmonic and rhythmic support. The melody-carrying cornet was the dominant instrument in these early New Orleans Dixieland bands.

The great cornetists of New Orleans were a legacy of the post-Civil War period, when many black and white musicians played in commu-

---

LISTENING ASSIGNMENT

"Dinah," Red Nichols and His Five Pennies. *Smithsonian Collection of Classic Jazz*, side C, #1 ▪ This is an example of a smoother style of Dixieland that developed in Chicago in the 1930s. It is more characteristic of white jazz groups. What differences can you hear between this recording and the Dixieland classic, "Potato Head Blues," discussed on page 95? Which instruments do you hear in "Dinah"?

nity bands. Buddy Bolden was the first great New Orleans jazz cornet soloist. He was followed, first, by King Oliver and Freddie Keppard, and then by Bunk Johnson and the great Louis Armstrong.

Some other early New Orleans jazz players included Johnny Dodds and Sidney Bechet on clarinet; Kid Ory and Miff Mole on trombone, Pops Foster on string bass, Baby Dodds and Zutty Singleton on drums, Johnny St. Cyr on banjo, and Jelly Roll Morton and Fate Marable on piano.

The instant popularity of early instrumental jazz, captured on record, quickly made national stars and entertainers out of many of the top New Orleans bands that migrated to Chicago in the 1920s. Of that era, probably the most influential, popular, and important early Dixieland recordings were made by King Oliver, Louis Armstrong and his Hot Five and Hot Seven, Freddie Keppard, and Jelly Roll Morton and his Red Hot Peppers.

SUMMARY

Folk art is a functional art, handed down within a subculture by rote, and without formal schooling. It is the first stage in the maturing of an art form, followed by commercial art and later by fine art.

The origins of folk-art jazz can be found in the music that immediately preceded it. *Ragtime* was a solo piano style involving heavily syncopated rhythms and varying degrees of improvisation. Scott Joplin's famous rags, including *Maple Leaf Rag* and *The Entertainer*, have become classics.

The *blues* was a secular vocal style with roots in black gospel. Rural, or "country," blues was popular from the Civil War through the 1930s, and could be divided into two regional styles—the Texas Panhandle and the Mississippi Delta—both of which combined personal emotional catharsis with the preservation of events and legends of the community.

The *brass bands*, which originated in New Orleans, drew on both the French and African traditions of marching bands and parades. The result was a syncopated dancing beat, rather than a walking march, and the beginnings of collective improvisation—both important features of later jazz bands.

There is much speculation and little agreement regarding the origins of the word "jazz." Theories cite a number of possibilities, from local abbreviations of an individual name to modified translations from the French to sexual slang.

Dixieland jazz, the first important instrumental jazz style, grew directly out of the marching-band tradition in New Orleans. In addition to rags, blues, and popular songs, Dixieland bands played street marches and religious music in the style of the brass band. This early instrumental jazz was instantly popular and made national stars out of the top performers.

■ Questions on Chapter 5

A. *In your own words* write one or two sentences describing each of the terms listed in Questions 1–10.

1. ragtime _____

_____

2. blues _____

_____

3. juke joint _____

_____

4. personalization _____

_____

5. cool jazz _____

_____

6. free jazz _____

_____

7. Third-Stream jazz _____

_____

8. Dixieland _____

_____

9. street music _____

_____

10. obbligato _____

_____

In Questions 11 and 12 fill in the blanks.

11. A musical piece with a measured, regular rhythm in duple time is a _____

_____.

12. The red-light district of New Orleans where early jazz and blues developed was called _____.

B.   13. What is "folk art"? How did ragtime, the blues, and early Dixieland jazz exhibit the characteristics of folk art?

14. What social conditions encouraged ragtime to develop?

15. What important stylistic contributions did the blues make to the development of jazz?

16. What was special about New Orleans and its traditions in the development of jazz?

17. Describe a New Orleans funeral ceremony.

18. Discuss the statement,

Jazz is the most significant American folk-art form.

Do you agree or disagree with the statement? Why?

■ Topics for Further Research

A. Read the play, *The Piano Lesson* by August Wilson. Discuss the piano as a symbol in this play. How does this play help you understand why so many young, intelligent blacks were attracted to careers in music?

B. Research the work of Scott Joplin. How does his work compare with that of other American musicians of the late nineteenth and early twentieth centuries?

C. Research the life and works of one of the following blues or ragtime composers:

a) Eubie Blake   b) W. C. Handy   c) James P. Johnson
d) Robert P. Johnson   e) Joe Jordan   f) Ben Turpin

■ Further Reading

Oliver, Paul, Max Harrison, and William Bolcom. *The New Grove Gospel, Blues and Jazz.* New York: W. W. Norton & Co., 1986. (Chapters 1–3)

Schuller, Gunther. *Early Jazz: Its Roots and Musical Development.* New York: Oxford University Press, 1986. (Chapters 1–2)

Southern, Eileen. *The Music of Black Americans: A History*, 2nd ed. New York: W. W. Norton & Co., 1983. (Chapters 9–12)

■ Further Listening

American Musical Theatre, The. Smithsonian.

Music of Jelly Roll Morton, The. Smithsonian (vol. 1–2).

Smithsonian Collection of Classic Jazz, The. Smithsonian (sides A and B).

■ Films and Videos

Cotton Club, The (1984).

Crossroads (1986). Blues.

Jazz Parades (video). Narrated by Alan Lomax.

Leadbelly (1976).

New Orleans: 'Til the Butcher Cuts Him Down (1971).

Pete Kelly's Blues (1955).

Piano Legends (video). Hosted by Chick Corea.

Sting, The (1973). Ragtime.

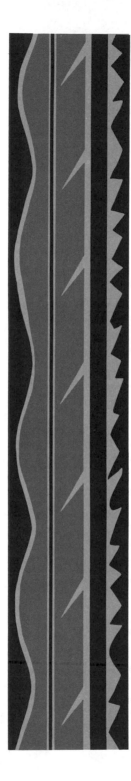

6
AFRO-AMERICAN MUSIC AS COMMERCIAL ART

/■/

You can hear the music
long before you get there,
easing its way through
the trees and a warm
summer night.

Soon the smooth sound of the
saxophones soothes you,
only to be interrupted by
the sudden smash of a tightly packed
brass-section chord,
reinforced by an alert drummer.

A cooking rhythm section
stirs up a special concoction
called "swing" and pours its
contents onto the dance floor,
for jitterbug enthusiasts
to slip and slide around upon.
Everybody's smiling,
Everyone's happy,
Fans are enjoying
a summer night,
a great big band,
and jazz.

—JW

commercial art: art created for the marketplace

Roaring Twenties: the 1920s, regarded as a boisterous era of prosperity and social change

speakeasy: a nightclub where alcohol was served illegally during Prohibition

race records: subsidiary record labels specializing in music by and for black Americans

*C*OMMERCIAL ART is art created for a mass market. A primary motivation for commercial artists is the desire for money and fame.

In the eighteenth century, many composers lived in service to churches or courts and produced work to order. By the nineteenth century, the system of patronage was beginning to break down and the composer began to work freelance; but wealthy people still supported some musicians. By the twentieth century, musicians were completely on their own, and *success* had come to mean "commercial success."

One of the reasons why commercial art produces so little that is original and enduring is that competition tends to breed conformity. In the race to make a buck and be "successful," everyone imitates the current pop champion (money maker). Experimental and innovative styles and artists are hard to sell to producers and distributors. They want a sure thing.

■/■ THE ROARING TWENTIES

Just as the classic period of jazz seemed to be ending in New Orleans, a new opening for jazz was just making its appearance in Chicago.

When prohibition came in, Chicago became the national capital for live jazz. Luxurious speakeasies provided an elegant atmosphere in which patrons could drink while listening to the new, exciting, loud, and naughty music that was becoming a symbol of social rebellion. Because the energy, sensuality, and brashness of the music seemed to match the mood of the times, F. Scott Fitzgerald christened the twenties the "Jazz Age." The American novelist not only wrote about the Roaring Twenties, he and his wife lived it—to the hilt. If "sex, drugs, and rock 'n' roll" was the popular slogan for the 1960s and '70s, then "booze, broads, and jazz" could have been the slogan for the 1920s. Chicago, along with New York, was also the center of the record industry in the '20s, and it was recordings and radio that introduced black music to the vast American audience.

Race Records. The mass migration of blacks from the rural South to the northern industrial cities during and after World War I created a whole new market for records. *Race Records* were subsidiary record labels turned out by major recording companies specifically for this previously untapped market in African-American music for black Americans. They were introduced after the phenomenal success of *Crazy Blues* and *It's Right Here for You*, recorded by Mamie Smith in 1920. This first vocal blues recording by a black artist sold millions of copies, and Mamie

The Roaring Twenties. From a painting by Otto Dix. [Picture Collection, The Branch Libraries, The New York Public Library.]

Smith, who had been substituted at the last minute for an ailing white vocal star, Sophie Tucker, became popular overnight. The record companies had almost accidentally discovered an audience hungry for blues in the black working-class neighborhoods of northern industrial cities.

The success of this record set off a talent search for new black singers and musicians. Record-company talent scouts were also anxious to re-

---

LISTENING ASSIGNMENT

"Crazy Blues," Perry Bradford's Jazz Hounds with Mamie Smith. *A History of Jazz: The New York Scene.* Folkways Records ▪ Why is this record important? What story is told in the lyrics? Which instruments accompany Mamie Smith?

Mamie Smith. [Photofest.]

TOBA circuit: a vaudeville booking agency for black talent in the South and East in the 1920s and '30s

cord some of the already popular male rural-blues singers, like Leadbelly, Robert P. Johnson, and Blind Lemon Jefferson. Over the following eight years (1920–1928), the OKeh label alone made thirteen trips to Atlanta, looking for rural-blues talent for its "Original Race Records." As a result, many blues singers and New Orleans-style jazz bands were brought to New York and Chicago to record. For almost fifteen years, OKeh was the leading label in the race-records market. In later years, Columbia assumed the lead, primarily on the strength of two discoveries—Bessie Smith and Clara Smith.

Bessie Smith, a young protege of the black vaudeville singer-entertainer Ma Rainey, eventually became the most popular blues singer of the time as well as the most successful pop-music performing artist on the basis of single-record sales. She was also responsible for the start of the "blues craze" that lasted until the late 1930s.

Clara Smith became the principal featured female blues singer on the *TOBA circuit*, a vaudeville booking agency that booked black talent throughout the East and the South. In 1923 she moved to New York, where she recorded and worked with some of the top jazzmen of the times. In 1924 she opened a theatrical club in New York, but continued touring. She recorded for Columbia records, where she was often in the shadow of Bessie Smith, "Empress of the Blues." Clara was known as the "Queen of the Moaners"—a stylistic characteristic most obvious in such recordings as *Awful Moanin' Blues.* Clara liked slow tempos that featured her deep, rich contralto voice and allowed her full emotional range for her songs. She was one of the most important of the vaudeville and classic blues singers.

A record catalog cover from the '20s. [Picture Collection, The Branch Libraries, The New York Public Library.]

A 1936 flier advertising hillbilly and race records. [Picture Collection, The Branch Libraries, The New York Public Library.]

Ethel Waters. [Photofest.]

"Classic" Blues Singers. The 1920s was the era of the black female blues singer. The record industry did a good job of finding, recording, advertising, and distributing the music of these singers to the black community, and it was even beginning to sell, though modestly, in the white record market, largely due to the commercial success of *Crazy Blues*, which made a fortune for Mamie Smith and her promoter, Perry Bradford.

> Over 211 black female blues singers were signed by record companies in the early '20's. In 1921, and again in 1922, at least 50 blues records were issued without nearly meeting the demand. Between 1920 and 1942, approximately 5,500 blues and 1,200 gospel records were released involving over 1,200 artist-performers.*

---

*Lou Curtiss, "The Birth of Black Blues and Jazz," *Jazz Link Magazine*, February 1991.

Fats Waller. [Photofest.]

Vaudeville launched the careers of most of the early great classical blues singers like Ma Rainey, Bessie Smith, Ethel Waters, Ida Cox, and Alberta Hunter, as well as black composers like Eubie Blake and Thomas "Fats" Waller. These "classic" blues singers recorded and performed with jazz musicians. The backing for these singers often included well-known musicians such as Louis Armstrong, Earl "Fatha" Hines (piano), and Sidney Bechet (clarinet).

The lyrics of most "classic" blues were more urban and sophisticated than were the lyrics of rural-blues songs and, most typically, dealt with problems of male-female relationships. The lyrics were often sexually risqué, and the use of double-entendre lyrics was common. A typical example was Alberta Hunter's recording of *My Man is Such a Handyman*, which suggests more than a man handy with a saw and hammer. Glamorous, sophisticated black women thus slowly began replacing cotton-mouthed rural-blues singers, and Chicago-style Dixieland began replacing the raw New Orleans style.

Sidney Becket. [Photofest.]

Fatha Hines.
[Drawing by Shirley Tanzi.]

The introduction of talking motion pictures in 1926 allowed Hollywood to produce lavish musicals, which eventually put traveling shows out of business. The classic blues singer also began to decline in popularity. By the late 1920s, radio had become the most popular form of entertainment in the United States, followed by the movies and ballroom dancing.

Bix Beiderbecke. Early jazz and blues recordings fascinated some white musicians. Learning to play jazz by playing along with the records of the top black jazz musicians and singers, some of these white musicians went on to form their own jazz bands. The most influential of

Bix Beiderbecke. [Picture Collection, The Branch Libraries, The New York Public Library.]

Great Depression: the
period of economic crisis
and stagnation following
the stock-market crash in
1929

these white jazz musicians of the 1920s was Bix Beiderbecke, a smooth-playing cornetist-composer born in Davenport, Iowa, in 1903.

Leon Bismarck "Bix" Beiderbecke first heard jazz—live Dixieland-style jazz—as it was played on the steamboats that came up the Missouri River from New Orleans during the summers—and it changed his life. From then on, all he wanted to do was play jazz. This was an unheard-of goal for a member of an affluent, white, upper-middle-class family in Iowa; and his parents never accepted his new life style and art. Shortly before he died, he wrote in one of his letters that when he visited his home town, he found all of the records and articles related to his career in a closet, unopened.

Beiderbecke was the first white jazz musician to influence jazz. His soft, lyrical style was very different from the brilliant, high-note style of Louis Armstrong, the other influential jazz trumpeter of the era. Beiderbecke impressed not only white audiences but also black players and audiences. The great King Oliver is said to have cried when he first heard Beiderbecke play. Even Louis Armstrong said when he first heard Beiderbecke, "I felt his pretty notes go all through me!"[*]

Despite a family background that was hostile to his ambitions, Beiderbecke's commitment to jazz was firm. In the words of jazz historian, Arnold Shaw,

> Bix approached jazz with all the respect and dedication that any Western European artist would do with classical music. He never (saw) jazz as inferior music, produced by a group of semi-literate blacks. It never entered his mind to think of jazz as anything else but the most important new music to come along in his lifetime.[†]

■/■ THE GREAT DEPRESSION

The stock-market crash in 1929 and the depression that followed signaled the end of the Roaring Twenties. The depression almost destroyed the pop and jazz record industry. Record production was reduced to a trickle, and many smaller labels were forced to drop the contracts on all but their best-selling artists.

A good example is Bessie Smith. In 1929, she was earning over two thousand dollars a week. She also starred in a low-budget film that year.

---

[*]Arnold Shaw, *The Jazz Age: Popular Music in the 1920s,* p. 35.
[†]Ibid, p. 36.

swing: *v.* to produce the rhythmic element that encourages dancing, clapping, etc.

scat: *v.* to imitate a jazz instrument vocally

vibrato: a rapid alternation between two very close pitches

By the mid-1930s, her normal three-thousand-dollar fee to record two sides of a record had been reduced to fifty dollars per side. John Hammond, one of her staunchest supporters, said later that even at that fee, the record sales after 1936 did not justify their costs.

Money was not readily available to buy records. The motion-picture theater and the ballroom were about the only affordable forms of entertainment for most Americans during this period. Americans wanted to escape the reality of their bleak surroundings—and did so in the exotically designed motion-picture theaters and the huge and grandly decorated public ballrooms.

Jazz barely remained alive. Live performances, motion-picture theater appearances, and occasional club work kept the better groups going; but most jazz combos and almost all forms of Dixieland disappeared. Radio had so glamorized the big band that it survived the hard times better than did most other jazz styles. Dance bands were kept busy playing for the growing ballroom-dancing crowds across the country. Many fans were lured to the ballrooms after first hearing a particular dance band on radio, which often created a desire to see a favorite band live.

Pop Singers. Pop-music vocalists of the 1930s originated the jazz singing style. Mildred Bailey, Sophie Tucker, and Bing Crosby were among the earliest popular commercial singers who could "swing" and "scat."

Billie Holiday, who started her career as a big-band pop singer, went on to establish jazz singing as a permanent and legitimate jazz style. Holiday was the first important female jazz singer, and her style continues to be a major influence on young jazz singers. Her peculiar manner of singing—beginning her notes slightly under pitch, with *no* vibrato, and then, at the last possible second, bringing them into tune and *with* vibrato—is similar to the style of singing used in the Islamic call to prayer from the high minarets above the mosques throughout the Middle East and North Africa. She also had the peculiar characteristic of often being as much as a whole step too high in pitch at the end of phrases, suddenly adjusting to the right note at the last second.

The three greatest influences on her vocal style were Bessie Smith, Louis Armstrong, and, later, Lester Young. The subtlety of her delayed rhythmic delivery is traceable to Louis Armstrong. However, even though these influences were present, they were subtle; most of what she accomplished was through her own innate creativity and sensitivity. According to esteemed jazz critic Leonard Feather, "The sound of her

Billie Holiday, wearing her trademark gardenia.
[Photofest.]

voice, despite its gradual deepening through the years, remained unique even when her sense of pitch began to falter, as it did in the later years."*

Urban Blues. The tough times of the Great Depression forced many blacks to turn inward for solace and entertainment. The many small blues clubs that sprang up on the South Side of Chicago and the Kansas City cabarets in the early 1930s attested to this fact.

The Chicago urban-blues style was born in these small, smoky clubs, where the new sound of the amplified guitar and electric bass gave a more modern sound to the blues. Improved microphones and public-address systems made it possible for singers to whisper and shout in the course of the same performance.

The falsetto voice is used a lot in this style. There was a return, after the urban sophistication of classic blues, to a more aggressive and emotional presentation of the blues. The harmonica, a holdover from the

---

*Leonard Feather, *The Encyclopedia of Jazz in the '60s*, p. 258.

LISTENING ASSIGNMENT

"I've Got a Right To Sing the Blues," Louis Armstrong and His Orchestra. *Smithsonian Collection of Classic Jazz*, side B, #7 ▪ Although technically, this is not a blues, this example is close enough to illustrate the urban style of blues—a male singer with a big band or combo behind him, playing a much more complicated and sophisticated style than the earlier rural blues. What differences do you hear in this recording compared to the earlier examples of classic and rural-blues styles?

big-band shouters: Kansas City-style urban blues singers with strong voices

rural-blues style, was used occasionally. The rural, country sound of the harmonica helped to link this new style of blues with the past.

The lyrics to songs, like Howlin' Wolf's *Little Red Rooster*, Muddy Waters's *Catfish Blues*, and John Lee Hooker's *Black Snake*, reflected back on the more nostalgic, slower-paced life-style of the rural South.

At the center of this development in Chicago was urban-blues singer Big Bill Broonzy. Besides Broonzy, great singers of this Chicago version of urban blues include Muddy Waters, James Brown, B. B. King, Albert King, Amos "Junior" Wells, and Eddie "Cleanhead" Vinson. Today, B. B. King is probably the most representative of the true Chicago-style urban blues.

Kansas City-style urban-blues singers were all men. They were sometimes called *big-band shouters* because of their ability to be heard over the local bands of twelve to eighteen players behind them. They favored faster and more energetic blues, usually with a boogie-woogie or shuffle beat. Slow, soulful blues ballads were rare in Kansas City. The music was obviously for dancers and catered to the new jitterbug craze.

Many of these singers, like Big Joe Turner, were capable of a wide range of blues styles—something many of them proved over the years. Though he was best known as a blues shouter, Turner had a musical voice and and was also a sensitive singer in slow blues. He is credited by many with providing the basic format and style, as well as many of the early definitive records, of what was to be called *rock 'n' roll*. Big Joe Turner's *Shake, Rattle and Roll* became one of the monster rhythm-and-blues hits of the fifties.

Kansas City urban-blues singers had strong voices. A honking tenor saxophone behind the singer was another characteristic of this style of blues, particularly when the back-up band was a smaller group, and the singer had to be heard over the sax.

Big Joe Turner. [Photofest.]

fox-trot: a couples dance with various combinations of slow and quick steps

The classic combination of the great Count Basie and his orchestra with the legendary bluesmen Jimmy Rushing ("Mr. Five-by-five") and Joe Williams is a good example of the Kansas City urban-blues style. Joe's recording of *Everyday I Have the Blues* with the Basie band is a Kansas City urban-blues classic. Today, Ernie Andrews and Joe Williams are two of the most popular artists still singing in this style.

■/■ THE SWING ERA

New Orleans- and Chicago-style Dixieland combos were not "big" enough to fill the large new dance halls being built throughout the nation in the 1920s and '30s. Dixieland music was too formalized by the mid-1930s and couldn't adapt quickly either to the larger halls or to new dances, like the fox trot, that were becoming popular.

swing: *n. or adj.* a jazz style popular in the 1930s and early '40s, often performed by big bands, having a smoother beat and more flowing phrasing than Dixieland

drum: a percussion instrument consisting of a hollow body, covered by a tightly stretched membrane which is struck with hands or sticks

vibes: also called *vibraharp* or *vibraphone*; a melodic percussion instrument played by striking small metal bars with hammers

Dance bands playing in increasingly larger dance halls had to enlarge themselves to be heard by all the dancers. Many of these new ballrooms, like the famous Roseland Ballroom in New York City, could handle a thousand or more dancers at a time. The large swing bands of the 1930s developed in response to the new ballroom-dancing craze that swept America after World War I.

Big bands can be divided into three sections:

1. The rhythm section always includes piano, string bass, and drums. Count Basie added an acoustic guitar, and Benny Goodman added a set of vibes. Bands that played Latin jazz added a conga drummer to the rhythm section.

2. The reed section usually includes three or four saxophones. Early dance bands often required their saxophonists to double on clarinet. After 1945, saxophonists were also often asked to play flute, bass clarinet, and other woodwind instruments. The sax section in some big bands might include as many as five players—two altos, two tenors, and one baritone.

3. The brass section includes trumpets and trombones. Early dance-band brass sections had three trumpets and one trombone. Players were gradually added until the maximum was reached with five trumpets and five trombones (Stan Kenton orchestra). The standard brass section in a jazz big band today includes four trumpets and four trombones. The fourth trombone is often a bass trombone, allowing for a lower bottom in the brass section.

The formally dressed band on stage, the large dance floor filled with dancers, the exotically decorated ballrooms, and the exciting new dances all contributed to the appeal of the big bands of the swing era.

Network radio broadcasts of bands from the ballrooms and casinos across the country added to the glamour. The Woody Allen film *Radio*

LISTENING ASSIGNMENT

"Sweethearts on Parade," Louis Armstrong and His Orchestra. *Smithsonian Collection of Classic Jazz*, side B, #6 ▪ Once again, we hear Armstrong singing and playing, but this time, he has behind him a smooth big band consisting of four saxophones, two trombones, three trumpets, piano, bass, and drums. Listen carefully to the difference between this recording and the earlier Dixieland style recording, "Potato Head Blues" (page 95). Besides the additional instruments, what other differences do you hear?

Ethel Waters with Tommy Dorsey. [Photofest.]

Days captures the power and glamour of the big-band broadcasts in the 1930s. This nostalgic motion picture also accurately portrays the big band in the typical lush hotel ballroom and on the stage of a magnificent motion picture palace (Radio City Music Hall in New York City).

By 1941, over four hundred dance bands were playing and traveling across America. The most popular radio show of the time was the *Chesterfield Hour*, featuring the famous Glenn Miller band. Bands had not yet become just backup groups for singers. That change was to happen after World War II.

Record companies discovered an enthusiastic market for big-band records, adding to an already popular image of jazz during the swing era. Not all of these dance bands played jazz, although most occasionally featured jazz soloists.

There emerged four types of big bands in the swing era:

1. Commercial big bands,
2. MOR big bands,
3. White jazz bands, and
4. Black jazz bands.

Commercial Big Bands. Commercial dance bands played little that could be called *jazz.* They even occasionally added a string section. Most commercial big bands featured male and female singers and vocal ensembles. The most popular early band of this type was the Paul Whiteman orchestra, which was extremely popular with high society from the early 1920s up until 1941. Other bandleaders in this category included Ted Fio Rito, Guy Lombardo, Eddie Duchin, Jan Garber, Kay Kaiser, and Lawrence Welk.

MOR Big Bands.

MOR is record-company slang for Middle-Of-the-Road. MOR bands split their programming between top-quality jazz arrangements featuring outstanding jazz soloists, and very smooth, but very commercial, dance arrangements. They tried to please the pop-music fan as well as the jazz fan. Most of these bands featured great jazz soloists and arrangers. The most popular MOR band of all time was the great Glenn Miller orchestra. Other popular MOR bandleaders included Artie Shaw, Tommy Dorsey, Jimmy Dorsey, Harry James, Les Brown, and Claude Thornhill.

White Jazz Bands.

Until after World War II, there were separate black and white musicians' unions. As a result, most of the early jazz big bands could be separated according to color. Some white big bands began moving more in the direction of jazz arrangements. This was a commercial risk for them because the "big money" was in playing the more watered-down arrangements and styles of commercial bands. There were some adventurous white bandleaders, however, who braved the economic storms that occurred.

The earliest important band in this style was the Benny Goodman band. In 1936, Benny Goodman became the first white bandleader to lead an unabashed, full-blown jazz band. Other pioneers in this category

A big band. [Drawing by Shirley Tanzi.]

A French article on Benny Goodman. [Picture Collection, The Branch Libraries, The New York Public Library.]

included Woody Herman, Gene Krupa, Charlie Barnet, Stan Kenton, Elliot Lawrence, and Don Ellis.

Black Jazz Bands. Since black bands played mostly for black audiences, and black audiences wanted jazz, all black dance bands could be categorized as *jazz bands*. Until the 1960s, most black communities in America were proud to support jazz, claiming it as their own.

Jazz solo instrumentalists were given more prominence in the arrangements for these bands, and the arrangers were driven by one primary purpose: to swing, to create excitement, to create jazz.

The Fletcher Henderson and Duke Ellington orchestras in New York City in the late 1920s were probably the most important and most prominent early black jazz bands. They were followed quickly by other pioneer bands, including those of Earl Hines, Jimmie Lunceford, and Louis Armstrong.

LISTENING ASSIGNMENT

"The Stampede," Fletcher Henderson and His Orchestra. *Smithsonian Collection of Classic Jazz*, side B, #11 ▪ There are three sections in a big band: the reed or sax section (sometimes including clarinet), the brass section (trumpets and trombones), and the rhythm section (piano, bass, and drums). Which sections do you hear featured? How often does the entire band play? Which instruments are given solo parts?

Count Basie's band came out of Kansas City and went on to become one of the greatest jazz bands of all time. Other late-developing black jazz bandleaders included Bennie Moten and Jay McShann. In the 1930s and '40s, other important black big bands emerged, led by Cab Calloway, Erskine Hawkins, Billy Eckstine, and Dizzy Gillespie.

Gene Krupa.

Woody Herman.
[Drawings by Shirley Tanzi.]

▪ Big Bands ▪

The most important big-band leaders of the swing era and beyond include:

Early **(1920s–'30s)**	Duke Ellington, Fletcher Henderson, Jimmie Lunceford, Luis Russell, Chick Webb
Middle **(1930s–'40s)**	Count Basie, Cab Calloway, Duke Ellington, Benny Goodman, Woody Herman, Gene Krupa
Late **(1940s–'70s)**	Toshiko Akiyoshi, Duke Ellington, Don Ellis, Gil Evans, Maynard Ferguson, Dizzy Gillespie, Lionel Hampton, Woody Herman, Thad Jones with Mel Lewis, Stan Kenton, Rob McConnell, Buddy Rich

The Early Jazz Arranger/Composer. As jazz bands increased in size, the informal collective improvisation so typical of the New Orleans Dixieland bands became impossible. Someone had to write out the parts for thirteen to twenty musicians. Jazz was forced to be increasingly preconceived, rather than spontaneous. The basic concepts in style came increasingly from the pen of the arranger and less and less from the soloists.

The arranger had to have some formal musical training in order to be able to organize and put his musical ideas down on paper. A new jazz star was thus born: the arranger. Some of the more important early arranger/composers included Fletcher Henderson, Duke Ellington, Don Redman, Sy Oliver, Benny Carter, and Jimmie Lunceford.

LISTENING ASSIGNMENT

"East St. Louis Toodle-oo," Duke Ellington and His Orchestra. *Smithsonian Collection of Classic Jazz*, side D, #10 ▪ This recording demonstrates the moody, colorful "jungle" music of Duke Ellington. How does this example contrast with "The Stampede" (page 119)? What jungle sounds do you hear? What's "African" about them?

---

stride piano: a jazz piano style that evolved in Harlem from ragtime, characterized by a smooth left hand and a trumpet-like right hand

boogie-woogie: a popular jazz piano style before World War II which evolved from the blues; also called "barrel house" after the New Orleans saloons in which it was born

walking tenths: the left-hand style often used in stride piano, involving a ten-step interval in which the upper and lower notes move simultaneously upward or downward in a scalelike fashion

block chord: four or more chord tones all within an octave

arpeggio: a chord in which the notes are played up or down in rapid succession, rather than simultaneously

countermelody: an additional melody that complements the main melody

The Keyboardists. The solo pianist was an important figure in the swing era (1935–1946). Brief appearances in Hollywood films by Fats Waller, Duke Ellington, Nat "King" Cole, Hoagy Carmichael, and others helped to keep solo piano styles alive and popular with the American public.

Two keyboard styles were dominant in this period. The first was *stride* piano. The other was *boogie-woogie*. Harlem stride piano was a refinement on the earlier ragtime style, whereas boogie-woogie evolved from the blues.

The left hand in *stride* alternates between bass notes and chords, as in ragtime, but the phrasing is smoother, the chords bigger, and the line is occasionally interrupted by walking tenths and octaves. The right hand, meanwhile, imitates the trumpet, the clarinet, or the saxophone. Block chords, octaves, and rapid arpeggios occasionally fill in for contrast.

One of the secrets of good stride piano playing is the creation of countermelodies simultaneously with the operations just described. This creates the illusion, when listening, that the pianist has three hands instead of two. Stride piano is sophisticated, yet rhythmic; commercial, yet inventive.

The father of stride piano was New York pianist and teacher, James P. Johnson, but the most accomplished ever in this style, and perhaps the greatest pianist jazz ever produced, was Art Tatum. His genius still influences keyboard players today.

Tatum, who died in Los Angeles on November 5, 1956, at the age of forty-seven, was originally from Toledo, Ohio. It was John Lewis, the leader of the Modern Jazz Quartet, who called Tatum the greatest jazz player that ever lived. His style was so complex and so unique that to this day no player has ever consistently and correctly imitated his style. His technique and innovative harmonic and melodic ideas were so far ahead of his time that the public had no real idea of the depth of artistry he was demonstrating.

LISTENING ASSIGNMENT

"Willow Weep for Me," Art Tatum. *Smithsonian Collection of Classic Jazz*, side C, #11 ▪ Art Tatum took stride piano to its zenith, paving the way for all other modern piano styles. Notice how it sounds like he's got three hands when he's playing. Notice also the constantly shifting chords accompanying the solo. How does this piece differ from the example of stride in "Weather Bird" (page 122)?

funky: having an earthy "blues-based" quality

Other early great stride pianists include Fats Waller, Duke Ellington, Count Basie, Teddy Wilson, Earl Hines, and Phil Napoleon.

Next to ragtime, *boogie-woogie* is probably the most commercially successful solo keyboard style ever. Boogie-woogie grew out of the blues, the way the blues were played on the piano in New Orleans and other parts of the South.

The constantly moving left hand in boogie-woogie gives a steady "eight-to-the-bar" forward-moving sound to the music. This is supposed to be symbolic of the restless nervous energy that existed in America in the early part of this century. The fact that the sound was somewhat similar to the sound of a moving train has also led some sociologists to speculate that it represents the railroad, as well.

The right hand in this style usually borrows liberally from blues singers, jazz combos, and even big bands in its attempt to create a colorful big-band sound. It sounds like the brass section of a big band or the smooth, flowing sound of a good sax section and is supposedly wailing, moaning, and punching out aggressively at fate and life itself.

Billy Taylor describes the evolution of the early jazz pianist into what came to be called boogie-woogie:

In the South there were the "funky" players who worked in the low-down dives of cities such as New Orleans and Charleston. In the Southwest there were powerful players who entertained the tough workers from the levee, turpentine, and sawmill camps.

These early black keyboard artists travelled on what was known as the "barrel-house" circuit. Often the camps were far from towns, and the company would typically set up a shack where the workers could drink, dance and relax. The bar was often just a wooden slab supported by barrels, but there was usually a beat-up piano in the corner for an itinerant musician to play.*

---

*Billy Taylor, *Jazz Piano* (Dubuque, Iowa: Wm C. Brown Group, 1982), p. 60.

The sound of boogie-woogie can get tiresome because there is little variation in style or form. However, it is exciting and very rhythmic, and it is the foundation on which rhythm-and-blues developed.

Early great boogie-woogie pianists include Clarence "Pine Top" Smith, Meade Lux Lewis, Freddie Slack, Pete Johnson, Mary Lou Williams, Sammy Price, Albert Ammons, and Jimmy Yancey.

Boogie-woogie and blues-style piano later became highly energized in the ultra-extreme performances of Jerry Lee Lewis and Little Richard in the early rock 'n' roll era of the 1950s and '60s. Even today, rock keyboardists use a boogie-woogie keyboard style when playing the blues.

LISTENING ASSIGNMENT

"Honky Tonk Train Blues," Meade Lux Lewis. *Smithsonian Collection of Classic Jazz*, side C, #4 ▪ Notice the continual eight-to-the-bar rhythm in the left hand. How does boogie-woogie differ from ragtime and stride? Can you hear how this pianist is trying to sound like a big band all by himself?

■/■ **NEW YORK**

In the late 1930s and early '40s, the center for jazz shifted to New York City. In fact, New York became the center for the entire American entertainment industry. It was the booking center for vaudeville, the new headquarters for network radio, the center for the music-publishing industry, and eventually, the headquarters for most of the new and rapidly growing record industry.

All-black musical revues began appearing annually on Broadway, and the Roseland Ballroom became the Mecca for jazz big bands. The only major entertainment center outside of New York at that time was the film industry in Hollywood.

By the 1930s, America had begun to rely increasingly on mass media in the form of records, radio, and motion pictures for most of its entertainment. Ballroom dancing was the only other major form of recreation for many Americans in this period. The increasing popularity of radio, records, and talking films (cinema) replaced earlier popular live forms of entertainment, like vaudeville and burlesque. As was mentioned, only ballroom dancing resisted this assault successfully. As a result, fewer artists were performing for more people. This gradual attrition put hundreds of singers, musicians, dancers, and comedians out of business.

Dancing in Harlem, 1935. [Picture Collection, The Branch Libraries, The New York Public Library.]

Harlem Renaissance: a period of great artistic productivity in the 1920s and '30s in the black community of Harlem, New York City

Harlem. New York City had been attracting black jazz musicians since the 1890s. Part of this had to do with the size and sophistication of the black community called Harlem. This large concentration of modestly affluent blacks (compared to poor Southern sharecroppers) guaranteed large and enthusiastic black audiences for most jazz groups. This community exploded with creativity in the 1920s and '30s in what has since been called the *Harlem Renaissance*. African-Americans were

art song: a song having interdependent vocal and piano parts, meant to be sung in recital

determined to remove the last vestiges of racism from America by producing art and literature of such high quality that there could no longer be any question as to their equality with the white majority.

During this renaissance, which was partially financed by a few successful black businessmen and women, composers used black poems in their art songs and African rhythms and dances in their ballets and symphonies; and classical singers and conductors insisted on programming music by black composers in their recitals and concerts.

Harlem was *the* place to be. New entertainment centers like the famous Cotton Club catered exclusively to all-white audiences. This club, and others like it in Harlem, presented exciting big-band jazz music, gorgeous showgirls, comedians, tap dancers, and masters-of-ceremony. It was at the Cotton Club that the careers of jazz greats like Duke Ellington, Cab Calloway, and Lena Horne were launched. A weekly radio broadcast from the nightclub gave America an opportunity

A program from the Cotton Club. [Picture Collection, The Branch Libraries, The New York Public Library.]

An ad for Cab Calloway at the Harlem Opera House. [Picture Collection, The Branch Libraries, The New York Public Library.]

to hear this exciting new urban jazz and dream of going to the Cotton Club themselves some day. These broadcasts helped to make superstars of Duke Ellington, Cab Calloway, and Lena Horne.

■/■ POSTWAR JAZZ

The swing era, which lasted from 1935 to 1946, might be considered the high-water mark in the general popularity of jazz. Jazz was then in its commercial phase, and swing took it as far as it could go. It was the new mass-marketing techniques and the glamour of ballroom dancing, radio, records, and film that helped make this era the most commercially successful for jazz.

This was also the high-water mark in popularity for ballroom dancing, in part because of radio. The glamour given to jazz bands by their late-night appearances on network radio broadcasts from ballrooms and theaters across the country helped to make jazz and its practitioners media stars in much the same way that television today has made media stars of athletes. Listeners actually wrote to NBC radio during this period demanding to hear more of the Glenn Miller band and less of the singers on the very popular network radio show, *The Chesterfield Hour.*

jam session: an informal or impromptu gathering and performance of jazz musicians which encourages experimentation with new sounds and new styles

cutting contest: a competition between players of like instruments during a jam session

fine art: art created for aesthetic purposes

But an art form can be more endangered by success than by failure. Jazz was threatened by success in the 1930s, but managed to survive and move into the next era with many new revolutionary ideas—ideas that would not be as commercially successful, but would raise jazz to a new level of expression and, eventually, bring international recognition.

Jam Sessions.   Much of the credit for the survival of the art of jazz improvisation must go to the after-hours jam session, which gave jazz musicians during this period an opportunity to experiment with new ideas, improvise freely without the commercial restraints imposed on them during working hours, and test their skills against the giants. Showdowns between two players were called *cutting contests*. Even when the competition was intense, however, the atmosphere was friendly. As long as you played well enough to keep up with the rest of the players, you were okay; but jam sessions were not for amateurs. Poor playing was not tolerated.

In the movie *Bird*, a cymbal is thrown at the feet of the as-yet-unformed Charlie Parker by drummer Jo Jones because the young Bird goofed on one of his solos. This incident, more than any other, drove him to practice so that he would never again be humiliated or embarrassed at a jam session. Bird, of course, became one of the greatest jazz saxophonists of all time.

Jazz at the Philharmonic. The intimate excitement generated by jam sessions was seen by some as a commercial opportunity. In 1953–1956, impresario Norman Granz organized the best jazz solo instrumentalists he could get, most of them award winners from *Downbeat* and *Metronome Magazine*'s annual readers poll, and put them into the recording studio. He also booked this group of all-stars into concert halls and auditoriums around the world and told them to start jamming. They did, audiences went wild, and Granz ended up calling the experience *Jazz at the Philharmonic.*

These jam-session concerts after World War II helped to change jazz's image. The concert format made the listener and the country realize that jazz could stand on its own as concert music.

Jazz at the Philharmonic was the root from which later sprang every major jazz festival both here and abroad. Norman Granz's experiment was successful both artistically and commercially. Jazz began to be booked into top concert halls around the country.

Jazz thus survived its greatest threat—success—and, by the mid-1940s, it had taken Step Three in the evolution of any art form: It had become a fine art.

▪ Big-Band Swing-Era Standards ▪

1930–36

Blue Skies, Benny Goodman
Casa Loma Stomp, Glen Gray
Four or Five Times, Jimmie
    Lunceford
I've Found a New Baby, Benny
    Goodman
Ja-Da, Tommy Dorsey
King Porter Stomp, Benny
    Goodman
Mood Indigo, Duke Ellington
Muskrat Ramble, Bob Crosby
Rockin' in Rhythm, Duke
    Ellington
Rosetta, Earl Hines
St. Louis Blues, Tommy Dorsey
Sometimes I'm Happy, Benny
    Goodman
Sophisticated Lady, Duke
    Ellington

1936–37

Bugle Call Rag, Benny Goodman
Caravan, Duke Ellington
Christopher Columbus, Fletcher
    Henderson
Down South Camp Meetin',
    Benny Goodman
I'm Gettin' Sentimental over You,
    Tommy Dorsey
In a Sentimental Mood, Duke
    Ellington
Marie, Tommy Dorsey
Moonglow, Benny Goodman
Moten Swing, Andy Kirk
My Blue Heaven, Jimmie
    Lunceford
One o'Clock Jump, Count Basie
Organ Grinder's Swing, Jimmie
    Lunceford
Prisoner's Song, The, Bunny
    Berigan
Royal Garden Blues, Bob Crosby

Song of India, Tommy Dorsey
Stompin' at the Savoy, Benny
    Goodman
Topsy, Count Basie

1937–38

Annie Laurie, Jimmie Lunceford
Blue and Sentimental, Count Basie
Boogie Woogie, Tommy Dorsey
Dipsy Doodle, The, Tommy
    Dorsey
Don't Be That Way, Benny
    Goodman
For Dancers Only, Jimmie
    Lunceford
I Can't Get Started, Bunny Berigan
I Let a Song Go Out of My Heart,
    Duke Ellington
Sleepy Time Gal, Glen Gray
South Rampart Street Parade, Bob
    Crosby
What Is This Thing Called Love?,
    Artie Shaw

1938–39

And the Angels Sing, Benny
    Goodman
Begin the Beguine, Artie Shaw
Boy Meets Horn, Duke Ellington
Carioca, Artie Shaw
Hawaiian War Chant, Tommy
    Dorsey
Jumpin' at the Woodside, Count
    Basie
Memories of You, Glen Gray
My Reverie, Larry Clinton
Softly, As in a Morning Sunrise,
    Artie Shaw
Undecided, John Kirby
What's New?, Bob Crosby
Woodchopper's Ball, Woody
    Herman

1939–40
After Hours, Erskine Hawkins
Concerto for Trumpet, Harry James
Cotton Tail, Duke Ellington
Harlem Nocturne, Ray Noble
Honeysuckle Rose, Benny Goodman
In a Persian Market, Larry Clinton
Jack the Bear, Duke Ellington
No Name Jive, Glen Gray
Pennsylvania 6-5000, Glenn Miller

1940–41
Big Noise from Winnetka, Bob Haggart
Bizet Has His Day, Les Brown
Cherokee, Charlie Barnet
Ciribiribin, Harry James
Frenesi, Artie Shaw
In the Mood, Glenn Miller
Let's Dance, Benny Goodman
Little Brown Jug, Glenn Miller
Lonesome Road, The, Tommy Dorsey
Moonlight Serenade, Glenn Miller
Music Makers, Harry James
Redskin Rhumba, Charlie Barnet
720 in the Books, Jan Savitt
Snowfall, Claude Thornhill
Stardust, Artie Shaw
Sunrise Serenade, Glenn Miller
Swanee River, Tommy Dorsey
Take the "A" Train, Duke Ellington
Temptation, Artie Shaw
Tuxedo Junction, Glenn Miller
Two o'Clock Jump, Harry James
You Made Me Love You, Harry James

1941–42
Air Mail Special, Benny Goodman
American Patrol, Glenn Miller

Autumn Nocturne, Claude Thornhill
Basie Boogie, Count Basie
Blue Flame, Woody Herman
Chattanooga Choo Choo, Glenn Miller
Dancing in the Dark, Artie Shaw
Don't Get Around Much Anymore, Duke Ellington
Don't Sit under the Apple Tree, Glenn Miller
Flyin' Home, Lionel Hampton
I Cried for You, Harry James
Jersey Bounce, Benny Goodman
Perdido, Duke Ellington
Song of the Volga Boatman, Glenn Miller
Strictly Instrumental, Harry James
String of Pearls, A, Glenn Miller
Summit Ridge Drive, Artie Shaw
Swing Low, Sweet Chariot, Tommy Dorsey
Warm Valley, Duke Ellington
Well, Git It!, Tommy Dorsey

1943–44
After You've Gone, Gene Krupa
Chelsea Bridge, Duke Ellington
C-Jam Blues, Duke Ellington
Elk's Parade, Bobby Sherwood
Hamp's Boogie Woogie, Lionel Hampton
It's Been a Long, Long Time, Harry James
I've Got a Gal in Kalamazoo, Glenn Miller
Leap Frog, Les Brown
Mission to Moscow, Benny Goodman
On the Alamo, Tommy Dorsey
On the Sunny Side of the Street, Tommy Dorsey
Rockin' Chair, Gene Krupa
Skyliner, Charlie Barnet
Sleepy Lagoon, Harry James

Slipped Disc, Benny Goodman
Southern Scandal, Stan Kenton
Straighten Up and Fly Right, Nat Cole
Tampico, Stan Kenton
Things Ain't What They Used to Be, Duke Ellington
Tippin' In, Erskine Hawkins
Trumpet Blues, Harry James

1944–45

Apple Honey, Woody Herman
Carnival, Harry James
Eager Beaver, Stan Kenton
It's Only a Paper Moon, Nat Cole
Northwest Passage, Woody Herman
Opus One, Tommy Dorsey
Sentimental Journey, Les Brown
Sweet Lorraine, Nat Cole
's Wonderful, Artie Shaw
Taps Miller, Count Basie
Twilight Time, Les Brown
Wildroot, Woody Herman

1946–50

Artistry in Rhythm, Stan Kenton
At Sundown, Tommy Dorsey
Autumn Serenade, Harry James
Bijou, Woody Herman
Concerto to End All Concertos, Stan Kenton
Dream, Glenn Miller
The Good Earth, Woody Herman
Intermission Riff, Stan Kenton
I've Got My Love to Keep Me Warm, Les Brown
Lover, Gene Krupa
Lover's Leap, Les Brown
Man with A Horn, Randy Brooks
Midnight Sun, Lionel Hampton
Route 66, Nat Cole
September Song, Harry James
Sherwood's Forest, Bobby Sherwood
Tenderly, Randy Brooks

1950s

Across the Alley from the Alamo, Stan Kenton
All of Me, Billy May
April in Paris, Count Basie
Artistry Jumps, Stan Kenton
Continental, The, Tommy Dorsey
Cute, Count Basie
Diminuendo and Crescendo in Blue, Duke Ellington
Early Autumn, Woody Herman
Four Brothers, Woody Herman
Hot Toddy, Ralph Flanagan
Interlude, Stan Kenton
The Kid from Red Bank, Count Basie
Laura, Stan Kenton
Lean Baby, Billy May
Li'l Darlin', Count Basie
Night Train, Buddy Morrow
Ol' Man River, Ted Heath
Peanut Vendor, The, Stan Kenton
St. Louis Blues March, Glenn Miller
Satin Doll, Duke Ellington
September Song, Stan Kenton
So Rare, Jimmy Dorsey

1960s

Blues in Hoss' Flat, Count Basie
Carlos, Gerald Wilson
Cuban Fire Suite, Stan Kenton
Exodus, Si Zentner
I Can't Stop Lovin' You, Count Basie
Lazy River, Si Zentner
Love for Sale, Buddy Rich
Malagueña, Stan Kenton
Mercy, Mercy, Mercy, Buddy Rich
The Opener, Stan Kenton
Pussywiggle Stomp, Don Ellis
Sweet Georgia Brown, Count Basie
West Side Story, Stan Kenton
West Side Story, Buddy Rich

rhythm-and-blues: a popular-music style with strong repetitive rhythms and simple melodies, often using blue notes

Country-and-Western: a popular-music style with roots in American folk, hillbilly, and cowboy music

rock 'n' roll: a popular-music style, derived from rhythm-and-blues and Country-and-Western, characterized by a heavily accented beat and repetitive phrase structure

Motown: an upbeat popular style of rhythm-and-blues which originated with black vocalists and groups in Detroit in the 1950s; also, the record company that defined this style

hillbilly music: the folk music of the mountains of the South

bluegrass: an instrumental country-music style

After World War II, American popular music was transformed through the meeting of black rhythm-and-blues and white Country-and-Western music. The new sound that emerged, which was to have huge consequences for jazz, was rock 'n' roll.

Rhythm-and-Blues. *Rhythm-and-blues* had its roots in the traveling male gospel quartets in the South in the late 1930s. Later, some of the quartets broke away from the gospel tradition and in the '40s began what was later to be called "rhythm-and-blues." This style of ensemble blues singing eventually developed into the early Motown style in the 1960s, featuring groups like the Temptations, Smokey Robinson and the Miracles, and the Supremes. Tired of constantly being ripped off by unfair agents and record companies, record-shop owner and songwriter Berry Gordy, Jr. founded the Motown complex in Detroit in 1959. This black-managed record company, which helped to elevate unknown gospel, pop, big-band, and rhythm-and-blues artists to their rightful place in the American entertainment picture, had its first big success in 1961.

Black musicians, singers, and composer/arrangers were suddenly free to create black music for black audiences—without restriction. The fact that this new music appealed to white audiences as well is just another indication that the time was right for a new direction in pop music.

Some very creative music was recorded by Motown—a new style that definitely has jazz roots. Without gospel, blues, and earlier jazz traditions, Motown wouldn't have seen the light of day. Among the outstanding early Motown stars and groups were Martha and the Vandellas, Stevie Wonder, The Contours, Mary Wells, The Marvelettes, Marvin Gaye, and The Four Tops.

The walls between musical styles were breaking down. It was becoming apparent that American pop music was moving more in the direction of gospel, blues, rhythm-and-blues, and jazz.

Country-and-Western. The *hillbilly* music of the '20s had its roots in the folk music that settlers brought with them from the Old World. It developed in inaccessible mountain regions, essentially free from outside influences. The melodies were simple, and the lyrics told stories of everyday events. Hillbilly music might be called "white blues," and was part of the oral tradition of the rural white Southerners who sang it. The combination of acoustic guitar, harmonica, violin, and sometimes a string bass eventually led to a very creative instrumental musical style called "bluegrass."

Cajun music: the folk music of the Cajuns of Louisiana

Norteño music: the folk music of northern Mexico

Hillbilly music developed into what we call today *Country-and-Western* music, beginning in the 1930s, and was influenced by such performers as Jimmie Rodgers, Ernest Tubb, Hank Snow, Eddy Arnold, Hank Williams, Sr., and Johnny Cash. Country-and-Western incorporated Appalachian music—the mountain-style fiddling and singing from Tennessee and other Southeastern mountain regions—with the distinctive sounds from Texas—the singing cowboy and the square-dance fiddle music. In addition, the polkas and waltzes of German, Bohemian, and other European settlers, the Cajun music of Louisiana, and the Norteño music of northern Mexico added spice to Country-and-Western music. Motion pictures with singing cowboys, like Gene Autry and later, Roy Rogers, helped to popularize this style.

When rock 'n' roll began, it began in the South (Memphis), and it brought together the diverse styles of rhythm-and-blues and Country-and-Western into one new style of music.

From a Jimmie Rodgers album. [Picture Collection, The Branch Libraries, The New York Public Library.]

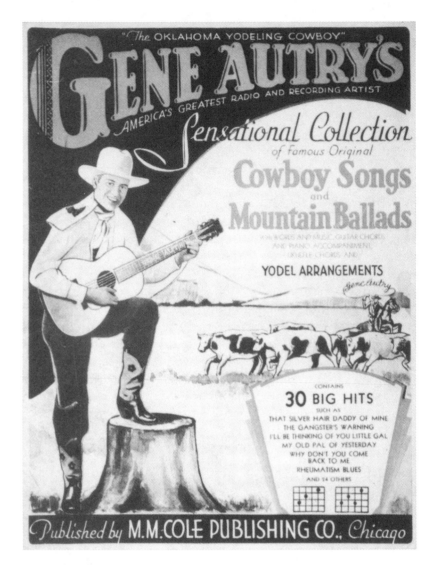

A Gene Autry songbook.
[Picture Collection, The Branch Libraries, The New York Public Library.]

disc jockey: the person who conducts a radio broadcast of recorded music

Rock 'n' Roll. In the early 1950s, rhythm-and-blues started attracting a large white audience, and a few disc jockeys began playing it for a general audience, not just the black community. Alan Freed, a popular DJ in Cleveland, began playing exclusively rhythm-and-blues, and the response was enormous. In 1951, he changed the title of his program from "Record Rendezvous" to "The Moon Dog Rock 'n' Roll House Party." Bo Diddley claims that he gave Alan the name when asked to define the style of music Bo was playing and recording at that time. Another theory says that Freed coined the term from the 1947 rhythm-and-blues hit, *We're Gonna Rock, We're Gonna Roll*, by Wild Bill Moore.

rock: a popular-music style that developed from rock 'n' roll in the 1960s

Rock 'n' roll was a fusion of rhythm-and-blues, pop, and Country-and-Western elements. It swept the nation and made superstars of Elvis Presley, Bill Haley, Jerry Lee Lewis, Chuck Berry, Bo Diddley, and other artists. Little Richard (Richard Penniman), Chubby Checker, and Fats Domino preserved the original "black" sound in rock 'n' roll.

From the beginning rock 'n' roll was a very commercially influenced music. In an age of mass media, as their fame spread worldwide, the financial success of some individuals was phenomenal. Rock 'n' roll entered the scene at the zenith of American economic prosperity, as the post-World War II baby boomers emerged into adolescence and early adulthood. Never had so many young adults had so much time, money, and freedom to explore new musical horizons. Rock, the increasingly popular style that emerged from rock 'n' roll in the 1960s with the Beatles and The Rolling Stones, quickly grew from a teenage fad to an explosion in the general population.

Rock artists kept turning back toward the earlier roots of jazz, blues, and gospel for their material. This caused resentment among some jazz and blues artists, who had blazed the trail many years earlier, but with less financial and popular reward. They felt that their creative efforts were being exploited without proper recognition and remuneration. As rock matured, rock artists began to pay respect more and more to these original jazz and blues pioneers, both in the liner notes of their albums and, often, by inviting these earlier artists to record with them.

From one of the many Elvis Presley albums. [The Hugh Jones Collection.]

A Bill Haley album. [The Hugh Jones Collection.]

Rock was and is primarily a vocally oriented music, and the beat is built for dancing. This caught short many jazz musicians, who had deemphasized both vocal music and dance beats beginning in the late 1940s with the birth of bop. Many were forced to return to this earlier format to survive.

Rock helped to preserve the essence of jazz during the '60s and '70s and reintroduce it to a wide audience as well. For that we can be thankful. On the other hand, rock just about destroyed the traditional pop-music industry and had a widely felt negative impact on jazz. For instance, the great swing-era bandleader Stan Kenton, who recorded for Capitol Records, left Capitol to form his own record company during this period because he felt that Capitol was so busy making money with its top rock artists (like the Beatles) that it no longer was promoting or paying attention to jazz artists. Frank Sinatra left for similar reasons during the same period and created his own label called "Reprise."

Commercial art, created for a mass market, is motivated largely by monetary considerations. Imitation of the most popular artists tends to breed conformity, thus producing little that is original and enduring.

The Roaring Twenties saw a shift to Chicago as the capital of live jazz and the center (along with New York) of the record industry. *Race Records* tapped a large audience of black blues and jazz fans, sold in the millions, and set off a talent search for new black singers and musicians. *Classic blues* introduced more urban and sophisticated lyrics than rural blues, and the urban styles of Chicago and Kansas City began replacing the raw New Orleans style.

In the Swing Era of the 1930s and early '40s, larger dance halls gave rise to big bands with enlarged sax sections, additional trumpets and trombones, and a rhythm section consisting of piano, bass, and drums. Big bands of this period often had to choose between smooth commercial dance arrangements (where the big money was to be found), and less financially successful, but top-quality, jazz arrangements. Bands that trod the fine line between both types were nicknamed *MOR* (Middle-Of-the-Road) *Bands* by record companies.

The solo pianist was an important figure in this period, and two keyboard styles were dominant—Harlem *stride* piano, which grew out of ragtime, and *boogie-woogie*, which evolved from the blues.

The careers of several jazz greats were launched at the Cotton Club in New York City during the Harlem Renaissance of the 1920s and '30s, and the national center for jazz shifted to New York in the 1930s and '40s. Mass-marketing techniques and ballroom dancing helped make this the most commercially successful era for jazz.

In the 1950s, Norman Granz booked *jam sessions* of jazz notables in concert halls around the world. These concerts, called *Jazz at the Philharmonic* by their promoter, helped change jazz's image and give it credibility as concert music—paving the way for its transition to a fine art.

Other developments in popular music at this time were the growth of rhythm-and-blues and the Motown style, and the emergence of rock 'n' roll from rhythm-and-blues and country roots. These commercially successful forms interacted with jazz to their mutual benefit and also competed with jazz in the marketplace to jazz's detriment.

■ **Questions on Chapter 6**

A. *In your own words* write one or two sentences describing each of the terms listed in Questions 1–20.

　　1. race records _____

　　_____

　　2. scat singing _____

　　_____

3. vibrato _____
_____

4. urban blues _____
_____

5. swing music _____
_____

6. commercial big bands _____
_____

7. MOR big bands _____
_____

8. stride piano _____
_____

9. countermelody _____
_____

10. art song _____
_____

11. Harlem Renaissance _____
_____

12. cutting contest _____
_____

13. Jazz at the Philharmonic _____
_____

14. rhythm-and-blues _____
_____

15. Country-and-Western _____
_____

16. rock 'n' roll _____
_____

17. Motown _____
_____

18. hillbilly music _____
_____

19. bluegrass _____
_____

20. Norteño music _____
_____

In Questions 21–26 fill in the blanks.

21. The term _____ refers to the boisterous era of prosperity that followed World War I.

22. A _____ was a nightclub where alcohol was served illegally during Prohibition.

23. The period of economic crisis following the stock-market crash of 1929 was called the _____.

24. To _____ is to produce the rhythmic element that encourages dancing and clapping.

25. Four or more chord tones all within an octave are known as a _____ _____.

26. An _____ is a chord in which the notes are played up or down in rapid succession, rather than simultaneously.

In Questions 27–32 write a sentence or two identifying each of the following artists.

27. Mamie Smith _____
_____

28. Bessie Smith _____
_____

29. Clara Smith _____
_____

30. Bix Beiderbecke _____
_____

31. Billie Holiday _____
_____

32. Art Tatum _____
_____

B. 33. Why was the "Roaring Twenties" called the "jazz age"?
34. How does "commercial art" differ from "folk art"?
35. Why did jazz move up the river from New Orleans to Chicago?
36. What technological inventions helped launch jazz into a mass-media format by the late 1920s?
37. What effects did the Great Depression have on commercial music of the 1930s?
38. What conditions brought about the development of the big bands?
39. What influence did commercial pressures exert on the big bands of the Swing Era?

Topics for Further Research

A. Discuss the social and cultural changes in America in the Roaring Twenties.

B. What effects did Prohibition have on American culture, socially and economically?

C. How did the rock era transform the popular-music scene?

D. Discuss the evolution of radio from a communications technology to an entertainment media, and trace the effects of radio on popular music in the twentieth century.

Further Reading

Charlton, Katherine. *Rock Music Styles: A History*. Dubuque, Iowa: Wm C Brown Group, 1990.

Gitler, Ira. *Swing to Bop: Jazz in the 1940s*. New York: Oxford University Press, 1985. (Chapters 1–4)

Oliver, Paul. *The Meaning of the Blues*. New York: Collier Books, 1972.

Schuller, Gunther. *Early Jazz: Its Roots and Musical Development*. New York: Oxford University Press, 1986. (Chapters 5–6)

_____ . *The Swing Era: The Development of Jazz, 1930–1945*. New York: Oxford University Press, 1989. (Chapters 4, 5, 7)

Shaw, Arnold. *The Jazz Age: Popular Music in the 1920s*. New York: Oxford University Press, 1987. (Chapters 1–3)

Further Listening

Big Band Jazz: From the Beginnings to the Fifties. Smithsonian.

Dizzy Gillespie: The Development of an Artist (1940–1946). Smithsonian.

Duke Ellington, 1938. Smithsonian 2003.

Experiment in Modern Music, An: Paul Whiteman at Aeolian Hall. Smithsonian 2028.

Fletcher Henderson: Developing an American Orchestra (1923–1937). Smithsonian.

Singers and Soloists of the Swing Bands. Smithsonian 2601.

Smithsonian Collection of Classic Jazz. Smithsonian (sides C, D, E).

Films and Videos

Benny Goodman Story, The (1955).

Blues for Central Avenue (video). Jazz in Los Angeles.

Elvis (video).

Gene Krupa Story, The (1959).

Glenn Miller Story, The (1954).

Lady Sings the Blues (1972). Life of Billie Holiday.

Memories of Duke (video).

Motown 25: Yesterday, Today, Forever (video).

New York, New York (1977).

Radio Days (1987). Golden Age of radio.

Young Man with a Horn (1950).

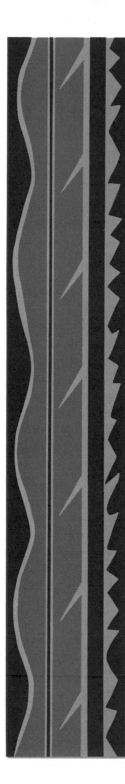

7

AFRO-AMERICAN MUSIC AS FINE ART

/ ■ /

There they were,
so prim and proper,
sittin' up straight in the concert hall
while we were on stage,
havin' a ball!
Who would've thought
that we'd get this far.
No more entertainers—
now we're the stars!
Hallowed concert halls
that featured "pure" sounds
now invite us in
and tell us "get down!"
"Le jazz hot"
has become OK
and now our musicians
sing and play
in places where before
only Bach broke ground.
Now it's time for jazz
to go to town!

—JW

Jazz entered the third stage of a maturing art form, that of a fine art, in the 1940s. The attitude of the true jazz artist during this period changed. Jazz moved out of the arena of novelty music and dance music, and into a more serious aesthetically motivated approach. This approach emphasized the inner concerns and musical expression of the artist, and was less concerned with public acceptance. Artists such as Bill Evans and Cecil Taylor maintained their artistic direction, despite commercial pressures.

Fine art is art for art's sake, and has a more esoteric appeal than commercial and folk art. It demands attention, intelligence, sensitivity, and background. Its rewards are great, but it is no longer pure entertainment. Fine art is obliged to deal will *all* of the emotions and *all* human experience. Music that expresses an unpleasant emotion may actually *sound* unpleasant. It holds a mirror up to society and says, "This is what you look like!" Society may not be pleased with its own reflection, but may very well appreciate the honesty of its artists.

The artist also has the responsibility to warn society of impending danger. Such warnings are not always appreciated. The fine artist feels the need to reach for new levels of excellence regardless of the public's reluctance to accept change.

The "why" of music has changed dramatically since 1940. Music is now used to heighten or change our moods, help sell products, and modify stressful environments. Music is today's nonprescription tranquilizer. It can even change the chemicals in our bodies that affect everything from our moods to our blood pressure.

Music has become the great escape from the necessity of dealing with ourselves and with reality. Constant music playing, behind radio and television commercials, in restaurants, grocery stores, banks, filling stations, gyms, doctors' offices, and hundreds of other locations, has made us all increasingly insensitive to changes in musical style. We listen less and feel music more.

Today's contemporary jazz artist is forced to use daring and innovative ways to get audiences to listen to new styles. Serious jazz can't sound like elevator music. It has to be able to move from the background to the foreground of our attention. This has forced jazz artists to search for sounds that have not been overused by the mass media.

In their constant search for new sounds, jazz groups have explored the world of ethnic music, new electronic sounds, and even the sounds found in nature. The Paul Winter Consort has incorporated whale, eagle, wolf, and migrating-bird sounds into their musical arrangements. Bernie Krause, a San Francisco composer, has successfully produced a jazz-rock album based entirely on sounds from the ocean, including whale sounds.

impressionist: a composer who uses unusual tone colors, rich harmonies, and subtle rhythms to evoke a mood or impression

innovator: an artist who experiments with new forms and ideas

synthesist: an artist who works with and perfects existing ideas, styles, and works

preserver: an artist who keeps older styles alive and refines them

Bill Evans, an impressionist who brought a lovely sound to the piano, was to jazz what Debussy was to classical music. His innovative harmonies created a shimmering sound that was both new and yet familiar. His melodic inventiveness was constant and his rhythmic creativity highly subtle. He changed the very concept of the jazz pianist from being either a time-keeper or smokin' soloist to an introspective intellectual with lovely ideas to share with the world. The gentleness of his compositions, among the best-known of which are *Waltz for Debbie* and *Blue in Green*, underlines these concepts.

Practitioners of fine art can be divided into three groups, all of which are important: innovators, synthesists, and preservers.

LISTENING ASSIGNMENT

"Blue in Green," Bill Evans Trio. *Smithsonian Collection of Classic Jazz*, side I, #1 ▪ The introspective, mysterious, and mystical sounds of Bill Evans' jazz-piano style created a whole new direction for jazz pianists. Why is this called *jazz impressionism*? How does Evans's style differ from those of Art Tatum and Bud Powell?

■/■ **INNOVATORS**

The type of artist that is hardest for most of us to understand and appreciate is the innovator. *Innovators* are experimenters. Although 90 to 95 percent of what they produce as art may disappear, the 5 to 10 percent of new ideas that live on can give new life and a new direction to an art form. Innovators may shock, disturb, bore, or confuse the public. Their job is not to entertain, but rather, to make the listener aware and to force the audience to confront often disturbing realities and hidden truths— about themselves, their society, and their world.

Strong emphasis on innovation and change in the arts indicates that a society has begun to search for new truths and is getting ready to dump the old ones. When you attend an avant-garde jazz concert, you may be previewing coming social and economic changes. Society must encourage its innovators. It must make room for those willing to take great artistic risks.

Weird Sun Ra, with his Myth-Science Arkestra, is a good example of an innovator. This philosopher-musician, who has been on the general scene for a long time, wants a music full of Africa. To create the appropriate "mood," members of the band dress in gold velvet. The lights go

Sun Ra. [Photofest.]

out during some tunes or flash on and off. Sun Ra lives in a mystical musical world all his own. His highly theatrical concerts, described by him as "cosmodramas," are by turns serious and surreal, raw and ritualistic, enigmatic and entertaining, unusual and unforgettable. Hard to describe, they are guerrilla theater with a bit of comedy shop and Mardi Gras thrown in. They often conclude with a serpentine conga line through the concert hall or club, led by Sun Ra, with the band chanting, "We're traveling the spaceway from planet to planet. Second stop is Jupiter!" Meanwhile, the saxophonists lie on their backs on stage, kicking their legs furiously in the air while playing hard-core blues licks on their horns. Sun Ra refuses to join the New York Musicians' Union. He claims that since he is from the planet Saturn, the union has no jurisdiction over him.

Resistance to change seems to be built into the human psyche. But when an art form fails to listen to or support its innovators, it is on its way to extinction, to becoming another historic relic, ready to frame and hang in some museum of the mind.

■/■ SYNTHESISTS

Tenor saxist Sonny Rollins is a good example of a synthesis player. Rollins's credits over the past thirty years read like a jazz *Who's Who*. Charlie "Bird" Parker, Thelonious Monk, Bud Powell, Dizzy Gillespie, Miles Davis, and Max Roach are just some of the players with whom he has worked or recorded. But unlike many of the names mentioned, he offers little in the way of innovation. What he offers is synthesis. He takes existing ideas and polishes them, perfects them, and raises them to higher artistic levels.

Sonny Rollins. [Photofest.]

Renaissance: the period of the revival of art and learning in Europe, from the 14th through the 17th centuries

The *synthesist* is a craftsperson. He or she takes what is best from the innovators and tries to perfect it. Michelangelo Buonarroti, the Italian sculptor, perfected the innovations of the Renaissance painters. J. S. Bach perfected the ideas of the baroque style of music. He used the new ideas created by baroque innovators. William Shakespeare pulled together new ideas from English playwrights and poets of his time and perfected them. Frank Lloyd Wright brought together new ideas developing in American architecture during the early part of this century.

In jazz-rock, a fairly recent example would be the Blood, Sweat & Tears recording of an early rock hit by The Rolling Stones, *Sympathy for the Devil.* If you compare these two versions of the same song, you will see how the synthesist takes raw, crude material and raises it to a higher level of expression.

The synthesist is a creative, but conservative, craftsperson who devotes his or her creative endeavors to perfecting existing ideas and concepts. The greatest synthesists keep polishing these ideas and concepts until they are close to perfect.

■/■ PRESERVERS

Great music transcends time and space. It transcends its original social and political implications. Great solo performers and great recordings can't be placed on the dusty shelves of time just because they come from a different era. Tenor-saxist Coleman Hawkins's version of *Body and Soul,** recorded in 1939, is still among the greatest solo performances ever recorded. There will always be those who hear it for the first time and find it as magnificent and exciting as did those who heard it when it first came out.

The preserver's role is to keep "alive," to preserve, important styles, refine them, and look for new ideas within older formats. Caught up in the frenzy of the twentieth century, jazz has been too eager to discard old styles in pursuit of the new. It's time for jazz to mature to the point where it is as concerned about preserving older styles as it is about promoting new ones. Each generation must have the opportunity to hear how early styles sounded.

Today, young jazz players like tenor saxist Scott Hamilton and Armstrong-influenced trumpeter Warren Vaché fall into this preserver category. They have devoted their skills to preserving and perfecting early jazz styles like swing.

---

*See the LISTENING ASSIGNMENT on page 255.

Artists frequently fit into more than one category. Louis Armstrong, for example, originated a style, took it to the top, and concentrated on preserving it in his later years.

Innovators, synthesists, and preservers are all necessary for the continued growth of jazz as a fine art.

■/■ THIRD-WORLD INFLUENCES

The third world had much to contribute to American artists. The ideas of black Islamic fundamentalists made black Americans more aware of their African heritage. Also, Alex Haley's popular book, *Roots*, and the television miniseries based on it, awakened a desire on the part of many black Americans to know more about their past. Between 1950 and 1970, there was a constant input of third-world influences on jazz—Latin America, the Middle East, and India, as well as Africa, all contributed. This influx of exotic new ideas from around the world reinforced jazz's position as the major musical style of the period. Just as the western European composers had absorbed and reinterpreted the peasant and gypsy folk music in their symphonies and concertos, jazz greats integrated worldwide musical ideas into their musical suites and production numbers. John Coltrane recorded his jazz albums *Africa* and *India* during this period. Duke Ellington wrote his *Far East Suite*, and John McLaughlin released his two albums, *Shakti I* and *Shakti II*.

Cuba was a Las Vegas type of playground for the east coast of the United States until Castro's regime. The jam sessions between American jazz musicians and local Cuban players, particularly Latin percussionists, helped to make these new sounds popular in the United States. The 1950s saw many new works for jazz orchestra in a Cuban-Latin style. Johnny Richard's *Cuban Fire* for Stan Kenton is a classic example of early Cuban big-band jazz.

LISTENING ASSIGNMENT

"India," John McLaughlin. *Shakti with John McLaughlin*. Columbia (CD) CK46868 ▪ This ensemble is an interesting combination of West (guitar and violin) and East (tabla and sitar). In this selection, the two tabla (small hand-held Indian drum) players sing the rhythmic patterns they are going to play before they play them. Note the virtuosity of the violin solo. How does this music differ from African tribal music? What are the similarities?

In Argentina, Lalo Schifrin, son of the concert-master of the Buenos Ares symphony orchestra, was drawn into the jazz world by the exciting music of Dizzy Gillespie. Lalo brought his training as a European composer (he studied under Madame Boulanger in Paris) to such works as the featured concerto for Dizzy called *Gillespiana* in the early 1950s. The most meaningful and popular inroads into the mainstreams of jazz by Brazilian-Latin music came through the collaboration of acoustic guitarist Charlie Byrd with jazz tenor-saxophonist Stan Getz and a Brazilian singer by the name of Astrud Gilberto.

Lalo Schifrin.
[Photofest.]

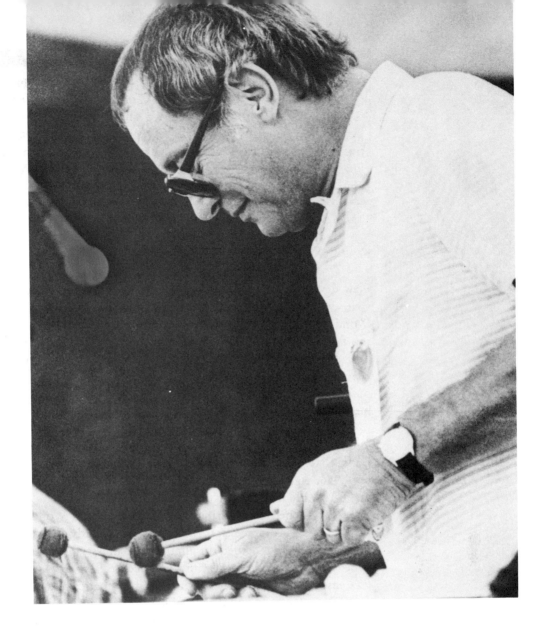

Cal Tjader.

These early collaborative albums, with their soft, sensual, and very lyrical melodies, caught hold in the 1960s. Their hauntingly beautiful melodies were composed by brilliant new Brazilian composers like Antonio Carlos Jobim (*Girl from Ipanema, Corcovado, Wave*) and Luiz Bonfá (*Mahna di Carnival, Samba di Orfeo*).

This period also witnessed the development of the Latin jazz combo. Artists like Machito, Mongo Santamaria, Willie Bobo, Cal Tjader, Chui Reyes, Eddy Cano, and Tito Puente became increasingly popular.

"Samba de Una Nota So" (One Note Samba), Stan Getz, Charlie Byrd, and Astrud Gilberto. *Jazz Samba*, Polygram 810-061 • Brazilian jazz is a combination of fiery, layered rhythms accompanied by a beautiful, lyrical melody with interesting chord progressions. Listen to the tenor saxophone (Getz), the voice (Gilberto), and the acoustic guitar (Byrd). How do they complement each other? What other instruments do you hear?

■/■ POST-WORLD WAR II BIG BANDS

New developments came from already established American forms as well, even in periods of decline. The big bands began breaking up after World War II. By 1970, very few full-time big jazz bands were left. The top four—those of Duke Ellington, Count Basie, Woody Herman, and Stan Kenton were still on the road and actively recording. Charlie Barnet, Boyd Raeburn, and Billy Eckstine also made the transition to modern jazz. But only their loyal fans kept these bands going; all were heavily dependent on overseas bookings for economic survival.

Of all the famous swing-era orchestras, Ellington's held on the longest. Lunceford's collapsed much earlier, in the early 1940s. Bandleaders like Goodman and Dorsey hung on a bit longer, but in December 1946, eight big bands called it quits. Basie was also a survivor, but just barely. He was still active until his death in 1984.

Most of the new big bands that developed after World War II were not full-time jazz orchestras. Many played regularly in their local areas and occasionally recorded an album. Jazz musicians were increasingly dependent on outside sources for their income. The cost of taking a large jazz ensemble on the road had increased dramatically and was by now prohibitive. Even with all these problems, several new leaders were willing to give it a try. These preservers, the successful new big-band leaders of this period, included:

Don Ellis.   The Don Ellis orchestra was the most innovative big band since Stan Kenton. Fascinated by the intricate rhythms and scales of the music of India, trumpet player Don Ellis made his band exciting. The Ellis band found an enthusiastic audience among young people and appeared at rock concerts and rock clubs, as well. Don's band was a west-coast band, working out of Los Angeles. Most of his players were top studio recording artists or talented college students. His band played once a week in a small club in Santa Monica, recorded several albums, and made a few short concert tours.

Buddy Rich. Most jazz experts agree that Buddy Rich was the finest big-band drummer of all time. Buddy needed a big band as a vehicle to showcase his tremendous talent. His band was a mainstream late-swing band, but the arrangements were fresh, the soloists outstanding, and the ensemble playing impeccable.

Buddy was a disciplinarian and required the best at all times from his musicians. His band worked out of Los Angeles and Las Vegas, but was on the road regularly for at least twenty-five weeks a year from the late 1960s until the mid-'70s. A favorite recording was his *West Side Story Medley.*

Maynard Ferguson's Big Band. Modern jazz trumpeter, Maynard Ferguson was one of the few successful new big-band leaders. His early band, a commercial jazz band, played proms, college dances, and concerts on the east coast. In the 1960s, Ferguson disbanded his band and moved to India to study yoga. He returned two years later and started a new band, this time on the west coast.

Today, his band is the only new big band that is touring full time. Ferguson lives in California and tours thirty to forty weeks a year. His daughter is his booking agent, and his band is very popular on both high school and college campuses. Ferguson has become one of the greatest trumpet players in the history of jazz due to his phenomenal range, fiery tone, and masterful technique.

Gerald Wilson. Gerald Wilson played trumpet and arranged for the Jimmy Lunceford band from 1939 to 1942. Settling in Los Angeles, Gerald arranged for Ella Fitzgerald and soon became active as a studio arranger/composer. In the 1960s, Gerald decided to form his own big band.

Made up of top studio players, the new band is a loose ensemble with lots of room for extended solos and a strong emphasis on Latin jazz. Their album *Viva Tirado* was one of the top-selling big-band albums of the 1970s. Because of studio commitments, the band seldom makes an appearance outside of California, but its recordings have been very successful.

Thad Jones–Mel Lewis Big Band. Although Jones and Lewis have died, this top New York City band continues to play every Monday night at the Village Vanguard in Greenwich Village. In the '60s, the band was the hottest and the most promising of all the new bands on the scene. Featuring the inventive, hard-driving, and explosive writing of Thad Jones and composer/trombonist Bob Brookmeyer, it has featured many of the top recording jazz artists in New York, giving it a creative balance not achieved in big bands since the famous Woody Herman "Herd" bands. Some jazz critics picked this as the best big band since Count Basie.

Arranger/Composers. The improvement in recording techniques and in particular, the advent of the long-playing record reinforced the importance of the role of the arranger. With more time to stretch out on a recording (up to twenty-two minutes per side) modern jazz required careful preplanning to avoid repetition and monotony.

Jazz began to seep into the airwaves, first through network AM radio in the 1930s and then through the advent of FM radio in the '60s. By the '50s, jazz had been used to underscore several Hollywood films. Duke Ellington was nominated for a Pulitzer Prize for his musical score to the film *Anatomy of a Murder*. Elmer Bernstein wrote an all-jazz score for the film *The Man with a Golden Arm*. Television followed quickly, with a light and clever jazz score by Henry Mancini to the series "Peter Gunn." All of these developments only further emphasized the importance of the arranger/composer in modern jazz.

Post-World War II educational opportunities, made accessible to veterans through the GI Bill, produced a number of well-trained jazz arrangers and composers. Most writers for jazz were as capable of writing a sonata or a symphony as a jazz arrangement. A partial list of great arranger/composers of this period includes Allyn Ferguson, Bill Holman, Stan Kenton, Oliver Nelson, Quincy Jones, Don Ellis, Johnny Mandel, Thad Jones, Bob Brookmeyer, Lalo Schifrin, Benny Carter, Pete Rugolo, Marty Paich, and Nelson Riddle.

■/■ BOP

Bob, or *bebop*, was the first jazz-style that could truly be called fine art. Divorced completely from dance and novelty music, mainly instrumental and wildly independent, bop burst upon the public like a space ship landing on the lawn of the White House. Bop was born in the after-hours jam sessions where serious, involved jazz musicians had the opportunity to experiment and try new ideas.

Charlie Parker. [Drawing by Shirley Tanzi.]

Basically a combo style, bop freed the drummer from the role of timekeeper. He became a co-soloist, with the freedom to accent solo ideas at any time and to "drive" the soloist. The bassist became the primary timekeeper in the rhythm section, keeping a relentless four-beat bass line, except for solos and Latin tunes. The chords that the pianist comped (played rhythmically with the left hand) were full of alterations and extensions, giving the harmony a bright, but aggressive and dissonant sound. The horn soloists, generally the alto sax and trumpet, often shared a complicated version of an original Broadway show tune, followed by explosive virtuosic solos.

Charlie "Bird" Parker, one of the most influential musicians in the development of bop, was a gigantic creative, yet tragic figure in the field

"Parker's Mood," Charlie Parker All Stars. *Smithsonian Collection of Classic Jazz*, side F, #3 ▪ This slow, bluesy selection illustrates the legendary Bird's fantastic tone, technique, and concept. How does he maintain the frantic excitement with this slower tempo?

of jazz. His virtuosic style of playing is almost impossible to duplicate. His innovative compositions and dizzying solos thrust Bird into the post-World War II jazz world as its leading man.

Trumpet player Dizzy Gillespie, Bird's "alter ego," was no less significant in the birth and development of bop. Together, they successfully

Dizzy Gillespie. [Drawing by Shirley Tanzi.]

LISTENING ASSIGNMENT

"Shaw 'Nuff," Dizzy Gillespie's All Star Quintette with Charlie Parker. *Smithsonian Collection of Classic Jazz*, side E, #7 ▪ The complexity of the chords, the virtuosity of the players, the frantic tempos, and the iconoclastic style of bop excited and frightened its fans and critics. How does this example differ from the earlier combo examples? What are the solo instruments?

played off one another and inspired creativity and excellence in each other. Joining them in major contributions to this new style were pianist Bud Powell, drummer Max Roach, and bassist Charles Mingus.

Charles Mingus. [Drawing by Shirley Tanzi.]

▪ Bop ▪

Important bop musicians include:

Saxophone	Dexter Gordon, Charlie Parker, Sonny Stitt
Trumpet	Miles Davis, Dizzy Gillespie, Fats Navarro, Red Rodney
Piano	Tadd Dameron, Erroll Garner, John Lewis, Thelonious Monk, Bud Powell, Lennie Tristano
Drums	Kenny Clarke, Max Roach
Bass	Charles Mingus
Trombone	J. J. Johnson
Composer/ Arrangers	Tadd Dameron, Dizzy Gillespie, Thelonious Monk, Charlie Parker

cool jazz: a jazz style of the 1950s, laid back and with subtle rhythm, unusual harmonies, and simple solo styles

Probably the most highly regarded single bop recording was an album entitled *The Greatest Jazz Concert Ever*, which was recorded in Canada in the early 1950s, and featured all of these acclaimed artists. Outstanding bop tunes include *Koko*, *Anthropology*, and *Ornithology* by Bird, and *A Night in Tunisia* and *Bebop* by Dizzy.

▪/▪ COOL JAZZ/WEST COAST JAZZ

Between 1948 and 1950, there was a stylistic backlash, a musical reaction, to the frantic energy and aggressiveness of bop. Called *cool jazz*, it was lighter, less dissonant, and less aggressive than bop. It was also more introspective and intellectual.

Miles Davis is regarded as a sort of leader of the cool movement, which was also tied into the changing social roles of the black American. (To be *cool* was to be laid-back and unemotional.) Miles began as a protege of Charlie Parker. He soon emerged as his own man, almost single-handedly moving jazz from bop to cool in the 1950s. One of the most creative minds and influences in jazz from the '50s on, Miles must rank among the strongest contributors to jazz, with Ellington and Armstrong. The most continuously innovative jazz personality of all

Miles Davis.
[Drawing by
Shirley Tanzi.]

time, he refused to repeat himself, and his constant search for new
avenues of expression always put him on the cutting edge of jazz. Not
only did he end the bop era by giving birth to the cool era, he also
pioneered hard bop, jazz-rock, and fusion.

LISTENING ASSIGNMENT

"So What," Miles Davis Sextet. *Smithsonian Collection of Classic
Jazz*, side H, #5 ▪ Note how the tune, the solos, and the interaction
of the players in this *cool* group is different than in earlier swing and
bop combos.

West Coast jazz/ West Coast cool: cool jazz with some Latin influences, played predominantly by white studio musicians in the 1950s

The cool style, which lasted into the 1960s, was perfectly suited for the new technological breakthroughs in the record industry. The long-playing record, hi-fi, stereo, and FM radio were all innovations that helped the cool music become the most popular jazz style since swing, resulting in a return to commercialism that lasted until hard bop brought jazz back into the fine-art arena.

Not only did jazz change from "hot" to "cool," but jazz chord progressions and jazz scales changed, as well. New-sounding scales, plus linear chord progressions (moving scalewise, up or down), created a different mood. Jazz records featured a wider range of sounds and feelings.

A variant of the cool style was called *West Coast jazz* or *West Coast cool*. Jazz has always had shifting energy centers. New Orleans was first, then Chicago, then New York, and then Kansas City. By the early 1950s, the cultural energy of the United States began to shift to the west coast. Los Angeles and San Francisco became the major jazz energy centers in the '50s and '60s. Most of the players of West Coast jazz were active in the Los Angeles and San Francisco recording scenes, doing film and televi-

Gerry Mulligan. [Photofest.]

Dave Brubeck. [Photofest.]

■ Cool Jazz ■

The leading practitioners of cool jazz during this period include:

Saxophone	
Alto	Paul Desmond, Lee Konitz, Lennie Niehaus, Art Pepper, Bud Shank
Tenor	Buddy Collette, Bob Cooper, Stan Getz, Bill Holman, Richie Kamuca, Harold Land, Dave Pell, Bill Perkins
Baritone	Gerry Mulligan
Trumpet	Chet Baker, Conte Candoli, Miles Davis, Carmel Jones, Shorty Rogers
Trombone	Milt Bernhart, Bob Enevoldsen, J. J. Johnson, Frank Rosolino, Kai Winding
Flute	Buddy Collette, Paul Horn, Bud Shank
Guitar	Barney Kessel, Howard Roberts
Bass	Monty Budwig, Red Callender, Percy Heath, Carson Smith, Leroy Vinnegar
Piano	Dave Brubeck, Clare Fischer, Vince Guaraldi, Hampton Hawes, Ahmad Jamal, Pete Jolly, John Lewis, André Previn, George Shearing, Lennie Tristano, Claude Williamson
Vibes	Terry Gibbs, Milt Jackson, Cal Tjader
Drums	Larry Bunker, Chico Hamilton, Stan Levey, Shelly Manne, Joe Morello
Latin Percussion	Willie Bobo, Tito Puente, Mongo Santamaria
Composer/ Arrangers	Dave Brubeck, Gil Evans, Jimmy Giuffre, Bill Holman, Stan Kenton, Billy May, Marty Paich, Dave Pell, Nelson Riddle, Shorty Rogers, Pete Rugolo, Gerald Wilson

sion sound tracks during the day and playing jazz at night. Light touches of the Latin influence were often part of the new West Coast sound.

Among the characteristic architects and arrangers of this music were Gil Evans, saxist Gerry Mulligan, trumpeter Shorty Rogers, and pianist

Dave Brubeck. The sound associated with Brubeck—cool and understated—had wide appeal. The West Coast style that made him a star in the 1950s was supposed to be a white man's sound—the antithesis of the hard-driven bop style that had exploded a few years earlier—but even while Brubeck was playing the white college circuit, he was drawing overflow crowds to black jazz clubs as well, thus mitigating the influence of commercialism. Extremely versatile, Brubeck has also written ten symphonies and choral works on religious themes, a Broadway musical, *The Ambassadors*, and several ballets.

■/■ HARD BOP

When jazz drifts too far away from its roots in blues and gospel, it begins to lose touch with reality. When an artist begins speaking a language the audience can't understand, there is no communication, and therefore, no artistic experience. Many post-bebop jazz players became too cerebral in their performances and found themselves playing to a rapidly diminishing audience. As a result, there was a movement to bring jazz back to its gospel roots.

The essence of *hard bop* lies in its rhythmic "groove" and in its melodic simplicity. Harsher, rawer, more classic timbres returned to jazz, and melodic ideas became singable again. "Blue" notes were used more often—even in nonblues tunes.

Hard bop was, at least partially, a reaction to cool. West Coast jazz had been watered down and, as a result, was considered too simplistic, too nice, too polite, too "white." Born in Philadelphia, hard bop brought the jazz scene back from the west coast and toughened it up with aggressive east-coast rhythm sections and relentless, inspired soloists, such as John Coltrane.

Hard bop was a combination of something old and something new. The old was the return to bop drumming and a "front line" of trumpet and tenor sax (as well as piano, bass, and drums). The new was the hard-driving and sometimes "funky" blues as well as the more arranged *heads*, or melodies, of the tunes selected. Broadway and Tin Pan Alley were no

---

LISTENING ASSIGNMENT

"Bikini," Dexter Gordon Quartet. *Smithsonian Collection of Classic Jazz*, side F, #6 ▪ The major characteristics of hard bop are a driving tenor saxophone with a big tone and a driving rhythm section. How does this example differ from the cool-jazz and bop examples given earlier?

■ Hard Bop ■

The outstanding hard-bop artists include:

Saxophone	
Alto	Cannonball Adderley, Jackie McLean, Phil Woods
Tenor	John Coltrane, Teddy Edwards, Benny Golson, Dexter Gordon, Joe Henderson, Hank Mobley, Sonny Rollins, Wayne Shorter
Baritone	Pepper Adams, Nick Brignola, Cecil Payne
Trumpet	Nat Adderley, Clifford Brown, Donald Byrd, Miles Davis, Kenny Dorham, Art Farmer, Freddie Hubbard, Blue Mitchell, Lee Morgan
Trombone	Jimmy Cleveland, Curtis Fuller, J. J. Johnson
Guitar	Kenny Burrell, Wes Montgomery, Howard Roberts
Bass	Paul Chambers, Percy Heath, Sam Jones, Wilber Warren, Reggie Workman
Piano	Tommy Flanagan, Red Garland, Jo Jones, Wynton Kelly, Ramsey Lewis, Junior Mance, Thelonious Monk, Horace Silver, Cedar Walton
Organ	Richard "Groove" Holmes, Jimmy McGriff, Shirley Scott, Jimmy Smith
Vibes	Roy Ayers, Bobby Hutcherson, Milt Jackson
Drums	Art Blakey, Louis Hayes, Roy Haynes, Elvin Jones, "Philly" Joe Jones, Max Roach, Mickey Roker
Composer/ Arrangers	Cannonball Adderley, John Coltrane, Miles Davis, Kenny Dorham, Benny Golson, J. J. Johnson, Les McCann, Charles Mingus, Thelonious Monk, Oliver Nelson, Wayne Shorter, Horace Silver, Bobby Timmons, Joe Zawinul

longer the sources for new material, as they were for bop. Hard bop consisted mainly of original compositions by the players themselves.

Hard bop was mostly a combo style: trumpet, tenor sax, piano, bass, and drums. Besides the important work by the Miles Davis combo, drummer Art Blakey and the Jazz Messengers, Horace Silver (and later, Cannonball Adderley, Sonny Rollins, and the Max Roach-Clifford Brown quintet) contributed to the development of the style.

Since the tenor sax was the most prominent solo instrument, this might be called the era of the great tenor sax players: Sonny Rollins, Dexter Gordon, Sonny Stitt, Zoot Sims, Al Cohn, and Stanley Turrentine.

John Coltrane.   Hard-bop tenor saxist John "Trane" Coltrane first attracted attention as a member of Miles Davis's quintet in the late 1950s. He also played with Thelonious Monk's "wild" group in 1957 and, about 1959, began leading his own small groups. In his recent autobiography, Miles Davis comments on these changes in Trane.

> John Coltrane was only really concerned about improving his playing and writing, and growing as a musician-composer. Those goals became an obsession. Women, drugs, alcohol, money, power—all were secondary or had become irrelevant in his life. He was a totally "devout" musician.*

Other than Charlie Parker, who greatly influenced him, John Coltrane has had more of a stylistic effect on saxophone playing than anyone else in the second half of the twentieth century. The intensity with which he dedicated his life to his music raised the level of jazz virtuoso playing another notch, to a level unattainable by most players.

Others who influenced him were Thelonious Monk, Miles Davis, and Olantunji (the Nigerian master drummer and teacher). Trane's discoveries included the "sheets-of-sound" style, particularly on fast tunes. This was a technique in which he ran connecting arpeggios on the repeated chords of the tune—so rapidly that the single-note saxophone

---

LISTENING ASSIGNMENT

"Giant Steps," John Coltrane. *Giant Steps*, Atlantic (CD) SD-1311-2
▪ This recording revolutionized tenor-saxophone jazz playing, and has gone on to become a hard-bop classic. The continuous-note style of Coltrane on tenor sax creates an illusion of chords—a technique called "sheets of sound." How does Coltrane differ from other sax soloists you have heard? How does this hard-bop style differ from bop?

---

*Davis, Miles and Quincy Troupe. *Miles: The Autobiography*, p. 266.

John Coltrane. [Drawing by Shirley Tanzi.]

sounded like the harmonic guitar or piano.

The latter stages of his musical life were influenced by other cultures: India, the Middle East, and Africa. The playing of his instrument at these stages was an act of religious devotion. In a way, he was functioning as a musical "evangelist," allowing the notes spoken through his instruments to be his spiritual message to mankind.

John Coltrane once said in an informal interview, "I think the main thing a musician would like to do is to give a picture to the listener of the many wonderful things he knows of and senses in the universe."*

---

*Downbeat Magazine, February 1960.

dissonance: a combination of tones that together produce a harsh or discordant sound

visceral rhythms: earthy, emotion-based rhythms

John Coltrane's contribution to jazz went beyond his recordings and personal appearances. The depth of his commitment to his art was so intense that it inspired hundreds of musicians. He raised the expression of jazz to a new level, to a level of spiritual devotion and celebration of life itself.

Coltrane died in 1967, at the age of 41, from a stomach ailment. He is survived by his children and by his wife, Alice Coltrane, a gifted keyboard player who has kept alive the Coltrane mission through recordings and performances of her own group.

> In the early days, John Coltrane was one of the loudest, fastest saxophonists around. He could play very fast and very loud at the same time. That's difficult to do. When most jazz tenor saxophonists play loud, they cannot play fast. Most jazz saxophonists get hung up trying to play like John Coltrane but he could do it and he was phenomenal. No one had ever played that way before—the sound, the style and the concept—all were brand new. Trane played with such intensity, with such a passion it was like he was possessed. However, he was gentle, quiet and shy—when he was not making music. John Coltrane definitely raised the dedication and intensity of playing jazz to a new level. There was never any doubt about the seriousness of his commitment to his art form.
>
> (Miles Davis, *Autobiography*, p. 267.)

Thelonious Monk. Next to John Coltrane, pianist Thelonious Monk was the most influential jazz musician of this period. Monk bridges two musical styles: bop and hard bop. He was the pianist in the early pioneering sessions at Harry Minton's and Monroe's in New York City in the early 1940s that led to the birth of bop.

Relying greatly on dissonance, visceral rhythms, and unusual intervals in his melodies and solos, Monk's style is so unusual, it is almost impossible to imitate. He wrote some of the greatest jazz tunes of the latter part of this century, including the popular ballad, *Round Midnight*.

LISTENING ASSIGNMENT

"Criss Cross," Thelonious Monk Quintet. *Smithsonian Collection of Classic Jazz*, side G, #3 ▪ Monk was one of the most original pianist/composers to come out of jazz. He characteristically alternates simple passages with sudden dissonant intervals and chords and with jarring rhythms. How does this contrast with "So What," the cool-jazz example (page 157)?

Thelonious Monk. [Photofest.]

As a partial tribute to his contributions to jazz, Duke University today houses the Thelonious Monk Institute, a resource and learning center for jazz musicians, writers, scholars, and students.

Max Roach–Clifford Brown Quintet. A quiet, friendly school-teacher who played jazz trumpet and shunned heroin began knocking critics out in the mid-1950s. A combination of masterful technique, a warm, rich tone, and wonderful rhythmic and melodic ideas made Clifford "Brownie" Brown a much-heralded trumpet player.

He teamed up with the great bop drummer, Max Roach, and formed a quintet which went on to record some of the most memorable music of this decade.

Unfortunately, Brown was killed in a car accident in 1956, at the age of 25. A ballad composed in his honor by tenor saxophonist Benny Golson, *I Remember Clifford*, has become a jazz standard.

Max Roach. [Photofest.]

Shortly before he died, Brownie recorded an album with strings, similar to the one that Charlie Parker did a few years earlier, but more successful. This further established the fact that well-played jazz could be integrated into a classical format, given the proper arrangements and soloist.

Cannonball Adderley.   Saxophonist Cannonball Adderley kept alto jazz playing at a high level during the hard-bop era. An alumnus of the Miles Davis sextet, Cannonball had the fiery technique of Bird as well as a funky, down-home quality that reflected his background in rhythm-and-blues and in gospel.

After leaving Davis, he formed his own quintet, teaming up with his talented brother, cornetist Nat, and Austrian-born pianist Joe Zawinul to create a Top 40 commercial hit called *Mercy, Mercy, Mercy*. The soulful, heavily gospel-influenced quality of this recording, including a strong interaction with the audience, along with the new and appropriately funky sound of its electronic piano (played by Zawinul) made this one of the most commercially successful jazz singles of the decade.

Cannonball had a phenomenal technique and command of his instrument. Occasionally, he would depart from the blues- and gospel-influenced phrasing of his solos to show his audience that he could hold his own with anyone on fast tunes. Probably the best example of this is in his album *Live in Tokyo*, where he dazzles the audience with a rocket-propelled version of Cole Porter's *Easy to Love*.

Cannonball Adderley. [Photofest.]

free jazz: a free-form jazz style that disregards traditional structures

tempo: speed

meter: the grouping of accented and unaccented beats

duple meter: a grouping of beats by twos

triple meter: a grouping of beats by threes

tonal center/key: the pitch or tone on which a piece of music centers

Free jazz begins where Charlie Parker and other bop musicians left off. Just before his death, jazz seemed on the verge of moving totally away from any preconceived restrictive ideas. The cold facts of making a living forced jazz musicians back into a more commercial mode during the cool era. Gradually, jazz learned once again to throw off all restraint, and free jazz was born. Its melodies are based on its phrasing and are not restricted by regular measures, chord progressions, or traditional forms. Its phrasing is an extension of its interval and pitch concepts and is based upon the tune being played. Its pitch is not locked into twelve even half steps to the octave. In free jazz, there is no such thing as "playing out of tune" or "playing out of time."

Free jazz has two basic guidelines:

1. Cast off any and all previous restrictions in the areas of melody, pitch, rhythm, form, and harmony.
2. Guide your playing by your deep inner feelings, and always be as spontaneous as possible.

Traditional jazz, despite its emphasis on improvisation and freedom of individual expression, has been controlled by the preconceived restrictions of

1. *tempo* (how slow or fast you play),
2. *meter* (duple or triple pulsation),
3. *tonal center* (the "key" and scale you use to build your melodies), and
4. *chord progressions* (the type of chord, how, when, and to what it changes).

Free jazz removes these traditional restrictions—there are no boundaries to creativity. The movement began in the late 1950s, led by such innovators as alto saxophonist Ornette Coleman and pianist/composer Cecil Taylor. The style was definitely experimental, and most of the recordings of early groups did not sell well.

LISTENING ASSIGNMENT

"Enter Evening," Cecil Taylor. *Smithsonian Collection of Classic Jazz,* side I, #2 ▪ Constantly searching for new directions, jazz kicked out all the restraints and began a new style that was totally spontaneous. Which features do you notice that are unusual in this recording?

Ornette Coleman.
[Drawing by Shirley Tanzi.]

Two important innovators were Anthony Braxton, who added an intellectual approach to free-form jazz, and Albert Mingelsdorf, a German trombonist who startled European audiences with his brilliant free-form trombone playing. The Art Ensemble of Chicago and the World Saxophone Quartet made excellent use of a controlled free-form approach to jazz. This approach allowed both structure and free improvisation.

LISTENING ASSIGNMENT

"Steppin'," World Saxophone Quartet. *Live in Zurich*, Black Saint BSR 0077 ▪ Not totally free, this tightly rehearsed, but modern, saxophone ensemble is free of the rhythm section and must generate rhythmic excitement on its own. Do they do it? Do you like it?

■ Free Jazz ■

Important musicians in free jazz include:

Saxophone	Anthony Braxton, Ornette Coleman, John Coltrane, Eric Dolphy, Roland Kirk, Pharoah Sanders, Archie Shepp
Trumpet	Lester Bowie, Bobby Bradford, Don Cherry
Trombone	Bruce Fowler, Albert Mangelsdorff
Flute	Paul Horn, Jeremy Steig
Guitar	Pat Metheny
Bass	Charlie Hayden, Scott La Faro, Steve Swallow
Piano	Keith Jarrett, Horace Tapscott, Cecil Taylor
Violin	Jean-Luc Ponty
Drums	Eddie Blackwell, Billy Higgins, Paul Motian
Bandleader	Sun Ra
Composer	Anthony Braxton, Ornette Coleman, John Coltrane, Charles Mingus, Archie Shepp, Cecil Taylor

inside solo style: traditional solo style

outside solo style: free solo style, unrestricted by traditional notions of tempo, meter, tonal center, and chord progression

Today, one of the most creative free-form vocal jazz artists is Bobby McFerrin, who sings other jazz styles and some pop as well. He was one of the first jazz vocalists to divorce himself totally from the rhythm section and from preconceived ideas on melodies and chord progressions.

Free jazz is exciting to play, to see, and to hear because it is totally spontaneous. Because of its freedom of expression, the music often lacks coherence and organization. This new jazz style was especially popular among young intellectuals in Europe, particularly in countries that were at that time suffering from political repression. Stifled expression often seeks release in artistic anarchy.

Many mainstream jazz artists began using free-jazz styles in their performances. The terms *inside* (traditional) and *outside* (free) solo styles became part of the jazz vocabulary. Jazz soloists are playing inside when they operate within the normal restrictions governing tempo, meter, key, scale, and chord progressions. A jazz improviser is playing outside when one or more of these restrictions are ignored. Today, many jazz soloists who start off playing inside end up playing outside by the time the solo is finished. Jazz soloists who play consistently outside are rare.

■/■ THIRD STREAM JAZZ

Third Stream jazz: a style that combines elements of classical music and jazz

Third Stream jazz is a fusion of contemporary classical music and modern jazz. The seriousness of jazz composers and players was underlined in the 1950s and '60s with the growing emphasis on concert performances. The Los Angeles Music Center opened in the '60s with two resident orchestras, the Los Angeles Philharmonic, under the baton of Zubin Mehta, and the Los Angeles Neophonic, under the able direction of jazz big-band leader and composer Stan Kenton. Some of the biggest names in jazz composition quickly lined up to write feature works for this second resident orchestra.

Stan Kenton conducting the Collegiate Neophonic Orchestra.

fusion: a blend of blues, rock, bop, and ethnic music, along with electronics, and other musical influences; heavily dependent on synthesizer use

Third Stream jazz started with Paul Whiteman, a former violist in the San Francisco Symphony, who always dreamed of combining the sophistication and wide range of tone color of the symphony orchestra with the spontaneity, excitement, and raw animal energy of jazz. He started the Third Stream movement in 1924 with his commission of George Gershwin's "Rhapsody in Blue" for solo piano and jazz orchestra for a New York concert after a successful European tour with his jazz orchestra.

Unfortunately, the marriage of classical music and jazz has not been altogether successful. One or the other of these two musical styles usually gets lost in the attempt to combine the two. Very few Third Stream compositions have become a permanent part of the jazz legacy, but efforts are still being made. Some of the best-known Third Stream composers are Gunther Schuller, John Lewis of the Modern Jazz Quartet, J. J. Johnson, Charlie Mingus, Paul Jordan, Quincy Jones, Chick Corea, Duke Ellington, Johnny Richards, William Russo, Allyn Ferguson, Gil Evans, Stan Kenton, Harold Shapiro, Jimmy Giuffre, Alan Shulman, Lalo Schifrin, Don Ellis, and Milton Babbitt. Had he lived, Bix Beiderbecke might have been a force in the development of Third Stream jazz.

▪/▪ FUSION

Experimental fusion concepts began evolving in the 1970s, but it was in the '80s that *fusion*, a word coined by record companies to avoid use of the word *jazz*, matured into a major modern jazz style of its own.

Fusion jazz is a blend of the blues, rock, gospel, soul, pop, and new electronic sounds. It also includes ethnic musical styles from Spain, Africa, Latin America, and Asia.

Paul Simon's album *The Rhythm of the Saints* could, in a sense, be called fusion because it carefully and artistically integrates most of the aforementioned ingredients. Simon spent over two years putting this

overdubbing: adding other recorded sounds or another musical track to a recording

synthesizer: a computerized device that enables a composer to create and combine an unlimited variety of musical sounds electronically

drum machine: a type of sequencer that allows drum sounds and other percussive effects to be stored on a digital disk and later to be re-created

synth drums: small drum pads hooked up to a synthesizer that can be programmed to re-create a wide range of percussion effects

jazz samba: a modified Brazilian dance rhythm, favored by fusion groups

album together—writing, recording, editing, overdubbing, and carefully integrating authentic Brazilian street-band music into his final product. Simon's four trips to Brazil and his unwillingness to compromise by using studio musicians tapped a mother lode of authentic Brazilian music.

Most fusion is instrument-oriented and cannot be considered "dance" music. Like bop, fusion tempos are too extreme (too fast or too slow) to dance to. Also, to write or play fusion, the musician must have a broad musical background.

The synthesizer is at the hub of the standard fusion ensemble, which is usually small. Besides the synthesizer, these ensembles may include drums, electric bass, guitar, sax, and trumpet. Some fusion groups carry two keyboard players. Fusion bass players usually play the fretless electric bass. The flexibility of this instrument has made the bottom or bass voice one of the most important and creative parts of the fusion sound. The drummer may play on top of prerecorded drum-machine tracks or *synth drums*, (a pattern of small drum pads hooked up to a synthesizer that can be programmed to re-create a wide range of different-sounding percussion effects). By the end of the 1980s, there were an increasing number of fusion groups in live jazz performances playing on top of sequenced prerecorded sounds.

The fusion repertoire varies from soft-rock ballads to fast jazz sambas, like *Samurai Samba* by the Yellowjackets. An occasional funk song or blues tune may be programmed, as well. The versatility of the fusion ensemble is almost unlimited. The only limitations are

1. the imagination and creativity of the players,
2. their level of musical technique,
3. their familiarity with other musical styles, and
4. their familiarity with the new technology built into the instruments.

▪ Fusion ▪

Important names in fusion include:

Saxophone	
Soprano	Kenny G, David Liebman, David Sanborn, Grover Washington, Jr., Paul Winter
Alto	Charles McPherson, David Sanborn, Grover Washington, Jr., Paul Winter
Tenor	Michael Brecker, Tom Scott, Wayne Shorter
Trumpet	Randy Brecker, Miles Davis, Don Ellis
Flügelhorn	Art Farmer, Chuck Mangione, Bobby Shew
Flute	Paul Horn, Herbie Mann
Guitar	Larry Coryell, Al DiMeola, Earl Klugh, John McLaughlin, Pat Metheny
Bass	Jeff Berlin, Stanley Clarke, Jaco Pastorius
Keyboard	Chick Corea, Tom Grant, Herbie Hancock, Jeff Lorber, Dee Tomlin, Joe Zawinul
Synthesizer	Jan Hammer, Herbie Hancock, Bob James, Jeff Lorber, Joe Zawinul
Vibes	Roy Ayers, Gary Burton
Drums	Billy Cobham, Harvey Mason, Alphonse Mouzon, Lenny White, Tony Williams
Composers	Randy Brecker, Billy Cobham, Chick Corea, Miles Davis, Kenny G, Jan Hammer, Herbie Hancock, Bob James, Earl Klugh, Jeff Lorber, Chuck Mangione, Tom Scott, Grover Washington, Jr., Tony Williams, Joe Zawinul
Groups	Pieces of a Dream, Spyro Gyra, Steely Dan, Steps Ahead, Weather Report

Stylistically, fusion groups favor the jazz samba for their fast-tempo numbers and a modified funk beat for their slower-tempo selections. Commercially, fusion has probably been the most successful jazz style since the swing era of the 1930s.

■/■ JAZZ-ROCK

Modern *jazz-rock* groups usually have rock rhythm sections with an added horn line. The horn lines generally consist of two or three trumpets. The typical rock rhythm section consists of two guitars (one lead and one rhythm), an electric piano or synthesizer, an electric bass, drums, and sometimes Latin percussion instruments.

Unlike other fusion ensembles, jazz-rock combos are vocal- and dance-oriented. Most of their numbers feature a vocalist, and their tempos are danceable.

Although jazz-rock was an obvious move by jazz back to the safer world of commercialism, there were still some very creative groups and recordings to come out of the jazz-rock style. The most artistic and creative (but not necessarily the most popular) jazz-rock combos included Blood, Sweat & Tears, Chicago, Ten-Wheel Drive, Chase, Matrix, The Crusaders, and Tower of Power.

■/■ VOCAL JAZZ

Jazz vocal groups struck out in new directions between 1950 and 1970. The Swingle Singers gave Johann Sebastian Bach the jazz treatment in their popular album *Bach's Greatest Hits.* Some groups adapted film or television themes. Manhattan Transfer's *Twilight Tone* is a jazz version of the theme to the popular television show "Twilight Zone." Even the theme to "The Flintstones" received a jazz treatment.

Multitrack recording allowed clever arrangers to overdub one voice many times. This electronic process "cloned" the singer into two to six parts. Al Jarreau was particularly adept at this.

The old-timers—Ella Fitzgerald, Sarah Vaughan, Betty Carter, Carmen McRae, and Mel Tormé—continued to get better with age, but new voices—singers like Astrud Gilberto, Cleo Laine, Flora Purim, Eddie Jefferson, and Bobby McFerrin—challenged the old-timers.

■/■ JACUZZI JAZZ

By the 1980s, music had become a constant part of the American scene. It was the cheapest, most efficient environment modifier and mood adjuster legally available. Music was increasingly used to mollify pain and frustration and offer an escape into an acoustic fantasy land.

Betty Carter.   [Drawing by Shirley Tanzi.]

jacuzzi jazz: watered-down, unimaginative jazz used as background music

Muzak: a corporation that introduced recorded background music for commercial purposes in the 1950s

New Age music: mood

The jazz that developed to meet this need has been called *jacuzzi jazz*. Jacuzzi jazz is nonthreatening and nonaggressive, monotonous and predictable, like the elevator music that was introduced by corporations like Muzak in the 1950s. It can also be considered an offshoot of *New Age* music, a lush blend of synthesized and acoustic sounds staged within well-crafted song structures. This new type of watered-down jazz often uses familiar musical clichés, but without adding anything new. It lacks the raw energy, excitement, spontaneity, and guilelessness of hardcore jazz.

music whose primary purpose is to modify the acoustical environment

Jacuzzi jazz is never too loud or too soft, too abrasive or too syrupy smooth, too fast or too slow. It's never too complicated harmonically or rhythmically. It certainly never does anything too aggressively, nor does it challenge the listener to sit up and pay attention. Its primary purpose is to create a nonthreatening, intellectually nonstimulating mood, against which you can do a myriad of things without worrying about the music interfering. There are no memorable melodies, solos or special-arrangement effects.

Unfortunately, two very talented musicians, Bob James and Kenny G, have almost totally surrendered to the financial rewards of the marketplace, and are now producing mostly jacuzzi jazz. At the time of this writing, Earl Klugh seems headed in this direction.

Jacuzzi jazz was created for commercial purposes only, and it often crowds other forms of jazz off the airwaves, off the record-rack shelves, and out of the jazz clubs and concert halls. For this reason, it represents a threat to the survival of other styles of jazz.

▪/▪ COMMERCIAL PRESSURES

The greatest danger that jazz faced between 1950 and 1970 was the pressure from the marketplace. Financial considerations often made it impossible for jazz artists, particularly those in the more innovative groups, to continue playing and recording their exciting new music. Most fine art needs to be subsidized to survive because it doesn't appeal to a mass market. Jazz, however, has yet to find a sufficient amount of subsidy.

Financial pressures forced jazz artists to move in one of two directions: into the concert hall or back into the world of commercial music. The Modern Jazz Quartet is a concert jazz ensemble that has been successful for over forty years. On the other hand, jazz guitarist George Benson reentered the world of commercial music as a pop singer and became a superstar.

Some jazz artists lost their souls in the attempt to climb the ladder of public success. Others made it while still holding on to their jazz and blues roots. Successful transitions were made by Ray Charles, George

Benson, and B. B. King, but others, like Freddie Hubbard, Ahmad Jamal, and Hubert Laws, lost their way and had to start over.

Jazz clubs were rapidly going out of business. In the early 1950s, there were approximately 10,000 jazz clubs in the United States; by the late 1970s, there were fewer than 1,000. Television was reshaping the entertainment concepts of America and those who danced now danced to rock 'n' roll or rhythm-and-blues. FM radio formats were moving away from jazz toward more lucrative fields like rock, pop, and Country-and-Western. The black community itself started rejecting jazz as its music and returned to earlier African-American musical styles, eventually combining them with rock and rhythm-and-blues.

Record companies ignored jazz artists, favoring those of the much more lucrative rock and pop world. As a business, there wasn't a choice. Promotion and attention went where the money was.

But new ways were developed to sell jazz, including subscription concerts, jazz festivals, and jazz parties. The foreign market for jazz also expanded greatly during this time. Many American jazz greats today are able to survive primarily on the proceeds from overseas appearances and record sales. Federal grants also helped many of the more avante-garde groups stay alive.

The new trends were good for the traditional jazz artist; they were not so good for jazz innovators. Most jazz innovators were unable to support themselves on a regular basis by playing jazz. Many were forced to take daytime jobs to pay their bills. Most hoped to salvage enough time to practice and write the music to which they had devoted their lives. Jazz should be warned by what happened to western European music when it separated itself from the masses. Today, most contemporary classical composers can support themselves only by teaching, lecturing, or conducting. Few are household names, and their music is often misunderstood or unappreciated.

Performing jazz artists and composers must, however, meet their own standards of excellence, even if those standards are ahead of their times. As long as artists know *why* they are making music and what they are trying to say, they will be able to communicate with the audience.

SUMMARY

As jazz entered the world of fine art, its artists turned their focus inward and produced serious art that was true to their own direction, but often less popular with audiences.

Fine art is a mature art form, created for aesthetic purposes and primarily concerned with quality and meaning. There are three types of creative talents necessary to the existence of a fine art: *innovators*—those artists who experiment with new styles; *synthesists*—who take existing works, styles, and ideas and try to improve on them; and *preservers*—those who preserve and refine important earlier styles and keep them alive.

There were a great many innovations and changes in post-1940s jazz. American jazz innovators in the '50s and '60s drew from a large variety of third-world and other influences in their music. The fate of big bands in this period, however, was primarily in the hands of preservers, big-band leaders who brought new life to a dying form. Synthesists created new jazz movements, such as *bop*, *cool jazz*, and *hard bop*, which reflected changing attitudes and aesthetic concerns. *Free jazz* was an attempt to work outside of the traditional rules and restrictions, whereas *jazz-rock* and *third stream jazz* both attempted to combine different genres. These important new directions and styles established between 1950 and 1970 will continue to influence jazz artists throughout the '90s and into the twenty-first century.

The greatest obstacles to jazz, as well as to any fine art, were the commercial pressures inherent in an art without much mass-market appeal. Jazz artists turned to a number of different strategies to stay afloat, from formal concerts to jazz festivals. Some entered the market as commercial artists, others stayed with true jazz, but took day jobs to support themselves. Like all fine arts that face financial pressures, jazz is in need of more public subsidies.

■ **Questions on Chapter 7**

A. *In your own words* write one or two sentences describing each of the terms listed in Questions 1–13.

1. bop _____
_____

2. cool jazz _____
_____

3. West Coast jazz _____
_____

4. hard bop _____
_____

5. inside solo style _____
_____

6. outside solo style _____

_____

7. free jazz _____

_____

8. third-stream jazz _____

_____

9. fusion jazz _____

_____

10. jazz-rock _____

_____

11. jacuzzi jazz _____

_____

12. Muzak _____

_____

13. New Age Music _____

_____

In Questions 14–18 fill in the blanks.

14. A discordant or harsh sound is called _____.

15. A grouping of beats by twos is known as _____.

16. The pitch or tone on which a piece of music centers is its _____

_____.

17. _____ means adding other recorded sounds or another track to a recording.

18. _____ is a technique in which different sounds are electronically recorded on separate tracks and later mixed by the sound engineer.

In Questions 19–28 write a sentence or two identifying each of the following artists or groups.

19. Sun Ra _____

_____

20. Don Ellis _____

_____

21. Buddy Rich _____

_____

22. Maynard Ferguson _____

_____

23. Gerald Wilson _____

_____

24. Thad Jones – Mel Lewis big band _____

_____

25. John Coltrane _____

_____

26. Thelonious Monk _____

_____

27. Max Roach – Clifford Brown Quintet _____

_____

28. Cannonball Adderley _____

_____

B. 29. Define "fine art." In what ways do jazz styles since the 1940s exhibit the characteristics of a fine art?

30. Describe the differences between jazz *innovators*, *synthesists*, and *preservers*.

31. What social and technological changes have affected the development of post-1940s jazz?

32. What are the major stylistic differences between post-1940s jazz styles? What features do they share in common?

33. What are some of the commercial pressures jazz artists faced during the fifties and sixties?

34. Why is it difficult to find a widely accepted definition of "jazz"? How would *you* define "jazz"?

■ Topics for Further Research

A. Discuss the evolution of jazz in Latin America and its influence on North American jazz since the 1950s.

B. How did Broadway influence the popular-music scene in post-World War II America?

■ Further Reading

Davis, Miles and Quincy Troupe. *Miles: The Autobiography*. New York: Simon & Schuster, 1990.

Ellington, Duke. *Music Is My Mistress*. New York: Doubleday & Co., 1973.

Gillespie, Dizzy, with Al Fraser. *To Be or Not To Bop*. New York: Doubleday & Co., 1979.

Gitler, Ira. *Swing to Bop: Jazz in the 1940s*. New York: Oxford University Press, 1985. (Chapters 5–8)

Russell, Ross. *Bird Lives! The High Life and Hard Times of Charlie "Yardbird" Parker*. New York: Charterhouse Press, 1973.

Taylor, Billy. *Jazz Piano*. Dubuque, Iowa: Wm C Brown Group, 1982. (Chapters 8–11)

■ Further Listening

Art Tatum, Pieces of Eight. Smithsonian.

Brecker Brothers Collection, The. Novus 3075.

Jazz Piano. Smithsonian 7002.

Light as a Feather, Chick Corea. Polygram 827148.

Simple Pleasures, Bobby McFerrin. EMI-Manhattan E21Y-48059.

Smithsonian Collection of Classic Jazz. Smithsonian (sides F–J).

Symphony in Black, Duke Ellington. Smithsonian 1024.

■ Films and Videos

Bird (1988).

Dizzy Gillespie: A Night in Tunisia (video).

Grover Washington Jr. in Concert (video). Commercial fusion.

Miles in Paris (video).

Mo' Better Blues (1990). Soundtrack by Branford Marsalis and Terence Blanchard.

Oregon (video). Jazz-rock and folk.

Round Midnight (1986). Jazzman in Paris.

Thelonious Monk: Straight No Chaser (1988).

Trumpet Kings (video). Hosted by Wynton Marsalis.

Vintage Jazz Collection (video). vol. 1–2.

Woodstock (1970).

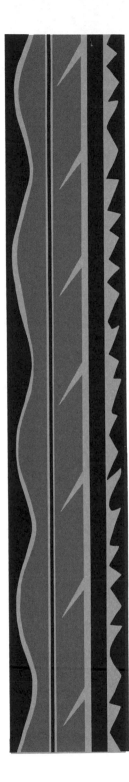

8
EARLY JAZZ ROYALTY

/ ■ /

Tap dancin' in the street
to a Bourbon Street beat,
skufflin' and singin' for tips
and things—
that's how Pops
started out
in New Orleans.

—JW

———

W E sometimes forget that most of the important things that happen in history happen as a result of individual effort. Too much has been credited to committees, groups, organizations, and political parties; too little has been credited to brave, creative, and inspirational individuals.

History is made by individuals. The movers and the shakers of the world have always been strong, talented people. This is just as true in the world of art and music as it is in the world of politics, religion, or science.

definitive practitioner:
an artist who takes the
art to new levels of excellence and expressiveness

product identification:
the association of an
image with a product

logo: a widely recog-
nized symbol or image
for easy identification

baton: a rod or staff
used to conduct an
orchestra

It takes courage to be creative. Challenging old ideas with new ones or trying to raise the standards of excellence for a particular artistic style takes discipline and courage. Gifted artists must have unshakable faith in what they are doing.

One of the signs that an art form has become a fine art is the emergence of *definitive practitioners*; that is, artists who take the art to new levels of excellence and expressiveness. By the time jazz entered the 1940s, it was already giving birth to many definitive practitioners, though some of them thought of themselves primarily as entertainers, not as artists.

Much of the music played, written, and recorded by jazz artists in the 1930s was startling in its depth of feeling and originality. But creating a public image that was glamorous and instantly recognizable was vital if these early artists expected to achieve commercial success. Today, creating this public image is called *product identification.*

A catchy, easy-to-remember name and an instantly identifiable musical logo would do much to make an artist recognizable, and so, in the 1930s, each popular big band and jazz or blues singer had a "show-biz" name and musical logo. In an attempt to raise the status of jazz in the eyes of the average American (and possibly to disguise the fact that jazz is the music of descendants of slaves), many of these early jazz artists gave themselves "royal" titles, such as Joseph "King" Oliver, and "Count" Basie.

Radio shows in the 1930s had memorable themes. Comedian Bob Hope's show, for example, had *Thanks for the Memory.* Even today, when audiences hear that tune they think of Bob Hope. Most children in American in the 1930s and '40s learned radio-show themes almost before they learned nursery rhymes.

The early jazz artists realized that their musical signatures had to be instantly recognizable, like Cab Calloway's "hi-dee-ho!," Duke Ellington's *Take the A Train*, Billie Holiday's *Lover Man*, Glenn Miller's *In the Mood*, and Satchmo's *Mack the Knife.* These early jazz artists couldn't afford press agents; they created their own public images by using their talent for mimicry and their understanding of their audiences. They understood that if they were strongly individualistic in their talk, walk, and dress, it would be easier for the public to pick them out from the crowd.

Either by design or by accident, all the early great jazz artists had some type of visual logo that quickly identified them. Louis Armstrong had his white handkerchief and ear-to-ear smile; Willie "the Lion" Smith had his derby and cigar; Duke Ellington had his elegant style in dress and manner; Cab Calloway had his extra-long baton, white tux, and big hat; Billie Holiday had the gardenia in her hair.

■/■ FERDINAND JOSEPH "JELLY ROLL" MORTON

Creole: a Louisiana native of French and black ancestry

When pianist/singer Jelly Roll Morton (1885–1941) moved to New York City in 1928, his business card claimed that he was the "inventor" of jazz. Though the claim was a bit exaggerated, it would be a mistake to dismiss this early jazz genius as just another loud-mouthed, lying braggart. He was the first important composer of this new music called *jazz* and one of the first jazz recording stars. He therefore played an important role in its early development.

Born into the sophisticated European Creole culture of New Orleans as Joseph Ferdinand la Menthe, this talented original quickly took to the musical sounds around him. His compositions reflect the tapestry of musical traditions to which he was exposed, from blues to African dance rhythms to classical European operatic and orchestral motifs.

Jelly Roll Morton. [Picture Collection, The Branch Libraries, The New York Public Library.]

Jelly Roll Morton and his Red Hot Peppers. [Picture Collection, The Branch Libraries, The New York Public Library.]

light opera: an operetta; a light, amusing opera with some spoken dialogue

He began to study piano at the age of ten. By the time he was seventeen, he was working in the Storyville bordellos, playing ragtime, French quadrilles, and light opera. Jelly Roll was also apparently active as a gambler, pool shark, card manipulator, nightclub operator, and pimp, though music remained his first "line of business."

New Orleans remained his home base, but he frequently traveled to Memphis, Chicago, St. Louis, and Kansas City, working for prolonged periods in minstrel shows. Eventually he traveled as far as New York and Los Angeles. During his early traveling years, Morton began to fuse a variety of black musical idioms—ragtime, folk, blues, minstrel-show tunes, field and levee hollers, and spirituals—with rhythms from the Caribbean and pop music from the white world. Morton's musical eclecticism reflected his absorption in the new sounds of jazz.

In 1923, Jelly Roll moved to Chicago and began to make his first jazz recordings. By 1926, he was recording for Victor with his Red Hot Peppers, a group of seven New Orleans jazz musicians familiar with Morton's style of writing. These early recordings were a triumphant fusion of composition and continuous improvisation.

four-to-the-bar: four notes to the measure—characteristic of swing music

His best ensemble work—especially with the Red Hot Peppers combo—reveals his belief that composed and meticulously rehearsed "head" arrangements are not incompatible with the spontaneity of improvised jazz, but, in fact, can retain and enhance this spontaneity. In this respect, his achievements may rank with those of Duke Ellington, Thelonious Monk, Charles Mingus, and Gil Evans. Morton also felt that most jazz was unnecessarily loud, raucous, and raw. He preferred jazz that was sweet and soft, with plenty of rhythm and a tone that was not too far removed from classical music.

In 1928, he moved to New York; but he was never able to adjust his concept of jazz to big-band arranging, and so he quickly faded from sight as the new big-band style of "swing" began to dominate jazz in the 1930s. This was particularly sad since Jelly Roll was one of the first jazz pianists to play with a four-to-the-bar "swing" feeling.

The folklorist Alan Lomax recorded Jelly Roll as part of an extensive series of musical interviews for the Library of Congress (May–July 1938). These important historical accounts, both verbal and musical, reveal Morton as jazz's earliest musician/historian and a perceptive theorist and analyst of the music. These fifty-two recordings have recently been rereleased through the Smithsonian in cassette and CD format.

Jelly Roll Morton died in 1941 in Los Angeles. He was one of the first musicians to realize the potential of jazz by recognizing its eclectic nature—its ability to absorb and adapt musical ideas and styles from many sources.

▪/▪ JOSEPH "KING" OLIVER

Born and raised in New Orleans, Joe Oliver (1885–1938) won the title "king" in a 1917 playing contest to decide who was the best cornetist in New Orleans. In 1918, he left for Chicago, where, in 1920, he formed his own group.

Oliver was Louis Armstrong's idol. Joe sent for the 23-year-old Satchmo in 1923, when he moved Oliver's Creole Jazz Band to the

King Oliver. [Picture Collection, The Branch Libraries, The New York Public Library.]

Lincoln Gardens dance hall in Chicago. His six-piece band, with Armstrong on second cornet, was the finest band of its day and the first important black jazz group to cut records (in 1923).

King Oliver was the first artist to popularize New Orleans jazz. Songs like *Livery Stable Blues*, recorded earlier by the Original Dixieland Jazz Band, were actually "novelty" songs and did not reflect authentic early jazz style.

King Oliver was an important jazz pioneer, not only because of his playing and bandleading, but because of his effect on Louis Armstrong, who called him "the best and only teacher I ever had." As a player his tone was strong and his vibrato controlled. He created rhythmic excitement by playing behind the beat, a stylistic device that Satchmo would later raise to the highest level of perfection.

LISTENING ASSIGNMENT

"Dippermouth Blues," King Oliver's Creole Jazz Band. *Smithsonian Collection of Classic Jazz*, side A, #5 ▪ Which instruments do you hear on this New Orleans Dixieland jazz recording? Can you hear the collective improvisation at the beginning and at the end?

Paul Whiteman. [Drawing by David Zuckerman.]

■/■ PAUL WHITEMAN

Bandleader Paul Whiteman (1890–1967), who looked like a chubby version of the little man on the top of the wedding cake, became known as the "King of Jazz" by accident. At a photo session, someone placed a crown on his head, a crown left over from some beauty queen's earlier session. It was meant as a joke, but the picture came over the Associated Press newswire and was picked up by newspapers all over the country. The caption under the picture read "Paul Whiteman, King of Jazz." From then on, as far as the public was concerned, Whiteman *was* the "king of jazz." After all, if you couldn't trust the newspapers, who could you trust? To his credit, Whiteman was always embarrassed by the title and contributed little to maintaining the legend.

Paul Whiteman's greatest contribution to jazz was his commissioning of the brilliant George Gershwin's *Rhapsody in Blue* (1924) for solo piano and jazz orchestra at a concert in Aeolian Hall in New York.* The premiere, with the composer as soloist, became one of those classic events in music history, like the Paris premiere of Igor Stravinsky's *Rites of Spring*. At the conclusion of the piece, there was stunned silence and then torrential applause. The music world realized that it had reached a milestone — the coming together of Western European and African musical art at its highest level of expression. The event was instantly transformed into legend.

By presenting jazz in concert format for the first time, Whiteman opened the door for others to follow suit and drew the attention of the American public to the fact that this new music called *jazz* was true art and not just entertainment. Although there had been earlier attempts at concert jazz, the attention created by Whiteman's New York concert gave the art form its first wide public acceptance.

Paul Whiteman was also well known for his kindness to and support of jazz musicians. He hired and encouraged many outstanding jazz artists, sometimes paying their bills when they were down and out.

The vast popularity of the Whiteman Orchestra also helped to bring the new sounds of jazz to America's upper-middle class, thereby giving jazz its first cultural stamp of approval.

▪/▪ FLETCHER HENDERSON

In the 1920s, New York began to play an increasingly important role in the evolution of jazz. It was in New York in 1923 that the nation's first big jazz band — the Fletcher Henderson Band — premiered. The leader of this band, composer-arranger-pianist Fletcher Henderson (1897-1952), is credited with starting the big-band swing movement in America.

---

*See the LISTENING ASSIGNMENT, "The Birth of 'Rhapsody in Blue': Paul Whiteman's Historic Aeolian Hall Concert of 1924," page 52.

Fletcher Henderson.
[Picture Collection, The Branch Libraries, The New York Public Library.]

Fletcher Henderson was the first important black jazz bandleader and arranger. He started as a piano accompanist for blues singers—including Bessie Smith—at a major record company. Later he started his own band, hiring many of the outstanding jazz players of the time, including Louis Armstrong and Coleman Hawkins.

His ensemble was one of the earliest to record big-band jazz arrangements, with recordings dating back to 1924. Although a gifted arranger, Henderson was less than successful as a bandleader. After breaking up his band in the early 1930s, Fletcher Henderson became the staff arranger for Benny Goodman. Classic big-band hits arranged or composed by Henderson include *Wrapping It Up, King Porter Stomp*, and *Down South Camp Meetin'*.

LISTENING ASSIGNMENT

"Wrapping It Up," Fletcher Henderson. *Smithsonian Collection of Classic Jazz*, side B, #12 • This is a good example of the early black big bands. Notice the balance between the ensemble and the soloist.

■/■ JIMMIE LUNCEFORD

If Ellington was the "Duke" of early big bands and Basie was the "Count," then Lunceford had to be the "Prince." From 1933 to 1943, the Lunceford band was one of the most creative jazz bands of all time.

Jimmie Lunceford.
[Picture Collection, The
Branch Libraries, The
New York Public Library.]

Jimmie Lunceford (1902–1947) liked creative arrangers. He carried
three on his payroll. Trumpeter Sy Oliver was one of Lunceford's arranger/
architects. Sy later wrote many well-known jazz arrangements for Tommy
Dorsey. Some of Lunceford's hits include *Organ Grinder's Swing*, *Harlem
Shout*, *For Dancers Only*, *Christopher Columbus*, and *Swanee River*.

He insisted on disciplined playing and rehearsing, bringing his band
to the highest possible level of musical and technical skill. This was no

---

LISTENING ASSIGNMENT

"Organ Grinder's Swing," Jimmie Lunceford. *Smithsonian Collection of
Classic Jazz*, side C, #13 ▪ The Lunceford band was one of the
smoothest and most exciting swing bands to come out of the 1930s.
Listen for the careful balance between soloists, sections, and ensemble passages. How does this differ from the earlier big-band examples?

---

semiliterate group of rural blacks, looking uncomfortable in tuxedos and playing loud, raucous jazz. This band was a highly oiled, highly sophisticated machine, challenging the classical orchestras of the country in its demand for excellence and professionalism on the part of its players.

Last, but not least, this band was fun to watch. Lunceford choreographed precise movements by each section of the band to complement the excitement generated by the arrangement. Glenn Miller patterned his band after the Lunceford band, copying many of the visual effects, such as up-and-down trumpets, side-to-side trombones, and scooping saxes.

Lunceford's career was cut short by an unfortunate fatal car accident in the early 1940s in southern California.

■/■ WILLIAM "COUNT" BASIE

The most predictable element about the Basie band was that *everything* it played had to swing. If a new arrangement did not have Basie tapping his foot happily by the second chorus, he threw it out, no matter how interesting its melody, harmony, or voicings. Basie's uncompromising commitment to swing made his band a favorite with countless jazz fans.

Count Basie (1904–1984) was discovered by jazz entrepreneur John Hammond at the Reno Club in Kansas City in May 1936. (Basie himself was from Red Bank, New Jersey.) Hammond brought the Basie band to New York, where they played the famous Roseland Ballroom and recorded for the Decca label. Except for a two-year period (1950–1952) when Basie toured with an octet, rather than with a big band, and once in the 1970s when illness forced him to cancel a season, the Basie band was on the road from 1936 until his death in 1984.

An uncannily balanced band (arrangements, solo instrumentalists, and singers); understated piano playing; hard driving, tight rhythms; and tight, but explosive, ensemble choruses are all Basie trademarks.

LISTENING ASSIGNMENT

"Taxi War Dance," Count Basie. *Smithsonian Collection of Classic Jazz*, side D, #6 ▪ This is a good example of Kansas City *shuffle blues*, a big-band style, with a rolling beat, developed by Count Basie. How is this similar to boogie-woogie? Note the excellent tenor-saxophone playing by Lester Young and the rhythm piano of Count Basie.

Count Basie. [Drawing by Shirley Tanzi.]

The "Count" appeared in over thirteen films (*Blazing Saddles* was his last), recorded numerous albums, and was regularly showcased at major jazz festivals. His band was also the home of some of the greatest jazz solo instrumentalists of all time, including tenor saxophonist Lester Young, trumpeters Buck Clayton and Harry Edison, drummer Jo Jones, trombonists Dicky Wells and Vic Dickenson, and saxophonists Herschel Evans and Buddy Tate. The Basie band also kept alive the exciting Kansas City blues style of singing with legendary bluesman Jimmy Rushing, "Mr. Five-by-five."

vibraharp: also called *vibraphone* or *vibes*; a melodic percussion instrument played by striking small metal bars with hammers

Benny Goodman. [Photofest.]

The mass media crowned Benny Goodman (1909–1986) the "King of Swing" in the 1930s. Benny and the majority of jazz fans and audiences worldwide have acknowledged that he earned the title many times over.

Benny Goodman's was the first white dance band to play nothing but jazz, the first white jazz band to appear at Carnegie Hall (in 1938), and the first white jazz band to tour with blacks (pianist Teddy Wilson in 1936 and vibraharpist Lionel Hampton in 1937). The band was chosen to represent America in the Soviet Union on a State Department-sponsored tour in 1962.

Benny Goodman launched the swing era of the 1930s and '40s. Made up of some of the greatest jazz players of the time, the Goodman orchestra, between late 1934 and 1942, when it finally broke up, was one of the most acclaimed big bands in the business. The recording of their 1938 Carnegie Hall concert is among the greatest live-concert jazz albums ever to be recorded. Only Benny's recurring bouts of ill health forced his band into early retirement.

Born Benjamin David Goodman in Chicago, he was a relentless perfectionist, demanding and getting nothing but the best from himself and his band. Many jazz experts feel that Benny Goodman's clarinet playing made him the greatest nonkeyboard soloist of the swing era. Some consider him to have been the finest clarinetist jazz has seen.

Peggy Lee, one of the best jazz singers of all time, started her career with the Goodman orchestra. Also out of Goodman's band, and partially financed by him, came three future great jazz bandleaders: Lionel Hampton, Harry James, and the great drummer and showman Gene Krupa.

▪/▪ LESTER "PREZ" YOUNG

Lester Young (1909–1959) and Coleman Hawkins were the two most important influences in the early history of tenor-sax playing. Of the two, Lester is probably the more significant, because he almost single-handedly turned jazz saxophone playing in a new direction in the 1930s.

Many jazz critics and historians have given Lester credit for inventing what came to be known as *cool jazz.* Certainly his playing, though no less rhythmical than that of Coleman Hawkins and others, was more laid-back and subtle, and less emotional.

Lester won his nickname in a 24-hour jam session in Kansas City in the mid-1930s when he bested four of the greatest tenor saxophonists of that time, including the great Coleman Hawkins. The title "The President" was later shortened to "Prez."

Lester Young was from a musical family. Raised in New Orleans, he played drums in his dad's band as a very young child. He later switched to saxophone, and it became his main instrument. His light, airy sound anticipated the switch from "hot" to "cool" jazz. Lester Young was the crowning jewel of the Basie band. He played briefly with Ellington, and also led his own combo.

Several traumatic encounters with racism and brutality while in the army in World War II left him sensitive, shy, and vulnerable to alcohol, depression, and frequent nervous breakdowns.

Lester Young.
[Drawing by
Shirley Tanzi.]

Lester was later married to Billie Holiday. They admired each other's musical styles enormously and remained cohorts and soulmates, but their marriage was brief. Lester supposedly was the first to refer to Billie as "Lady Day." Lester Young remained a strong influence on tenor saxophonists until the 1960s, when John Coltrane revolutionized jazz tenor-saxophone style and took things in a new direction.

LISTENING ASSIGNMENT

"Lector Leaps in," Lester Young (with Count Basie). *Smithsonian Collection of Classic Jazz*, side D, #7 ▪ This blues was written and performed by one of the most important tenor-saxophone soloists of the 1930s. Lester Young created a whole new style of tenor-sax playing. Notice the light, lyrical, "floating" approach to soloing.

■/■ GERTRUDE "MA" RAINEY

Ma Rainey (1886–1939) toured as a minstrel-show singer while still in her teens. She was one of the first to realize the importance of the blues.

In the early 1920s, the discovery of the blues record market led to a search for new talent in this style. Record companies sent talent scouts to black vaudeville houses, rural dance halls called *juke joints*, and cabarets—anywhere there might be a great blues singer. In their search, they

Ma Rainey with her Rabbit's Foot Minstrels. From left to right: Gabriel Washington, drums; Al Wynn, trombone; Dave Nelson, trumpet; Ma Rainey; Eddie Pollack, saxophone; Thomas A. Dorsey, piano (and gospel songwriter). [Picture Collection, The Branch Libraries, The New York Public Library.]

discovered Ma Rainey, who came out of the touring black vaudeville troupe called the Rabbit's Foot Minstrels.

Paramount Records began recording Madame Rainey, as she was sometimes called, in 1924, modestly touting her as "the greatest blues singer ever known." Her early recordings for Paramount Records helped to establish her as a pioneer in the new classic-blues style.

Ma Rainey recorded over a hundred records between 1924 and 1929. After 1930, her fame diminished rapidly, and by the end of the '30s she had retired from active performing and recording.

▪/▪ BESSIE SMITH

Bessie Smith (1894–1937), the Empress of the Blues, was the best of the classic blues singers. There never was one like her and there'll never be one like her again. Even though she was raucous and loud, she had hidden deep within her voice the collected misery of over three hundred years of slavery and racism. Although the misery was there, so was the triumph and the strength—the overcoming of adversity and the sound of freedom were also heard in her voice.

John Hammond, who discovered and helped launch the careers of many top jazz artists, makes the following comments on Bessie Smith in Leonard Feather's *Encyclopedia of Jazz*:

> To my way of thinking, Bessie Smith was the greatest artist American jazz ever produced; in fact, I'm not sure that her art did not reach beyond the limits of the term *jazz*. She was one of those rare beings, a completely integrated artist capable of projecting her whole personality into her music.
>
> (1966 edition, p. 423.)

Bessie Smith was a large woman whose talent and energy overpowered everyone in her immediate presence. After a rough start (she

Bessie Smith. [Photofest.]

was fired from her first recording date for spitting on the floor), Bessie Smith went on to become perhaps the most famous of all the classic blues singers. For years, she toured the United States with her own vaudeville troupe, living aboard her private train partially to avoid the racial hassles that accompanied black artists on their tours in those days.

By the end of her first year as a recording artist for Columbia Records in 1923, Bessie had sold over two million records and was a headliner in Milton Starr's Negro vaudeville circuit. Bessie recorded with some of the best jazz musicians of the time, including Louis Armstrong.

LISTENING ASSIGNMENT

"Lost Your Head Blues," Bessie Smith. *Smithsonian Collection of Classic Jazz*, side A, #4 ▪ Bessie Smith created this song spontaneously in the studio when it was discovered that she was one song short in the recording session. It is an excellent example of her creativity and inventiveness as well as of her powerful voice.

She appeared briefly in an early Warner Brothers film, *St. Louis Blues*, in 1929. Bad health, problems with alcohol, the disastrous effects of the Great Depression on the recording industry, and changing tastes among urban blacks brought about a decline in Bessie's popularity in the early 1930s. During this period she continued starring and touring with her own vaudeville show, the Midnight Steppers. Death came in the form of a grisly car accident in 1937, cutting short her life and career.

Bessie Smith's powerful voice, masterful phrasing, and subtle musicality placed her along with Louis Armstrong as one of the two most brilliant and influential early jazz artists. A recent book on her life (*Bessie*), and a Broadway show based on her life (*Me and Bessie*), along with countless recorded tributes to her by other artists, have helped to keep her music and memory alive.

■/■ BILLIE HOLIDAY

In 1948, Frank Sinatra remarked that Billie Holiday (1915–1959) was "unquestionably the most important influence on American popular singing in the last twenty years."

Nicknamed "Lady Day" by Lester Young, Holiday was the principal bridge in vocal style between the earlier female blues singers like Bessie Smith and later jazz singers like Ella Fitzgerald.

She solidified that transition, staked out the basic concepts of good jazz style, and went on to record most of the definitive examples of female jazz singing in the 1930s and '40s. A great song writer as well as one of the greatest female jazz singers of all time, Holiday's phrasing and stylistic concepts are still influencing jazz and pop singers today.

Her personal life, however, was tragic and harrowing. As one jazz critic put it:

> Raped when she was 10, a star when she was 20, a heroin addict at 30, and an ex-con with a felony dope conviction during her last dozen years, Holiday had a lifetime pass on the death-wish roller coaster.

> (George Varga, *San Diego Union*, October 27, 1990.)

The movie *Lady Sings the Blues* introduced millions of Americans to the hardships in Billie Holiday's life while also acquainting them with her songs and her innovative vocal style.

At a time when many black singers were imitating the styles of the more popular white singers, Holiday continued to sing "black." The earthiness and sexuality of her voice were balanced by her impeccable phrasing. No one could deliver a lyric like Billie Holiday. She seemed to

Billie Holiday.
[Photofest.]

have an innate ability to reach inside each line of a lyric, touching the most important word and bringing it to life.

Sadly, toward the end of her career, some recordings were released that were not up to her earlier standards. Alcohol and drug dependency shortened both her career and her life. *Strange Fruit*, a powerful song about lynchings in the South, became Holiday's song. She insisted on singing it in most of her club and concert appearances. Many feel this was the first modern "protest" song, predating by decades Martin Luther King, the Civil Rights Movement, and *We Shall Overcome*.

Besides *Strange Fruit*, some of Holiday's best recordings include *God Bless the Child*, *Lover Man*, *Fine and Mellow*, *Don't Explain*, and *Ain't Nobody's Business*.

LISTENING ASSIGNMENT

"He's Funny That Way" and "These Foolish Things," Billie Holiday. *Smithsonian Collection of Classic Jazz*, side C, #8 and #9 ▪ What techniques does Billie Holiday use to deliver her lyrics? How does she personalize the song?

Ella Fitzgerald in 1960.
[Photofest.]

■/■ ELLA FITZGERALD

Discovered by jazz-great Benny Carter in an amateur contest at the Apollo Theatre in Harlem in the early 1930s, Ella Fitzgerald (1918–) went on to star with Chick Webb's band at the Savoy in Harlem when she was fourteen. When Chick died in 1939, she took over the band, becoming the first woman in history to lead a jazz band.

Her first smash pop hit in 1938, *A-Tisket A-Tasket*, brought her to the attention of millions of Americans. It was a novelty record, and had very little "jazz" feel to it, but her clear tone, clever phrasing, and infectious style of singing quickly made her a major recording artist. She has been able to walk the tightrope between pop and jazz over the past forty years more successfully than any other artist. She's gone on to win practically every jazz poll there is, and is internationally recognized as the "First Lady of Song."

Fitzgerald's recordings of *How High the Moon* (now a classic), *Lady Be Good*, *You'd Be So Nice To Come Home to*, and *Lemon Drop* are among the greatest examples of scat singing ever recorded. Her impeccable pitch, range, vocal flexibility, diction, and rhythmic inventiveness make her one of the greatest jazz singers of all time.

▪/▪ LOUIS "SATCHMO" ARMSTRONG

bugle: a brass instrument resembling a cornet, but without valves

Born in New Orleans in 1900, Louis Armstrong (1900–1971) became the most popular trumpeter-singer-bandleader in history. Unfortunately, the general public knows Satchmo (short for "Satchelmouth," supposedly a reference to his trumpet-scarred lips) primarily from his New Orleans jazz interpretations of pop tunes, show tunes, and ballads, like *Hello, Dolly!*, *Mack the Knife*, and *Blueberry Hill.* His gravel-choked voice and bubbling charm captured the hearts of millions of fans.

Relatively few people realize the extent of his musical genius and the depth of his contribution to American music. This former bugler from the Colored Waifs' Home in New Orleans went on to become one of the preeminent musical geniuses of American music and one of the most influential musical artists of the twentieth century.

By remodeling jazz in its early days, Armstrong had a permanent and critical effect on the musical styles evolved from it: rhythm-and-blues, Motown, and rock 'n' roll. Contemporary classical music was also influenced by Armstrong. Composers like Igor Stravinsky, Darius Milhaud, and many lesser composers heard him, marveled at his genius, and rushed to produce jazz-influenced works. Sophisticated Broadway show composers like Cole Porter couldn't resist writing for Satchmo. Porter wrote the clever *That's Jazz* for Louis Armstrong and Bing Crosby in the movie *High Society.*

Louis Armstrong was not only the most influential instrumental jazz soloist of the 1920s but also the first recorded scat singer. If these were his only accomplishments, it would be enough to put him in the Jazz Hall of Fame; but Satchmo went on to become a great deal more. He was the first definitive jazz soloist to attain worldwide recognition as a trumpeter, singer, entertainer, and show-business personality. His melodic and harmonic style was simple, but intensely rhythmic; and his lyric style and tone were warm and beautiful. His singing had a rhythmic intensity, guttural charm, and natural lyricism that made his voice the most imitated voice of the twentieth century.

The recordings made by his early groups—the Hot Five and Hot Seven—are among the greatest instrumental jazz recordings made in the

Louis Armstrong.

[Drawing by Shirley Tanzi.]

1920s. Armstrong's singing of *Ain't Misbehavin, Mack the Knife, What a Wonderful World*, and *Hello, Dolly!* are among the best examples of pop tunes sung in jazz style.

LISTENING ASSIGNMENT

"West End Blues," Louis Armstrong. *Smithsonian Collection of Classic Jazz*, side B, #4 ▪ This classic 1920s recording shows Louis Armstrong's startling brilliance as a trumpet soloist. This is one of the top ten recordings of early jazz.

Louis Armstrong did more than any other single human being to make jazz meaningful to the world. Loved in France, Japan, and Africa as he was in America, he was jazz's first truly international superstar. It is impossible to overestimate his importance to the history of jazz.

■/■ EDWARD KENNEDY "DUKE" ELLINGTON

Ellington composed incessantly to the very last days of his life. Music was indeed his mistress; it was his total life, and his commitment to it was incorruptible and unalterable. In jazz he was a giant among giants. And in twentieth-century music he may yet one day be recognized as one of the half-dozen greatest masters of our time.*

Duke Ellington (1899–1974) was born to an educated, well-to-do family in Washington, D.C. Started on piano at seven, he flirted with possible careers in athletics and art, but after his first musical composition, *Soda Fountain Rag* (1916), he never looked back. He wrote his first Broadway musical revue in 1924, a show called *Chocolate Kiddies*. He moved to New York, where he played and wrote for a variety of groups until he decided to front a six-piece band at Broadway's Kentucky Club. In 1927, the band began a five-year tenure at the Cotton Club in Harlem.

Duke's early period is referred to by some as his "jungle" period because many of the special effects used in the live shows at the Cotton Club became part of the band: the lewd shrieks, wah-wah brass, and other "junglelike" effects. The Ellington orchestra recreated many African sounds and introduced them to American audiences in a startlingly sophisticated and original format.

Ellington's recordings in the 1920s and '30s firmly established his reputation as a composer/arranger who balanced his written score withoutstanding improvised solos by members of his band. In fact, the fifteen-member Ellington band always had great jazz soloists. Johnny "the Rabbit" Hodges (alto saxophone), trumpeter James "Bubber" Miley, Joseph "Tricky Sam" Nanton (trombone), and Cootie Williams (trumpet) are just a few of the great names featured with Ellington. The Ellington band traveled to Europe for the first time in 1933, adding trombonists Juan Tizol and Lawrence Brown and vocalist Ivie Anderson to the ensemble.

---

*Gunther Schuller, *The Swing Era*, (New York, Oxford University Press, 1989), p. 157.

Duke Ellington. [Drawing by Shirley Tanzi.]

Some of Ellington's early hits include *East St. Louis Toodle-oo* (1927), *Black and Tan Fantasy* (1927), *Mood Indigo* (1930), *Sophisticated Lady* (1932), *Solitude* (1934), *Daybreak Express* (1934), and *In a Sentimental Mood* (1935).

In 1939, new personnel, like Ben Webster on tenor sax and the amazing bassist Jimmy Blanton (an eighteen-year-old whose musical and technical skills revolutionized jazz bass playing), as well as Cat Anderson, his "high-note" trumpet artist, and other new faces rejuvenated the Ellington band.

Some of the best recordings ever made by a jazz band were done in the so-called golden age of Ellington (1940–1942). Sharing the writing duties with recently arrived arranger Billy Strayhorn, Ellington played and recorded many of his classics, including *Jack the Bear, Bojangles, Take the A Train, Chelsea Bridge, Warm Valley*, and *Harlem Airshaft*.

During this time, the band participated in a Hollywood musical revue called *Jump for Joy*. Out of this revue came an Ellington classic, *I Got It Bad and That Ain't Good*. Jazz trumpeter Ray Nance and Cat Anderson, the fiery lead trumpet player, added salt and pepper to the band's brass section during this stay in Hollywood. Ray Nance's doubling on violin gave Ellington another sound to weave into his musical tapestry.

Ellington's most ambitious work, *Black, Brown and Beige*, premiered at Carnegie Hall in 1943, but was not recorded until thirty-five years later. This suite, his first attempt at extended composition, was 50 minutes long. From 1943 to 1950, the Ellington band made annual concert appearances at Carnegie Hall, with occasional performances in later years. Duke liked to showcase one or more of his extended works at these concerts. Besides *Black, Brown and Beige*, the serious works premiered at Carnegie Hall by Ellington included *Night Creatures* (1955), which combined his band and the New York Symphony, *Deep South Suite* (1947), and *Liberian Suite* (1947).

Drummer Louis Bellson, Willie Smith on alto sax, and Juan Tizol all joined or rejoined the Ellington band in the early 1950s, as did his great lead alto player, Johnny Hodges. The band's electrifying performance of *Diminuendo and Crescendo in Blue* at the Newport Jazz Festival (1956) as well as the television musical *A Drum Is a Woman* (CBS, 1957) encouraged Ellington to begin writing extended works again.

The band regained a lot of its popularity as result of its smash performance at Newport and the success of its television appearance. In 1958, Ellington performed at another Carnegie Hall concert, this one featuring guest vocalist Ella Fitzgerald. Following this concert, the band left on a European tour. In 1959, Duke turned his hand to writing music for films and won a Pulitzer Prize nomination for his brilliant musical underscore to the film *Anatomy of a Murder*.

In the 1960s and '70s, Ellington alternated lengthy overseas tours—visiting countries in Europe, Africa, the Middle East, Asia, and the Soviet Union—with record sessions, jazz-festival appearances, concerts, television appearances, and an occasional film score. Ellington's ever-listening ear captured the exotic sounds of the Far East in his *Far East Suite* (1964).

Beginning in 1965, Duke Ellington carried jazz into the church with his sacred jazz concerts. He produced three concerts of sacred music: the first, at the Grace Cathedral Church of San Francisco on September 6, 1965; the second, at the Cathedral of St. John the Divine in New York on January 19, 1968; and the third, at Westminster Abbey in London on United Nations Day, October 24, 1973. Many of Duke's extended musical works included spirituals and gospel songs.

> We will save this land if we can all agree on the meaning of that unconditional word—love.
>
> (Duke Ellington, *Music Is My Mistress*, p. 433.)

Ellington's genius lay in his ability to find, attract, and keep soloists and to weave their talents into the fabric of his compositions and arrangements. His recording career was aided by the stability of his band, which had few changes in personnel. The Ellington Band holds the record for the longest continuously organized jazz big band in history. Begun in 1926, the band never disbanded, even after Duke's death in 1974. His only son, trumpeter Mercer Ellington, now heads the band, which still tours and records.

A decline in ballroom dancing after World War II and the switch by record companies from big bands to singers made it almost impossible to sustain the costs of maintaining a big band on the road on a full-time basis unless the leader was willing to subsidize his own orchestra. Ellington invested most of his earnings from royalties and records in his band. It was essential to Ellington to have a band to compose for, so he kept his band going even when it did not make sense from a business standpoint. During its lean period in the 1950s and '60s, the constant exposure of the Ellington band in films, on television, on recordings, and in jazz-festival performances was of immeasurable importance in keeping big-band jazz alive.

His amazing output of extended works in the form of chamber music, suites, film scores, Broadway revues, religious works, and sketches for an opera place Duke Ellington among the great composers of the twentieth century, classical or jazz.

Duke Ellington was the most popular black songwriter in America until Stevie Wonder. He composed over 350 songs in 40 years and made over 1,300 recordings. Many of his tunes became standards. Ellington was a self-taught composer, but he had "big ears." He was able to hear

cross-section voicing: the combining of one or two instruments from each section of a big band

polychord: simultaneous sounding of two different chords

reversed-lead voicing: melody written for the lowest pitched instrument

tension note: a note added between chord tones to create harmonic tension

something new—pop, jazz, ethnic, or classical—analyze it quickly and adapt it to his own style.

Ellington's crucial role as pianist in his own orchestra is often overlooked. His rich and daring harmonies, use of the bass register, percussive use of the instrument, dramatic register changes, and repetitive riffs made Ellington one of the most innovative jazz pianists of all time, though he was not, and had no ambition to be, a major soloist, like Art Tatum, Thelonious Monk, Bill Evans, or Keith Jarrett.

Duke Ellington's constant experimentation placed him on the cutting edge of many important innovations in the development of jazz.

1. He was the first to use the voice as an instrument in a big band. (Adelaide Hall's wordless solo on *Creole Love Call*, recorded in 1928).
2. He was the first jazzman to write extended jazz works.
3. He was the first big-band leader to move the string bass to the front of the rhythm section and give it a more prominent role.
4. He was the first big-band leader to experiment with *cross-section voicings*, that is, the combining of one or two instruments from each section of a big band. An example would be two saxophones, one trumpet, and one trombone.
5. He was the first big-band leader to bypass the three-minute limit on the old 78-rpm recording by dividing a longer work into two parts.
6. He was the first modern black bandleader to present annual concerts at Carnegie Hall in New York.
7. His was the first jazz big band to tour the Soviet Union.
8. He was the the first black big-band leader to tour Europe.
9. He was the first big-band leader and composer to write and record a score for a dramatic film.
10. He was the first to write a series of "concertos" for individual players in the orchestra: *Echoes of Harlem* (*Cootie's Concerto*), *Clarinet Lament* (*Barney's Concerto*), *Yearning for Love* (*Lawrence's Concerto*), and *Trumpet in Spades* (*Rex's Concerto*).
11. He holds the record for the longest single selection ever performed at a major jazz festival (*Diminuendo and Crescendo in Blue* at the Newport Jazz Festival in 1956).
12. He was the first to use *polychords* (simultaneous sounding of two different chords), *reversed-lead voicing* (melody written for the lowest pitch instrument), and *tension notes*

Pulitzer Prize: one of several annual prizes in journalism, literature, music, and other arts, established by Joseph Pulitzer

(notes added between two interior chord tones) in traditional chords .

13. He was the first black American composer to be nominated for a Pulitzer Prize (for the musical underscore of the dramatic film *Anatomy of a Murder*).

14. He holds the record for the most jazz albums recorded by any jazz band or single artist.

15. He was the first black American composer to have a television musical built around his music ("A Drum Is a Woman," CBS, 1957).

How was Duke Ellington able to survive for fifty years as a composer and bandleader when jazz records never exceeded 10 percent of total record sales? Most feel that it was due to his songwriting and the shrewd managerial hand of Irving Mills, who pushed hard to get his music recorded and keep the Duke's name and music constantly before the public.

There are few courses in Ellington's music in our colleges and universities. His name is seldom mentioned in music-appreciation classes. He is almost totally ignored in books on twentieth-century music. Large sums of money are being granted by federal, state, and local arts councils and societies for the study of obscure, but acceptable, composers, while the music of Ellington lies dormant.

This great American musical genius will eventually be recognized as one of the greatest composers, bandleaders, and songwriters who ever lived. There is a street named for Duke in New York City. There is a school named for him in Washington, D.C. There are Ellington seminars, concerts, festivals, and clubs. The legend has not died.

■/■ STAN KENTON

White bandleader Stan Kenton (1912–1979) courageously and totally transformed the direction of big-band music in America. An early disciple of bop, he was one of the first to take a full jazz orchestra, including strings and woodwinds, on the road. And he was one of the first, if not *the* first, to propose and have accepted the concept of a resident jazz orchestra sharing the facilities and spotlight with the local resident symphony.

Stan Kenton was the first commercially successful big-band leader to move his band, formed at the start of the 1940s, totally into the arena of concert performances. He began the transition in the late '40s, a time

Stan Kenton.

progressive jazz: an experimental modern-jazz style characterized by often highly dissonant and rhythmically complex arrangements and solos

when there were efforts to resurrect the big-band sounds and styles of the '30s and early '40s. Kenton's band, relatively new on the scene, had already recorded several successful records by the late '40s, but Kenton was not satisfied. His dream was to convert the dance band of the '30s into a concert orchestra playing exciting, original, and, in most instances, nondanceable jazz.

His attempts to move the big-band ensemble into the arena of what he called "progressive jazz" were often met with hostility, even from musicians, but Kenton was not easily discouraged. Like Ellington, Kenton poured the profits from his successful commercial recordings back into this band.

Stan Kenton was both a successful and charismatic entertainer and a serious composer and musical visionary. He was among the first to see the direction in which big-band jazz was headed. His was the first widely known big band to add Latin percussion to the rhythm section. He also expanded the brass section by adding a fifth trumpet and fifth trombone. He was one of the first to introduce the rhythms and melodies of Cuba seriously into the mainstream of jazz.

Stan's daring Innovations Orchestra in the 1950s was the largest jazz ensemble ever to tour the country. Adding strings, French horns, and additional percussion, this huge jazz orchestra, playing original music by some of America's most talented composers, established the principle of the jazz orchestra as a legitimate means of contemporary musical expression.

In the late 1960s, Stan Kenton's Los Angeles Neophonic Orchestra became the first resident jazz orchestra in the country, sharing the spotlight and facilities of the Los Angeles Music Center with the Los Angeles Philharmonic. This set the stage for future full-time resident jazz orchestras in New York, Dallas, and elsewhere.

Kenton was among the first jazz personalities to realize that the future of jazz was in the hands of the youth of America. Kenton again became an innovator, subsidizing and promoting jazz instruction in high school and college "clinics" all over the country. The Kenton Collegiate Neophonic Orchestra has received many awards, including a Grammy. The success of these clinics eventually led to the beginning of the International Association of Jazz Educators, one of the most dynamic professional music-education organizations in the world today.

Like Ellington, Kenton was always able to bring out the best in his arrangers, composers, and instrumental soloists. The names of those associated with the Kenton Orchestra reads like a *Who's Who* of West Coast jazz—Lee Konitz, Bill Holman, Frank Rosolino, Shelly Manne, Conte Candoli, Stan Levey, Gerry Mulligan, Maynard Ferguson, Art Pepper, William Russo, Milt Bernhart, Shorty Rogers, and Pete Rugolo, to name just a few.

Stan Kenton was always ready to champion the importance of jazz. The intensity of his dedication is matched by few in today's jazz world.

LISTENING ASSIGNMENT

"Concerto To End All Concertos," Stan Kenton. *Comprehensive Kenton*, Capitol 4XVV-12016 ▪ This was one of Stan Kenton's first attempts at combining jazz and classical music. The form is that of a small concerto, while the playing is West Coast jazz. The style is dramatic, with extreme changes in tempo and dynamics.

Fletcher Henderson, Paul Horn, Jack Teagarden, Vido Musso, Corky Corcoran, Leonard Feather, Jerry Jerome, Murray McEachern, Red Ballard, John Hammond, Horace Henderson, Irving Goodman, Chris Griffin, Zeke Zarchy, Benny Goodman, Billy Butterfield, Big Sid Catlett, Ziggy Elman, Nick Fatool, Mel Powell, Lionel Hampton, Peggy Lee, Harry James. [The Marjorie Ball Collection.]

SUMMARY

The great jazz musicians who won national acclaim from the 1920s onward contributed immeasurably to jazz as an art form. Each was easily identified by a musical style or visual logo, and this distinctive image, combined with creative talent and artistic influence, made these musicians stand out and impact strongly on the growth of jazz. In an attempt to raise the status of jazz and, perhaps, to obscure its roots in the music of descendants of slaves, many early jazz greats, such as Joseph "King" Oliver and "Count" Basie, gave themselves titles of royalty.

Jelly Roll Morton, the first important composer of jazz, successfully fused his carefully composed and rehearsed arrangements with continuous improvisation, demonstrating that the two techniques are not incompatible and can, in fact, enhance jazz's spontaneity.

King Oliver, the first to popularize New Orleans jazz in Chicago in the early 1920s, was a superb cornetist and bandleader, and an important influence on Louis Armstrong. **Paul Whiteman** drew attention to jazz as a fine art through his successful combination of western European music and jazz in a formal New York concert setting.

Fletcher Henderson led the swing movement with the first big band in America. **Jimmie Lunceford** introduced sophisticated polish and choreographed movements for visual effect in his big band. **Count Basie**'s commitment to foot-tapping swing made him a favorite with jazz fans, and the "King of Swing," **Benny Goodman**, attracted some of the greatest jazz players of the time to his orchestra. **Lester "Prez" Young**, one of the most important tenor-saxophonists, is credited with inventing *cool jazz*.

Blues singers **Ma Rainey**, a pioneer in the classic blues style, and **Bessie Smith**, who projected all her strength and emotion into her voice and was known as the best of the classic blues singers, were followed by the great female jazz singers. **Billie Holiday** influenced numerous jazz and pop singers since the 1930s with her innovative vocal style, and **Ella Fitzgerald**'s infectious singing style and immense popularity in jazz and pop earned her the title, "First Lady of Song."

Louis Armstrong excelled in many areas —as an outstanding trumpeter, singer, and instrumental jazz soloist, as the first recorded scat singer, and as the force behind some of the greatest instrumental jazz recordings made and the best pop tunes sung jazz-style. Satchmo had a profound impact on jazz and the musical styles that evolved from it, and did more than any other artist to draw international attention to jazz.

Duke Ellington combined compositional genius with a talent for attracting outstanding soloists. He was the most popular black songwriter of his time in America and was renowned for his classical compositions as well as for jazz. He was one of the most creative and talented jazz pianists of all time, and his constant experimentation led to numerous innovations in the development of jazz.

Stan Kenton was the first to tour with a full jazz orchestra and to establish the concept of a local resident jazz orchestra. He was an innovative composer, a successful entertainer, and an active promoter of jazz education.

These jazz giants, through their various talents, their creativity, and their willingness to experiment, left their priceless mark on the ever-changing and growing world of jazz.

A. *In your own words* write one or two sentences describing each of the terms listed in Questions 1–7.

1. wa-wa brass _____

_____

2. riff _____

_____

3. cross-section voicing _____

_____

4. polychord _____

_____

5. reversed-lead voicing _____

_____

6. tension note _____

_____

7. progressive jazz _____

_____

In Questions 8–22 write a sentence or two identifying each of the following artists.

8. Jelly Roll Morton _____

_____

9. King Oliver _____

_____

10. Paul Whiteman _____

_____

11. Fletcher Henderson _____

_____

12. Jimmie Lunceford _____

_____

13. Count Basie _____

_____

14. Benny Goodman _____

_____

15. Lester Young _____

_____

16. Ma Rainey _____

_____

17. Bessie Smith _____

_____

18. Billie Holiday _____

_____

19. Ella Fitzgerald _____

_____

20. Louis Armstrong _____

_____

21. Duke Ellington _____

_____

22. Stan Kenton _____

_____

B. In Questions 23–27 choose three jazz personalities from this chapter.

23. Why is each person considered jazz "royalty"?

24. What stylistic influences did each have on contemporary and later jazz musicians?

25. For each musician, what social, technological, or personal influences helped shape his or her music and career?

26. What personal and musical characteristics did these three musicians share in common, and in what ways were they different?

27. Who is your favorite among them? Why?

28. Discuss the statement,

Duke Ellington was the most influential musician in American history.

Do you agree or disagree with the statement? Why?

■ Topics for Further Research

A. Choose an important jazz artist *not* discussed in this chapter. Can he or she be considered "jazz royalty"? Why?

B. How much influence did record companies and agents have on the careers of important jazz musicians discussed in this chapter and on the direction of popular music in general? Have the roles of these companies and agents changed with regard to today's popular music?

■ Further Reading

Arganian, Lillian. *Stan Kenton: The Man and His Music.* East Lansing, Mich.: Artistry Press, 1989.

Basie, Count and Albert Murray. *Good Morning Blues: The Autobiography of Count Basie.* New York: Donald I Fine, 1985.

Collier, James Lincoln. *Louis Armstrong: An American Genius*. New York: Oxford University Press, 1983.

Ellington, Duke. *Music Is My Mistress*. New York: Doubleday & Co., 1973.

■ Further Listening

Hot Fives and Hot Sevens, Louis Armstrong. Columbia CK 44253, CK 44422.

Lester Young in Tokyo. Pablo 2405-420.

Music of Jelly Roll Morton, The. Smithsonian (vol. 1–3).

Smithsonian Collection of Classic Jazz. Smithsonian (sides A–E).

■ Films and Videos

Duke Ellington Story, The (video).

Ladies Sing the Blues, The (video).

Satchmo: Louis Armstrong (video).

PART II

The
Development of
Listening
Skills

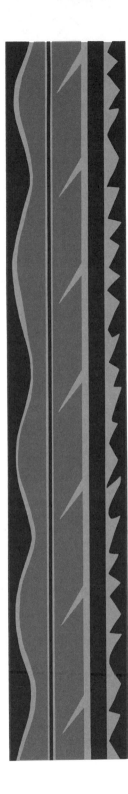

9
VOCAL STYLES

/ ■ /

Well, I drink to keep from worrying,
    and I laugh to keep from crying.
Yeah, I said I drink to keep from worrying,
    and I laugh to keep from crying.
I keep a smile on my face
    so the public won't know my mind.
Some people thinks I'm happy,
    but they sho' don't know my mind.
Whoo-ee, I said, some people thinks I'm happy,
    but they sho' don't know my mind.
They see this smile on my face,
    but my heart's a bleedin' all the time.

—RURAL BLUES SONG, early 1900s

THROUGHOUT history, when language was not sufficient to express our deepest feelings, we have cried out in song. Some anthropologists believe that singing preceded spoken language.

The voice and the drum are the two oldest musical instruments known. Even today, the essence of music is in its melody and rhythm. Even the most musically inexperienced person has sung songs and tapped rhythms at one time or another. Because singing is a natural act and because we are rhythmic creatures, melody and rhythm are the most

range: the scope of musical pitches (how high or how low) possible for an instrument or voice

dynamics: variations in volume

sotto voce: a very soft voice

tone color: the quality of sound of a particular instrument or voice; sometimes called *timbre*

soprano: the highest pitched female voice

alto/contralto: the lowest pitched female voice

coloratura: a high-pitched lyric soprano who specializes in runs and trills

lyric soprano: a soprano voice having a relatively low volume and modest range

mezzo soprano: a voice that falls between a soprano and alto in pitch

dramatic soprano: a mezzo soprano with a powerful voice

tenor: a male voice intermediate in pitch between the baritone and countertenor

baritone: a male voice that falls between the tenor and bass

bass: the lowest pitched voice

lyric tenor: a tenor voice having low volume and modest range

dramatic tenor/ Wagnerian tenor: a powerful tenor voice with a wide range

lyric baritone: a baritone voice having low

easily recognized and analyzed parts of any musical performance.

A great deal of African tribal music was just rhythm and melody. The wide range of vocal expression allowed for the African singer is one of the most instantly recognizable differences between African music and the classical music of western civilization. The African singer uses a palette of incredibly diverse and exciting sounds, from moans to shouts, growls, and high falsetto singing. The Afro-American spiritual, gospel, field holler, and work song also used such vocal devices.

A singer's musical framework, melodically speaking, is controlled by *range* (how high and how low) and *dynamics* (how soft and how loud) he or she can sing. Since music is a language of the emotions, the range and the dynamics needed are closely related to the emotions the music is meant to express. Some singers have a very wide range, three octaves or more, but the average nonprofessional has a range of around an octave and a half.

Some singers are limited in their dynamics: They can sing very softly or very loudly, but not both. Others can sing in a very soft voice (called *sotto voce* or *half voice* in classical music) and in a very loud (and sometimes even distorted) voice.

Besides a specific range and dynamics, every singer has a vocal *tone color*, which characterizes the quality of his or her voice. It can be bright, clear, dark, or raspy-distorted (like Louis Armstrong or Joe Cocker). Some singers use more than one vocal tone. Jazz singers, in particular, change their tone qualities often. Al Jarreau and Bobby McFerrin are two such singers who go from bright to clear to dark to raspy, often within the same song. They use these changes to emphasize and bring out the emotional content of the lyrics. Some singers, however, stay basically with one sound.

■/■ RANGE

In classical music, women's voices fall into two general categories: soprano and alto or contralto. There are several subheads within the soprano category—coloratura, lyric, mezzo, and dramatic soprano. The lower-pitched alto voice is favored in jazz and blues, largely because it sounds "sexier" and "earthier."

Most men's voices fall into three general categories—tenor, baritone, and bass—but there are lyric and dramatic or Wagnerian tenors, lyric and dramatic baritones, and basso and basso profundo voices. A countertenor is a rare voice—seldom heard in jazz—that is pitched higher than a tenor. Most male jazz and blues singers are baritones, although many of them vary their ranges for added emphasis.

Al Jarreau.
[Drawing by David Zuckerman.]

■/■ DYNAMICS

Dynamics are the variations in volume of singers' voices. Most good jazz singers have a wide dynamic range, being able to sing down to a whisper and up to a roar—depending on the mood of the music, the lyric, and the arrangement. In fact, one of the major differences between jazz and rock is that jazz has a much wider dynamic range.

■/■ TONE COLOR

Billie Holiday's voice was instantly recognizable and unmistakable. It was unlike the tone of any other popular or blues singer of her time. The more you listened to Billie, the more captured you were by the intimate tone of her voice.

Blues and jazz singers wail and moan, imitating musical instruments, environmental sounds, and often creating their own sounds. In

volume and modest range

dramatic baritone: a powerful baritone voice with a wide range

basso: a bass voice

basso profundo: a bass voice of the lowest range

countertenor: a rare voice that is pitched higher than a tenor; also called *male alto*

Tone Color ■ **223**

jazz singing, experimentation—particularly for the purpose of heightened emotional impact—is encouraged. The main difference between the jazz singer and the classical singer is the degree of personalization. We can all tell the difference between Louis Armstrong's and Frank Sinatra's singing; it is much harder to tell whether an aria is being sung by Placido Domingo or Luciano Pavarotti.

The idea of personalizing vocal tone is one of the primary characteristics of the Afro-American vocal style in jazz. Every jazz song is personally modified to fit the personality of the singer. A good example of this is Ray Charles's recording of *America the Beautiful*, in which the artist's unique vocal style is instantly recognizable.

There are four types of vocal tone colors.

▶ 1. **Bright.** Nell Carter and Patti LaBelle are two contemporary singers with very bright, almost metallic-sounding, tones. This bright edge is easily recognizable and can be heard on top of the loudest accompaniment. One early male blues singer who favored a bright tone was Robert P. Johnson, who usually sang with a high-pitched, metallic Texas twang.

LISTENING ASSIGNMENT

"Ain't Misbehavin'," Nell Carter. *Ain't Misbehavin'* (soundtrack), RCA 2965-2-RC ▪ An example of a bright vocal tone.

▶ 2. **Clear.** Whitney Houston, Ella Fitzgerald, Mark Murphy, and Mel Tormé are four contemporary singers who sing in clear vocal tones. Less "edgy" than the bright tone, this crystal-clear sound is pleasing, yet dynamic. B. B. King is a good example of a singer who uses this tone quality in the blues. Frank Sinatra has a clear tone most of the time. The clear tone is the one most commonly used by modern jazz singers.

LISTENING ASSIGNMENT

"Undecided," Ella Fitzgerald. *Singers and Soloists of the Swing Bands,* Smithsonian, side B, #5 ▪ An example of a clear vocal tone.

▶ 3. **Dark.** Sarah Vaughan, Joe Williams, Arthur Prysock, and Billy Eckstine are a few contemporary jazz singers with a dark, husky quality to their voices. Many blues singers favor

calliope: a harsh-sounding musical instrument consisting of a set of steam whistles that are activated by a keyboard

this darker tone. The recordings of Muddy Waters, the great South Side Chicago urban-blues singer, is another example of this dark vocal tone.

> **LISTENING ASSIGNMENT**
>
> "Stormy Monday Blues," Billy Eckstine. *Singers and Soloists of the Swing Bands*, Smithsonian, side C, #5 ▪ An example of a dark vocal tone.

▶ 4. **Distorted, raspy.** This is the "buzz tone" that was so popular in west African tribal music. The Africans' love of the buzz tone has been preserved through the raspy, distorted sounds of singers such as James Brown, Louis Armstrong, Joe Cocker, and Bruce Springsteen. Male singers seem to favor this sound in jazz and blues.

> **LISTENING ASSIGNMENT**
>
> "I've Got a Right To Sing the Blues," Louis Armstrong and his Orchestra. *Smithsonian Collection of Classic Jazz*, side B, #7 ▪ An example of a raspy vocal tone.

■/■ PERSONALIZING A SONG

One of the most startling examples of the wide range of vocal expression allowed the jazz singer is afforded by the singing of Bobby McFerrin. McFerrin can sound like anything from a broken-down wino to a high-note trumpet player to an ancient circus calliope. McFerrin also acts out his sounds—by jumping in the air, slapping his body, standing on his toes, or occasionally throwing himself on the floor. His creativity is what makes him the Number One male jazz singer today.

All jazz and blues singers have their own ways of "personalizing" their songs. There are many ways to

Bobby McFerrin.

modify a melody. You can modify the tone and range, the rhythm and lyrics, or the emphasis. Sarah Vaughan, the "Divine One," was one of the greatest at maximizing the potentialities of her incredible voice while personalizing a song.

Sarah had not only an incredible range (over three octaves), but a tone gearshift that allowed her to move from a dark and silky tone to a bright and brassy one. Her sense of timing and her pitch were almost perfect, and no intervals were difficult for her to sing. Her sliding glissandos always arrived just in time—never too late and never too early. Her vibrato was one of her most important stocks in trade, and no one could go from a high to a low note faster and smoother than could

Sarah Vaughan. [Photofest.]

Sarah. Her performance of Stephen Sondheim's *Send in the Clowns* cannot be duplicated or surpassed.

Jazz and blues singers never try to sound like anyone but themselves, and they never sing the same song in the same way twice. The following quote describes a typical performance by the great blues singer Bobby "Blue" Bland.

> He is resigned and reflective on his first slow blues, with its *Stormy Monday* type lyrics, and when he actually goes into the more passionate *Stormy Monday*, he walks out onto the dance floor and falls on bended knee, shouting, "LORD, HAVE MERCY!" He growls with such ferocity it raises the hair on the back of your neck. The raspy African buzz tone sounds like a thousand bumblebees all trying to get out of a shoebox at the same time. The band has already split, leaving only the guitarist to hold a musical dialogue with Bobby. He walks over to the guitarist as he begins his solo. "Take your time, baby," he says.
>
> (Garry Giddins, *Riding on a Blue Note,* p. 41.)

As you can see, it's hard to describe a personalized vocal style. It's like trying to describe the taste of a grape.

Another way to personalize a song is to personalize the lyrics. A singer may take a word or phrase out of the original lyrics and repeat it over and over, often interrupting the flow of the original melody in order to do so. Billie Holiday, for example, personalized the song *Lover Man* by changing the line, "I don't know why, but I'm feelin' so bad" to "I don't know why, I don't know why, baby, I don't know why, but I'm *feelin'* so—bad!"

Ray Charles is a genius at personalizing well-known songs. How many jazz or blues singers would mess with a simple Country-and-Western tune like *I Can't Stop Loving You* or the patriotic *America the Beautiful*? Ray delights in distorting and personalizing the lyrics to well-known songs. The trick is to personalize the words without destroying the original meaning. The technique seems to work best on ballads and slow blues.

■ Jazz Vocalists ■

Soloists	MALE	FEMALE
(1920s–'40s)	Louis Armstrong	Ivie Anderson
	Cab Calloway	Mildred Bailey
	Bing Crosby	Connie Boswell
	Jimmy Rushing	Ella Fitzgerald
	Jack Teagarden	Helen Forrest
	Fats Waller	Billie Holiday
		Peggy Lee
(1940s–'60s)	Louis Armstrong	Pearl Bailey
	Chet Baker	Betty Bennett
	Nat Cole	Betty Carter
	Billy Eckstine	June Christy
	Al Hibbler	Chris Connor
	Frank Sinatra	Ella Fitzgerald
	Mel Tormé	Lena Horne
		Helen Humes
		Abbey Lincoln
		Carmen McRae
		Anita O'Day
		Nina Simone
		Sarah Vaughan
		Fran Warren
		Dinah Washington
		Frances Wayne
(late 1960s to present)	Mose Allison	Ernestine Anderson
	Ernie Andrews	Rosemary Clooney
	Tony Bennett	Sheila Jordan
	Oscar Brown, Jr.	Cleo Laine
	Ray Charles	Flora Purim
	Harry Connick, Jr.	Dianne Reeves
	Jon Hendricks	Diane Schuur
	Al Jarreau	Janet Siegel
	Eddie Jefferson	Nancy Wilson
	Herb Jeffries	
	Bobby McFerrin	
	Mark Murphy	
	Mel Tormé	
	Joe Williams	

Vocal groups	Charlie Ventura and Bop for the People
	Double Six of Paris
	The Four Freshmen
	The Hi-Lo's
	Jackie & Roy
	Lambert, Hendricks and Ross
	The Manhattan Transfer
	The New York Voices
	The Pointer Sisters
	Rare Silk
	The Singers Unlimited
	The Swingle Singers
	Take Six

■/■ SCAT SINGING

scat singing: singing without a text or imitating a jazz instrument; vocal improvisation

nonimitative scat singing: using the voice in place of an instrument for the vocal sound quality

Scat singing, singing without a text, originated in a Chicago recording studio in 1927 when Louis Armstrong accidentally knocked the lyrics sheet off the music stand during a live recording session, but continued to sing by *scatting,* or singing sounds. This first recorded example of scat singing was the bestseller *Heebie Jeebies.* Satchmo later recorded *West End Blues,* in which he imitated the clarinet sounds of Leon Albany "Barney" Bigard. The idea of imitating an instrument with the voice quickly became very popular, with pop singers of the day, like Bing Crosby, using it from time to time.

Actually, the technique is not new. It was a common vocal practice in tribal Africa. The interplay between blues singers and their instrumental accompanists helped to develop the style. The singer might pick up where the instrumental soloist left off, imitating the sound of the instrument vocally before returning to the original melody and lyrics. The saxophone and the trumpet are the two most commonly imitated instruments. Today, jazz singers like Bobby McFerrin and Al Jarreau can mimic the sound of *any* instrument, including drums. The opening of the film *Round Midnight* and the theme to "The Cosby Show," recently on television, both featured scat virtuoso McFerrin. Some other great imitative scat singers are Ella Fitzgerald, Mark Murphy, Jon Hendricks, Mel Tormé, Eddie Jefferson, Sarah Vaughan, and George Benson.

Nonimitative scat singing is using the voice *in place of* another instrument. The voice floats on a neutral syllable like *ahh* or *ooh.* The first to record the voice this way was Duke Ellington, beginning with his early

Ella Fitzgerald in 1976.
[Photofest.]

recording of *Creole Love Call* and later in his orchestral suite, *A Drum Is a Woman.* Stan Kenton used June Christy's voice in this manner with his Innovations Orchestra in 1951 in an original work called *Christie.* Chick Corea's popular recording of *Spain* features Flora Purim using her voice as an instrument.* Scat virtuoso Bobby McFerrin's touring vocal ensemble, called a "voicestra," re-creates an entire orchestra vocally with both imitative and nonimitative scat-singing techniques. So does the recent Grammy Award winning *a cappella* group, Take Six.

■/■ VOCALISE

Vocalise is a musical technique in which a jazz singer actually writes lyrics to a previously recorded instrumental jazz solo and rerecords it vocally with the lyrics.

Vocalise did not begin to be widely popular until the late 1950s. One of its early pioneers was the Lambert, Hendricks and Ross trio with its bop vocals. Annie Ross's *My Analyst Told Me* was based on a well-known jazz tenor sax solo. Annie recorded it in the late 1950s and the pop singer Joni Mitchell rerecorded it in the 1970s, exposing this innovative style to the wider pop audience. The guitarist and singer George Benson helped spread the new concept by recording James Moody's solo rendition of *I'm in the Mood for Love* with clever new lyrics created by Eddie Jefferson. Finally, the popular jazz vocal group The Manhattan Transfer decided to do an entire album of these vocal re-creations of famous instrumental solos. The album is appropriately called *Vocalese.*

Unlike the previously described ways of personalizing a song, vocalise is usually not spontaneous. Lyrics must be carefully crafted so as to fit the original solo and to make sense. Although spontaneous im-

---

LISTENING ASSIGNMENT

"Four Brothers," The Manhattan Transfer. *The Best of The Manhattan Transfer*, Atlantic [CS] 19319 ▪ This arrangement was originally written by Jimmy Guiffre for the Woody Herman Orchestra in the late 1940s. The Manhattan Transfer added clever lyrics, duplicated the sax solos, and rerecorded it. Who else uses vocalise a lot as a jazz vocal style?

---

*See the LISTENING ASSIGNMENT, "Spain," page 289.

dramatizing the lyrics:
distorting the lyrics by
means such as repetition,
pitch change, or dynamic
changes

transactional analysis:
a school of psychology
emphasizing personal
relationships

provisation is not involved, it is a clever and creative use of the voice and demonstrates great imagination and skill on the part of both the lyricist and the singer.

■/■ DRAMATIZING THE LYRICS

In this vocal technique, the singer takes a phrase or word from the original lyrics and works with it (wailing, moaning, distorting the tone, scooping into a word, singing suddenly softer, louder, higher, or lower, and so on). This is different from the previously described technique of changing the lyrics. In this approach, the singer doesn't change the original rhythm or melody of the song or add or delete words from the lyrics. Billie Holiday was particularly good at dramatizing lyrics, as are B. B. King, the famous blues singer, and soul singer James Brown. In using this technique, the jazz or blues singer zeros in on the most important word in each phrase and "massages" that word, squeezing out every drop of meaning and emotion.

■/■ MUSIC AS A LANGUAGE

> My music always has followed me around, like a stray dog. I've tried to stop playing, particularly when I've been preparing my soul for Jesus. Never been able to shake that stray dog. He's always there, waiting to be scratched behind the ears. Pretty soon, he's the best and most loyal company I'll ever have. Just looks to me like I can't put my music down. By the time I get hold of one guitar and I maybe sell it to somebody, well, pretty soon that stray dog begins to whine and bark—forcing me to go back and buy another guitar.
>
> (Rural blues singer.)

We have shown that music is a language of the emotions. But what are the common emotions expressed in music? Dr. Eric Berne, creator of an American school of psychology called *transactional analysis*, identifies the four basic emotional states as

1. **Mad** (from slight irritation to full-blown rage);
2. **Glad** (from "Have a nice day" to uncontrollable joy);
3. **Sad** (from a slight case of the blues to deep sorrow); and
4. **Scared** (from slight apprehension to full-blown terror).

For an analysis of emotion in music, additional categories could include:

Al Jolson in the title role of *The Jazz Singer.*
[Picture Collection, The Branch Libraries, The New York Public Library.]

cantor: the chief singer and leader of prayer in a synagogue

5. **Sexual** (from light flirtation to full-blown lust);
6. **Humorous** (from a chuckle to an all-out belly laugh); and
7. **Inspirational** (religious, ideological, ecological, and humanistic).

When you listen to music, ask yourself what it means. Are the performers in tune with your concept of the meaning of the song? What is the overall feeling of the piece? Does it change? Are conflicting emotions being expressed? Is the emotional level on the order of "Have a nice day," or is it more like "If you leave me, I'll die"? How can you identify the emotion being expressed? Which musical cues help you? Focusing on the emotions expressed will intensify your enjoyment of music.

■/■ **THE JAZZ SINGER**

The first talking motion picture in 1926 was called *The Jazz Singer.* Typical of Hollywood, it wasn't about jazz. It was about a young Jewish man who was drawn to the world of theatrical entertainment rather than to being a cantor in a synagogue. The fact that the first talking film had the word "jazz" in the title did make people more aware of the growing importance of the art. It was also around this time that Louis Armstrong recorded the important vocal jazz tune mentioned earlier, *Heebie Jeebies.*

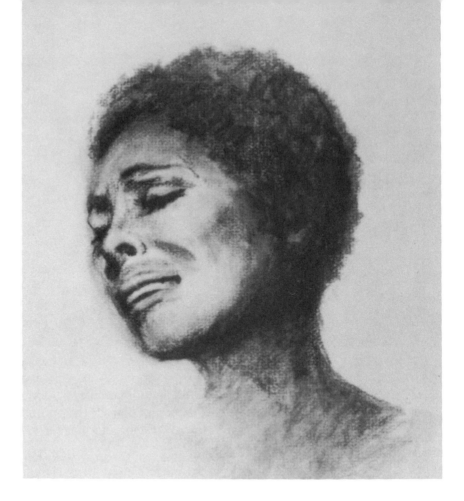

Carmen McRae.
[Drawing by Shirley Tanzi.]

Although Armstrong was probably the most influential jazz singer of the era, for the most part, women have dominated the style. Billie Holiday could be said to have established its ground rules, although she seldom sang scat.

The jazz singer may sing blues, pop songs, or Broadway show tunes, but the performance always involves some improvisation and the material is always personalized. No two jazz singers sing in exactly the same way. Ella Fitzgerald, Sarah Vaughan, Carmen McRae, Mel Tormé, and Mark Murphy are all notable jazz singers, as are Bing Crosby, Mildred Bailey, and Fats Waller. Most jazz singers started out as pop vocalists with big bands in the swing era of the 1930s and only gradually began to record songs that were more related to jazz than to pop.

There are certain characteristics by which you can recognize a jazz singer:

1. They may use a wide range of vocal techniques to get a point across.

2. They are rhythm-oriented in their interpretations and often use *syncopation* (displaced accents) and other rhythmic tricks to make a song more exciting. Singing slightly behind the beat is common.

3. They seldom sing the same song in the same way twice.

4. They are strongly influenced by the leading instrumental solo in their accompaniment.

5. They often distort pitch and tone in order to achieve an effect. They may slide into notes from below or above.

SUMMARY

The human voice is the instrument that we all have from birth. It is capable of an incredibly diverse range of sounds, including moans, shouts, growls, and the high falsetto voice, all of which have been used in Afro-American music. Individual voices can vary greatly in *range* (high-, medium-, or low-pitched), *dynamics* (loud or soft), and *tone* (bright, clear, dark, or raspy/distorted).

In addition to these natural differences, jazz singers make use of a variety of vocal devices to *personalize* their songs, to claim a singing style that is recognizably their own. Other vocal techniques that have added variety to the world of jazz are *scat singing*, which uses the voice as an instrument, without a text; *vocalise*, which involves carefully crafting lyrics to an instrumental solo; and *dramatizing the lyrics*, in which a singer works with a chosen phrase or word to fill it with meaning and emotion.

Music is capable of expressing emotions that vary greatly in mood, intensity, and clarity. Emotional states that characterize different types of music include: mad, glad, sad, scared, sexual, humorous, and inspirational.

Despite their natural differences, jazz singers share a number of recognizable characteristics in common. The most important of these shared features are the improvisation involved in their performance and the personalization of their material—characteristics that appear in all aspects of jazz.

■ **Questions on Chapter 9**

A. *In your own words* write one or two sentences describing each of the terms listed in Questions 1–16.

    1. range _____

    _____

2. dynamics _____

_____

3. sotto voce _____

_____

4. tone _____

_____

5. lyric soprano _____

_____

6. coloratura _____

_____

7. dramatic soprano _____

_____

8. mezzo soprano _____

_____

9. lyric tenor _____

_____

10. Wagnerian tenor _____

_____

11. lyric baritone _____

_____

12. dramatic baritone _____

_____

13. basso profundo _____

_____

14. scat singing _____

_____

15. a capella _____

_____

16. vocalise _____

_____

In Questions 17–22 fill in the blanks.

17. The highest pitched female voice is the _____.

18. The lowest pitched female voice is the _____.

19. The lowest pitched male voice is the _____.

20. A male voice between the tenor and bass is the _____.

21. A _____ is another name for a bass.

22. _____ means distorting the lyric by such means as repetition or pitch change.

B. Listen to a jazz singer and analyze his or her vocal style according to the guidelines in Questions 23–29.

23. What is the singer's *range* (soprano, alto, tenor, bass)?

24. How large a *dynamic* range does he or she employ?

25. What is the singer's *tone color* (bright, clear, dark, or raspy)?

26. Notice other factors affecting tone color (age, gender, dialect, or accent).

27. What techniques does the singer use to *personalize* the song?

28. Does the vocalist make use of *scat singing* or *vocalise*? What is the difference between these two techniques?

29. What *mood* is created by the music? Does the mood remain the same throughout or does it change? Useful terms include:

humorous	angry	dark	sexy
passionate	light-hearted	energetic	inspirational

■ Concert Report

Attend a live jazz concert and pay particular attention to the vocalist. Consider Questions 23–29 again, but add to your report an analysis of visual cues (performers' appearance and actions, staging, lighting effects), audience reactions and/or participation, and overall effect or mood. Which aspects of the concert were done well? In what ways could the concert have been improved?

■ Further Reading

Oliver, Paul. *The Meaning of the Blues*. New York: Collier Books, 1972. (Chapters 7–11)

—————, Max Harrison, and William Bolcom. *The New Grove Gospel, Blues and Jazz*. New York: W. W. Norton & Co., 1986. (Chapters 1, 3, 4)

Pleasants, Henry. *The Great American Popular Singers*. New York: Oxford University Press, 1959.

■ Further Listening

American Popular Song: Six Decades of Songwriters and Singers. Smithsonian.

Kings of the Blues. RCA RCX 202-204.

Singers and Soloists of the Swing Bands. Smithsonian.

Smithsonian Collection of Classic Jazz. Smithsonian (sides A–C).

■ Films and Videos

Crossroads (1986). Blues.

Eddie Jefferson (video). Vocalise.

Jazz on a Summer's Day (1959). Newport Jazz Festival of 1958.

Lady Sings the Blues (1972). Life of Billie Holliday.

Manhattan Transfer: Live (video).

Sinatra (video).

Bobby McFerrin: Spontaneous Inventions (video).

10
INSTRUMENTS AND INSTRUMENTALISTS

/■/

The piano is
    A good old beast—
Peaceful and meek, without complaint,
    It suffers much
    Abuse and such
In patient self-restraint.

—WILHELM BUSCH*.

Musical instruments expand the potential of the human voice (they have greater range, power, and changes of tone color) and offer new means of expression.

In identifying jazz instruments, it helps if you can recognize

1. their basic tone quality, or *timbre*,
2. their basic register (high, medium, or low), and
3. their basic function (solo instrument, rhythm-section instrument, or background instrument).

Practice trying to distinguish the instrument or section of instruments featured in the music you are listening to.

---

*Translation by Christiane Cooper.

■/■ TONE COLOR

tone color: the quality of sound of a particular instrument or voice; sometimes called *timbre*

register: the tonal range of an instrument from its lowest note to its highest

mute: a device used to soften the sounds of brass instruments

plunger: a device used by jazz brass players to distort sounds

flutter-tongue: the rapid repetition of tongue movements on a wind instrument producing a buzz tone

fuzz pedal and wah-wah pedal: foot-switches for distorting the tone of an electric guitar

synthesizer: a computerized device that enables a composer to create and combine an unlimited variety of musical sounds electronically

sampling: the process of recording and storing natural sounds electronically

pitch: the degree to which an instrument, voice, or sound is high or low

piccolo: the highest pitched instrument of the flute family

double bass/string bass/contrabass: the largest and lowest pitched instrument of the string family

contrabassoon/double bassoon: an instrument

Each instrument produces a basic *tone color*, or quality. These tone colors can be categorized as bright, clear, dark, or raspy/distorted.

Cornets, trumpets, soprano saxophones, and guitars and clarinets in their high registers produce bright tones. Flügelhorns, alto and tenor saxophones, trombones, and flutes produce clear tones. Clarinets in the low register, alto flutes, and baritone saxophones produce dark tones.

Tones can be modified to produce other sounds. Trombones or trumpets used with mute or plunger and saxophones or clarinets used with flutter-tongue produce husky or distorted tones. Saxophone players can also change the sound of their instruments by changing the type of mouthpiece, reed, and wind velocity. Rock guitarists can change the sound of their electric guitars by using a variety of tone-distorting foot switches (fuzz pedals, wah-wah pedals, and so on). Today's synthesizer-keyboardist has an almost limitless assortment of different tones and sounds available through electronic sampling, which allows the modern sampling synthesizer to capture any sound one-twelfth of a second or longer and translate it through the keyboard into a unified musical tone.

The drums and the bass are probably the least flexible instruments in choices of tone color.

■/■ REGISTER

An instrument's *register* is the range that it can produce from its lowest pitch to its highest. Register varies widely from instrument to instrument in the jazz ensemble. Instruments are classified as low-, medium- or high-pitched. In the symphony orchestra the piccolo is the highest-pitched instrument, whereas the double bass, also called string bass or contrabass, and the contrabassoon (double bassoon) are the lowest-pitched. In the jazz ensemble the flute, soprano sax, and trumpet are high-register instruments. The alto saxophone can play in both the high and medium registers. The tenor saxophone, trumpet, cornet, guitar, and flügelhorn in its low register are medium-register instruments. The trombone, tenor sax in its low register, and the baritone sax are low-register instruments.

The clarinet, piano, synthesizer, vibes, and harp are capable of playing in all the musical registers, top to bottom. (See the table at the top of the following page.)

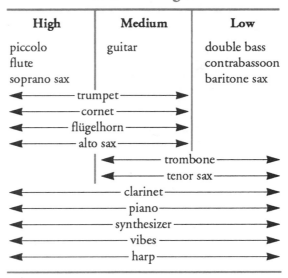

Instrument Register

High	Medium	Low
piccolo	guitar	double bass
flute		contrabassoon
soprano sax		baritone sax

←————— trumpet —————→
←————— cornet —————→
←————— flügelhorn —————→
←————— alto sax —————→

←————— trombone —————→
←————— tenor sax —————→
←————— clarinet —————→
←————— piano —————→
←————— synthesizer —————→
←————— vibes —————→
←————— harp —————→

■/■ SOLO INSTRUMENTS

that is an octave lower in pitch than the ordinary bassoon

vibes: a vibraharp

harp: an instrument consisting of strings stretched across a frame which are plucked with the fingers

player piano: a piano with prerecorded piano rolls and pump pedals

No one knows why certain solo instruments have been favored at certain times in the history of jazz. It may have to do with style, technology, and the listening habits of audiences in each period.

At the turn of the century, a piano could be found in a large number of American living rooms. It had become a popular status symbol. For those who lacked the time or inclination to learn to play the piano, however, the *player piano* was invented. Professional pianists prerecorded musical selections on piano rolls, which were then played at home on the player piano. To hear the music, all one had to do was pump the pedals that moved the roll and caused the hammers of the keys to strike the strings. It was the player piano that brought ragtime into American homes in the early 1900s, making it the first mass-produced, mass-media popular-music style.

The piano continued as the preferred solo instrument in America through the 1930s. Soon, however, this instrument had to vie for living-room space with the increasingly popular phonograph and radio, which were often housed in large cabinets.

After the piano, the cornet and trumpet were the most popular solo instruments of this era. These two instruments are almost identical; the only difference is that the tone of the cornet is mellower than that of its

From an ad for a player piano, 1913. [Picture Collection, The Branch Libraries, The New York Public Library.]

jazz violin: a violin used as a jazz instrument for an improvised solo

brighter, more brilliant-sounding cousin, the trumpet. The cornet carried the melody in the early Dixieland ensembles. It was heard as the principal voice in the early instrumental jazz ensembles. As the perform-ance arena for jazz gradually increased in size, the cornet was replaced by the trumpet, because of its ability to project its sound further.

The jazz violin became popular in the 1930s, thanks largely to the efforts of great players like Joe Venuti, Ray Nance, Stuff Smith, and Stephane Grappelli. Later, in the early stages of fusion, the jazz violin made a comeback when John McLaughlin added the young jazz violinist Jean-Luc Ponty to his Mahavishnu Orchestra.

The tenor saxophone became popular in the later 1930s. Successful tenor-sax recordings, like the famous 1939 performance of *Body and Soul* by Coleman Hawkins, contributed to its popularity, as did the improve-ments in recording techniques at this time, which allowed the more subtle sounds of the tenor sax to be faithfully captured and reproduced.*

*See the LISTENING ASSIGNMENT, "Body and Soul," page 255.

In 1992, the election of Bill Clinton, who is an amateur jazz tenor-saxophone player, drew attention to this instrument.

In the 1940s, the clarinet became very popular, largely because of the skills of great bandleaders and clarinetists like Benny Goodman, Artie Shaw, Jimmy Dorsey, and Woody Herman. The clarinet is an unusual instrument in that it has a range of over three octaves. The tone quality of the clarinet can vary from a dark, intimate sound in its low registers, through a clear sound in its middle registers, to a bright and exciting sound in its high registers.

Also in the 1940s, Charlie Christian became the first widely popular electronically amplified guitarist in jazz. From the 1950s on, the jazz guitar became increasingly popular as a solo instrument, with the diverse talents of Mundell Lowe, Joe Pass, Barney Kessel, Jim Hall, Wes Montgomery, Pat Metheny, Larry Coryell, Howard Roberts, George Benson, Kenny Burrell, and many others.

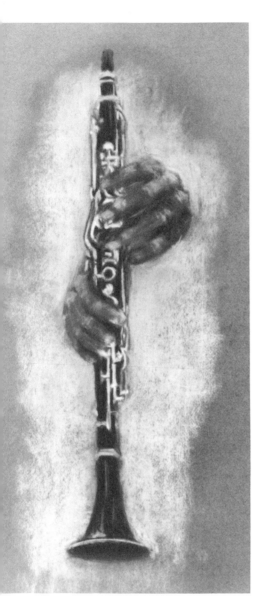

Clarinet. [Drawing by Shirley Tanzi.]

Mundell Lowe. [Drawing by Shirley Tanzi.]

Benny Goodman on clarinet, with Lionel Hampton on vibes. [Photofest.]

In the 1950s, Miles Davis made the muted trumpet one of the most dominant solo voices in jazz. The alto sax was also a popular jazz solo instrument through the 1950s, largely because of the virtuosity of such alto saxophonists as Johnny Hodges, Jimmy Dorsey, Charlie Parker, and Benny Carter.

New, more exotic-sounding instruments did not become popular in jazz until the 1960s, with the improvement of recording techniques and playback systems. Prior to that time, the subtle tone qualities or limited dynamic ranges of these instruments made them less than popular in the jazz world. Some of the new instruments were the soprano sax, flügelhorn, acoustic guitar, flute, and alto flute. The '60s also witnessed a resurgence of interest in the tenor sax as a solo instrument. It wasn't until the late '60s, however, that the "new kid on the block," the electric guitar, began to edge toward the center spotlight.

The 1970s was the era of the great guitar players and the beginning of the electric piano as an important solo instrument. In the '80s, the synthesizer began to revolutionize jazz with its ability to re-create any musical tone as well as to create many new sounds. The '80s also saw the soprano sax and the bass guitar emerge as dominant solo instruments.

The 1990s have seen a rediscovery of the beautiful sounds of acoustic instruments. Probably the most popular solo instrument in the early '90s has been the soprano sax. Wynton Marsalis has repopularized the trumpet as a solo instrument and there has also been a resurgence of interest in the acoustic guitar, led by the popular recordings of Earl Klugh. Again, improved recording techniques and playback systems (the compact disk (CD) and digital audio tape (DAT), for example) have lead to a more realistic reproduction of acoustic instrument tone in the recording studio.

Although there have been experiments with other common orchestral instruments in jazz—the French horn, oboe, bassoon, and cello—for the most part, they have remained experiments. These instruments, so common as solo voices in symphony orchestras, have not transferred well to the jazz world.

Another unusual solo instrument, but one with a better track record as far as popularity is concerned, is the vibraharp, or "vibes." One of the early jazz virtuosos on this instrument was Lionel Hampton. Later, vibraharpists like Red Norvo, Marjorie Hyams, Terry Gibbs, Milt Jackson, Victor Feldman, Tommy Vig, and Gary Burton increased the popularity of this rhythm-section instrument as a solo instrument.

Vibraharpists at a tribute to Lionel Hampton.

LISTENING ASSIGNMENT

"When Lights Are Low," Lionel Hampton Combo. *Smithsonian Collection of Classic Jazz*, side D, #3 ▪ Notice the use of a *vibraharp*, or *vibes*. Lionel Hampton, a West Coast jazz musician, was first featured on this instrument in the Benny Goodman Orchestra of the 1930s. What is the order of the solos in this example? Why do the vibes sound so "cool"? Which instruments do you hear?

comping: accompanying a soloist with a syncopated rhythmic pattern

trap set/traps: a drum set, a conglomeration of drums and cymbals played by a single drummer

bass drum: the largest and lowest pitched drum of a drum set

sock-cymbals: a pair of cymbals controlled by a foot pedal

snare drum: a drum with strings (snares) stretched across the bottom to add a reverberating effect and create a buzz tone

tom toms/toms: low-pitched drums of various sizes attached to a drum set

ride cymbal: a large suspended cymbal on a drum set

crash cymbal: a suspended cymbal on a drum set used for special effects

wood block: a simple percussion instrument consisting of a hollow block of hard wood struck with a stick or mallet

Chinese rivet "sizzle" cymbal: a large suspended cymbal on a drum set that creates a buzz tone

To the jazz musician, soloing over a good rhythm section is one of the peak experiences in life. Rhythm-section instruments produce a multi-layered supportive sound for the soloists in a jazz band. The importance of the rhythm section is thus hard to overestimate. No group can rise higher than the performance level and experience of its rhythm-section players.

The rhythm section in the standard jazz ensemble consists of piano, bass, and drums; but other instruments, like the guitar or vibes, may be added. Instruments like the guitar, banjo, and piano function as both melodic and rhythmic instruments.

Keyboard instruments have been the featured solo instruments in rhythm sections throughout the history of jazz—from ragtime to fusion. Occasionally, however, there have been groups that used a guitar in place of a keyboard instrument; and there have been groups that used neither, like the Gerry Mulligan Quartet of the 1950s, the Ornette Coleman Quartet of the 1960s, and the World Saxophone Quartet of the 1980s.

The musicians in rhythm sections must work as a team. However, there have been examples of some great piano, bass, and drum soloists that have not worked well together.

Throughout the history of jazz, it has been the rhythm section's job to provide the basic polyrhythmic conflict on accented beats that provides the feeling of excitement and "swing" in jazz. In addition, the rhythm section supplies the basic tempo, the basic "feel" for each tune and style, and the syncopated harmonic progression of chords over which soloists can improvise. The rhythmic pattern used in presenting or framing the harmonic structure for the soloist is called *comping*.

Drums. The drum set, sometimes called the *trap set* or *traps*, developed during the 1920s and was settled into its present form by the '40s. The essential parts of a drum set include the bass drum, the sock-cymbals, the snare drum, the larger tom toms (set on the floor, next to the bass drum), and the smaller toms (attached to the upper part of the bass drum), the ride cymbal, and the crash cymbal. Other, smaller items of equipment may include wood blocks, the Chinese rivet "sizzle" cymbal, and, occasionally, the samba whistle.

Great drummers, like Gene Krupa, Buddy Rich, "Big" Sid Catlett, Don Lamond, Mel Lewis, Art Blakey, Louis Bellson, and Max Roach, raised the art of drum-set playing to incredibly high levels.

Gene Krupa. [Photofest.]

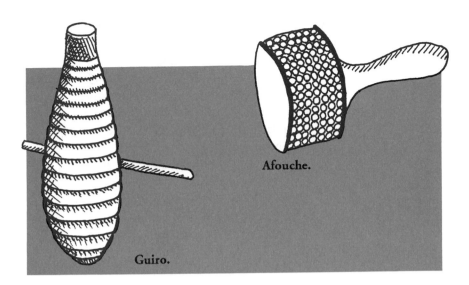

Afouche.

Guiro.

guiro: a Brazilian instrument consisting of a hollow gourd scraped with a stick

kettledrum: a drum shaped like a large pot or kettle, sometimes called *timpani*

afouche: a Brazilian instrument consisting of strands of metal beads wrapped around a wooden handle

Latin percussionists may use the conga, bongos, claves (cherry-wood sticks), guiro, cowbell, maracas, tambourim, kettledrum, and afouche. All of these Cuban or Brazilian percussion instruments originated in Africa.

These percussion instruments of African origin did not begin to become a featured part of the jazz rhythm section until the late 1940s. Trumpeter Dizzy Gillespie was responsible for introducing the great Cuban drummer Chano Pozo to American audiences. Later, Stan Kenton added a Latin percussionist (playing conga drums) to his band, as did Cal Tjader with his combo.

LISTENING ASSIGNMENT

"After You've Gone," Roy Eldridge and Gene Krupa. *Singers and Soloists of the Swing Bands*, Smithsonian, side E, #12 ▪ Notice how the drummer switches from keeping time, to being a co-soloist, to being the only soloist. Notice also the interplay between the trumpet soloist (Eldridge) and the drum soloist (Krupa).

Bass Instruments. The bass notes used in jazz were originally supplied by brass instruments. The tuba or sousaphone were the instruments used in the New Orleans marching bands.

When jazz moved indoors and up the river to Chicago and New York in the 1920s, the bass instrument used was a string bass, the bass instrument of the symphony orchestra. The introduction of the string

fret: a raised bar placed at regular intervals along the neck of some string instruments

chord voicing: the position of chord-tones within each chord

bass facilitated faster tempos and the steady bass rhythm necessary for swing and bop.

The third transition began with the invention of an electric instrument, the bass guitar. Since the 1950s, there has been an increasing use of the electric bass guitar as the bass-line instrument in modern jazz. The bass guitar or electric bass developed two styles of playing—traditional or fretless. The removal of the frets on the fingerboard of the bass allowed the bass player a much wider range of expression and special effects, but demanded a greater level of technique and musicianship. The fretless electric bass is very flexible and is capable of playing expressive melodic lines as well as traditional bass lines. From the 1970s on, the electric fretless bass became a new solo voice as well as a basic timekeeper in the jazz rhythm section.

The Guitar.

The guitar has been in and out of the rhythm section, depending on the latest trend. The guitar replaced the banjo in the rhythm section beginning in the late 1920s because its smoother sound blended better with the rest of the instruments in the rhythm section.

Django Reinhardt, a Belgian gypsy guitarist who took up jazz after damaging the last two fingers of his left hand in a fire, was one of the first great jazz guitarists. There are some wonderful early jazz recordings of the Quintette of the Hot Club of France, featuring Django Reinhardt on guitar.

Freddie Green, the great acoustic rhythm guitarist with the Count Basie band, was largely responsible for the tight, driving sound of the band. The guitar has always been a standard accompanying instrument for blues singers. After 1940, the electric guitar gradually began to replace the acoustic guitar in the jazz rhythm section. Some groups, like the George Shearing quintet in the 1950s, found new ways of using the electric-guitar sound, allowing the instrument to be reintroduced to the rhythm section. Shearing had the guitar "double" the melody an octave lower than the piano, thereby creating a lush, exotic sound.

One of the problems with the guitar in the rhythm section is that it changes the role of the pianist, who must move chord voicings up an octave to accommodate the guitar and coordinate comp patterns with the guitarist. After 1950, some jazz groups preferred to use either a guitarist or a pianist—but not both.

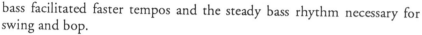

Acoustic guitar. [Picture Collection, The Branch Libraries, The New York Public Library.]

Django Reinhardt. [Drawing by Shirley Tanzi.]

■/■ IMPROVISATION

improvisation: spontaneous composition

developmental approach: an improvisational technique that emphasizes the development of a solo from the melodic and rhythmic ideas of a specific musical phrase

The heart and soul of jazz is *improvisation*, which is spontaneous composition. Using the form and chord progressions of the original tune, the jazz soloist spontaneously creates a unique melody, phrasing it in a highly personalized style.

Jazz artists like pianist Keith Jarrett, who replaced Chick Corea in the Miles Davis "fusion" group, suggest that the *idea* is the important thing, not the medium of expression. In other words, any musical instrument is just a means to an end.

There are three approaches to creating a jazz solo—the developmental, the lyrical, and the rhapsodic. Often, a jazz soloist will use all three during one long solo, switching back and forth for contrast. Each of these techniques is easy to recognize.

The Developmental Approach. This method concentrates on taking the essence of the melodic and rhythmic ideas from a short opening theme and developing them, much like taking characters in a novel or play and "developing" them while telling the story. This approach is easily recognizable because the listener will keep hearing parts of the original idea throughout the solo.

In classical music, one of the best examples of this is found in the first movement of Beethoven's Fifth. This famous symphony opens with three rapidly repeated notes followed by a fourth sustained note (*dut-dut-dut-daaah*). Beethoven built the entire movement, almost fifteen minutes of music, around this simple opening motif.

Louis Armstrong's recorded trumpet solos on his hit songs *Mack the Knife* and *Potato Head Blues* are also good examples of the developmental solo approach. In each case, Louis takes a simple, short melody and builds an entire solo around it.

The three distinguishing characteristics of this style are

1. the selection of a simple opening motif (a short musical idea) of the song,
2. the exploration of different ways to play and subtly change or expand that motif, and
3. usually, a final return to the original motif at the end of the solo.

> **LISTENING ASSIGNMENT**
>
> "Potato Head Blues," Louis Armstrong and His Hot Seven. *Smithsonian Collection of Classic Jazz*, side B, #1 ▪ Listen for the developmental solo style.

Louis Armstrong. [Photofest.]

lyrical approach: an improvisational technique utilizing a singable solo line and the dramatic use of rests

rhapsodic approach: a virtuoso improvisational technique involving double-time patterns, wide skips in register, and extreme dynamic and tonal variations

double-time pattern: a sudden increase in tempo to twice as fast as the original

The Lyrical Approach. This method is simple, adapting a "singable" approach to the improvised line, with dramatic use of musical rests. Miles Davis's solo on *Summertime* from his *Porgy and Bess* album with arranger Gil Evans is a classic example of the simple, dramatic, easy-to-sing lyrical approach to the solo. The four distinguishing characteristics of this approach are

1. a "singable" solo line,
2. a dramatic use of rests,
3. a limited range (usually less than two octaves), and
4. simple note values and rhythm patterns (few rapid passages).

LISTENING ASSIGNMENT

"Summertime," Miles Davis with the Gil Evans Orchestra. *Smithsonian Collection of Classic Jazz*, side G, #7 ▪ Listen for the lyrical solo style.

The Rhapsodic Approach. This might be better titled the "virtuoso" approach. Using this technique, the instrumental soloist can show off his skills with wide skips in register, fast-moving notes, *double-time patterns* (musical patterns that move twice as fast as the rhythm section), and extreme dynamic and tonal variations (soft to very loud, screaming, moaning, wailing, and so on).

The characteristics of this solo style usually include a lot of rapidly played notes over a wide range, with many tone-color transformations. This can easily become a show-off style, illustrating the soloist's technique. This solo style is not easy to sing and is usually very emotional and intense.

One of the greatest recordings of the 1960s was the unbelievable tenor-sax solo by John Coltrane on his tune *Giant Steps*.* This solo, Cannonball Adderley's *Easy to Love*, and Charlie Parker's *Koko* are good illustrations of the rhapsodic approach to improvisation.

The three distinguishing characteristics of this style are

1. fast-moving notes (sometimes in double-time patterns),
2. a wide range (usually unsingable), and
3. many tone-color distortions (even "squeals" and "honks").

LISTENING ASSIGNMENT

"Easy To Love," Cannonball Adderley. *Cannonball Adderley in Japan* Polygram C2793560 ▪ Listen for the rhapsodic solo style.

---

*See the LISTENING ASSIGNMENT, "Giant Steps," page 162.

■/■ INSTRUMENTALISTS

We're never really ready for the superstars of jazz when they appear. They always seem to come out of nowhere. Who would have thought that the skinny little alto player hanging around Count Basie's band in Kansas City in the 1930s would grow up to be Charlie "Bird" Parker, who descended on New York City in the '40s with a sound and a style that revolutionized jazz for the next twenty years? Or who would have bet that the tall, shy tenor saxophonist being carefully nurtured by Thelonious Monk in New York in the '50s would go on to become Trane, the musical giant who still has the jazz world spinning with the originality and intensity of his musical thought?

When will the next jazz giant appear, the one who will create new excitement, new controversy, new energy and a new direction for jazz?

Throughout the history of jazz, great instrumentalists, as well as great vocalists, have burst upon the scene unannounced. Artists like Louis Armstrong, Art Tatum, Duke Ellington, or the one-and-only Count Basie seemed to spring out of nowhere and take the jazz world by storm. Each era, each style of jazz seems to produce at least one world-class soloist, composer, or bandleader. Many jazz greats have set standards that will never be surpassed. We are fortunate to have on record or tape most of the great soloists and groups from each era.

> ## LISTENING ASSIGNMENT
>
> "Body and Soul," Benny Goodman Trio, and "Body and Soul," Coleman Hawkins Combo. *Smithsonian Collection of Classic Jazz*, side C, #5 and #6 ▪ Compare these recordings by two major jazz artists of the 1930s. How does the tone of the tenor saxophone differ from that of the clarinet? Which other instruments are used in each recording? Compare the solo styles. Note how the Coleman Hawkins recording begins with a solo—the original melody is never played.

The following well-known story will serve to illustrate the respect that jazz giants have for one another:

> Harry Myerson, a record-company executive, called Artie Shaw one day in the late 1930s or early 1940s and supposedly said something like "We want to record two completely different versions of the pop ballad *Stardust* on the same record, back-to-back, with your band and its version on one side and Tommy's band and his arrangement on the other side. You two guys are our biggest selling artists, and this should be a smash hit record. What do you think?"

Artie agreed to the deal, and his band recorded their version of *Stardust* in 1940. When Tommy Dorsey heard the Artie Shaw recording, he said, "I ain't getting on back of that!"

The Artie Shaw interpretation of *Stardust* went on to sell over 16 million records. Tommy Dorsey lost a bundle in royalties for honoring the great performance of the Artie Shaw band.

Dorsey later made a highly successful recorded version of the tune, but in no way approached the Shaw version, which many consider to be the finest example of a big-band ballad arrangement ever recorded. The three solos on the recording—the clarinet solo by Shaw, the trumpet solo by Billy Butterfield, and the trombone solo by Jack Jenney—all became classic instrumental solos of the swing era.

Poncho Sanchez.
[Drawing by Shirley Tanzi.]

■ Contrasting Jazz Stylists ■

Here are the names of several jazz instrumentalists whose solo styles are so radically different that it is hard to believe each one plays the same instrument. The names listed below have been selected because their solo styles vary so dramatically. They are not necessarily the top artists on their instruments.

BRASS

Saxophone Soprano	Sidney Bechet, John Coltrane
Alto	Johnny Hodges (with Duke Ellington), Louis Jordan, Charlie Parker
Tenor	John Coltrane, Stan Getz, Coleman Hawkins, Lester Young
Trumpet	Louis Armstrong, Chet Baker, Dizzy Gillespie
Trombone	J. J. Johnson, Frank Rosolino, Jack Teagarden

PERCUSSION

Piano Ragtime	Scott Joplin, Jelly Roll Morton
Stride	Earl Hines, Fats Waller
Bop	Thelonious Monk, Bud Powell, Art Tatum
Modern	Keith Jarrett, Cecil Taylor, McCoy Tyner
Synthesizer	Chick Corea, Tom Grant, Stevie Wonder
Vibes	Gary Burton, Lionel Hampton, Milt Jackson
Drums	Elvin Jones, Gene Krupa, Max Roach
Congas	Machito, Poncho Sanchez

STRING

Acoustic Bass	Ray Brown, Scott La Faro, Charles Mingus
Acoustic Guitar	Earl Klugh, Django Reinhardt

Like the human voice (discussed in Chapter 9), jazz instruments also vary in *tone* (bright, clear, dark, or raspy/distorted) and *register* (high-, medium-, or low-pitched).

As solo instruments, the popularity of the piano, trumpet, saxophone, guitar, and so on, rose and fell throughout jazz's history in response to changing jazz styles, influential musicians, new technology, and audience preferences.

The rhythm section, usually consisting of piano, drums, and a bass instrument, supplies the basic tempo and chord progression to back up the soloist. The drum set developed into its present form in the 1940s. Latin percussionists use various instruments of African origin, including the *conga*, *bongos*, and *claves*. The bass instrument of choice in the early New Orleans bands was the tuba or sousaphone. With jazz's shift to Chicago and New York in the 1920s, the string bass became popular. Since the '50s, there has been an increasing preference for the electric bass guitar.

The spontaneous composition that jazz soloists strive to create over the rhythm section is often a combination of three improvisational techniques. The *developmental approach* concentrates on developing a solo from a specific melodic and rhythmic idea, the *lyrical approach* makes use of a singable solo line and dramatic use of rests, and the *rhapsodic approach* involves notes played rapidly over a wide range with extreme tonal variations.

Each era in jazz's history has produced innovative jazz instrumentalists, hoping to dazzle the world with their originality and intensity. Like jazz singers, these instrumentalists work hard to produce a sound that will be all their own, a sound that their fans will immediately recognize as theirs.

■ Questions on Chapter 10

A. *In your own words* write one or two sentences describing each of the terms listed in Questions 1–8.

1. timbre _____

_____

2. register _____

_____

3. flutter tongue _____

_____

4. wah-wah pedal _____

_____

5. synthesizer _____

_____

6. fret _____

_____

7. chord voicing _____

_____

8. double-time pattern _____

_____

In Questions 9–16 fill in the blanks.

9. A _____ is a device for softening the sound of a brass instrument.

10. A _____ is a device used by jazz brass players to distort sounds.

11. The process of recording and storing sounds electronically is called _____ _____.

12. A _____ is a piano with prerecorded player rolls and pump pedals.

13. A conglomeration of drums and cymbals played by a single drummer is known as _____.

14. A _____ is a drum with strings stretched across the bottom for a reverberating effect and for creating a buzz tone.

15. A _____ is a Brazilian instrument that consists of a hollow gourd that is scraped with a stick.

16. A Brazilian instrument consisting of a large gourd covered with beads that rattle when shaken is a _____.

B. Listen to an instrumental jazz group and analyze it according to the guidelines in Questions 17–20.

17. In which jazz style (swing, bop, cool, etc.) is this group playing? How can you tell?

18. Which instruments improvise solos? Describe the *tone color* and *register* of each of these instruments.

19. Which improvisational approach (*developmental, rhapsodic, lyrical,* or more than one of these) does each soloist use? What is the difference between these three techniques?

20. Which instruments comprise the *rhythm* section? What is the role of each of these instruments?

■ Concert Report

Attend a live jazz concert of an instrumental group. Consider Questions 17–20 again, but (as in the Chapter Nine concert report) pay attention to visual cues (performers' appearance and actions, staging, lighting effects), audience reactions and/or participation, and overall effect or mood. Which aspects of the concert were done well? In what ways could the concert have been improved?

■ Further Reading

Jones, Leroi. *Black Music.* New York: William Morrow & Co., 1971.

Schuller, Gunther. *Early Jazz: Its Roots and Musical Development.* New York: Oxford University Press, 1986

——————. *The Swing Era: The Development of Jazz, 1930–1945.* New York: Oxford University Press, 1989.

Shaw, Arnold. *Fifty-Second Street: The Street of Jazz.* New York: Da Capo Press, 1977.

■ Further Listening

Smithsonian Collection of Classic Jazz. Smithsonian (all instrumental examples).

■ Films and Videos

Bird (1988).

Chick Corea: Keyboard Workshop (video).

Coltrane Legacy, The (video).

Miles in Paris (video).

Mo' Better Blues (1990). Soundtrack by Branford Marsalis and Terence Blanchard.

Piano Legends (video). Hosted by Chick Corea.

Thelonious Monk: Straight No Chaser (1988).

Trumpet Kings (video). Hosted by Wynton Marsalis.

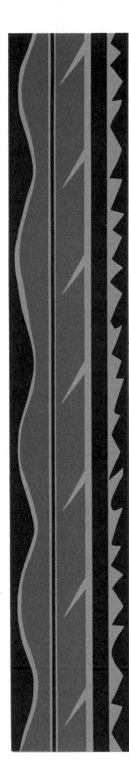

II
THE ANATOMY
OF MUSIC

/■/

I've got rhythm,
I've got music,
I've got my man—
Who can ask for anything more?

—GEORGE GERSHWIN*

W HAT is music? What is it made of? You don't have to be a musical theoretician to enjoy jazz, but it helps to know a little about the basics.

The Greeks believed that music was of divine origin. They also believed that it had supernatural powers to heal, arouse, and inspire. Along with the Native Americans, they believed that music even had some power over nature. Some early Greek philosophers claimed that music was the most powerful of the art forms. It could supposedly take control of your emotions against your conscious will. Plato said that "musical training is a more potent instrument than any other, because rhythm and harmony find their way into the inward places of the soul."†

---

*Excerpted from *Girl Crazy*.
† *The Republic*, Book III, 401.

rhythm: the pattern of long and short notes and accented and unaccented beats, encompassing both tempo and meter

form: the internal structure of a musical composition

melody: a succession of single notes producing a distinct musical idea

countermelody: an additional melody that complements the main melody

harmony: the combination of tones into chords and chord progressions

texture: the total effect produced by rhythm, chords, range, register, and tone color

style: the effect of subtle nuances in tempo, dynamics (volume), and articulation (length of notes) that distinguishes and identifies the music of a particular musician, region, cultural group, or time period

beat: the pulse or repetition of sound

Recent consumer studies have shown that customers are more likely to buy in a retail store with selected music playing softly in the background. Music can arouse us, energize us, even make us more aggressive. Research has also shown that music can help the mentally disturbed, the worker on the job, the student in the classroom, and the child in nursery school. Music is also being used today to modify stressful and ugly physical environments.

Just as all automobiles—regardless of their make or model—have an engine, a transmission, and an electrical system, nearly all music consists of seven basic parts. These are:

1. Rhythm.
2. Form.
3. Melody.
4. Countermelody.
5. Harmony.
6. Texture.
7. Style.

■/■ RHYTHM

In 1854, Eduard Hanslick, in *The Beautiful in Music*,* called rhythm "the main artery of the musical organism" and the regulator of both melody and harmony. We are more sensitive to rhythm than to any other part of music. We are rhythmical creatures. All of our involuntary systems—our nervous system, respiratory system, and circulatory system—function rhythmically. The heart, for example, the master organ of the body, maintains a normal rhythm of approximately seventy-two beats a minute.

Audiences may gloss over other weak areas in a musical performance, but they are unforgiving when it comes to rhythm. A pop group can have weak melodies, weak form, weak structure, or boring harmonic patterns, but successful groups have one thing in common: good rhythm. Rhythm is, perhaps, the most important element in any genre of music—particularly in the case of jazz. An improvised jazz solo is attractive to the listener so long as its rhythmic ideas are interesting. If the soloist's rhythmic ideas are repetitive, predictable, or otherwise unexciting, the listener will not be interested in listening.

Rhythm is what you *feel* when you listen to music, not what you *understand*. The rhythmic element is both the most important element

---

*Gustav Cohen (trans.), (New York: Liberal Arts, 1957), p. 47.

in music and the hardest to teach. Rhythmic sensitivity and creativity are what separate the great from the mediocre talent in music, whether that talent be for playing, composing, or singing.

Most art forms rely on the tension-release factor to create excitement. The typical cop movie, for instance, usually starts with a tense situation (a murder?), immediately followed by some sort of release. The plot then usually travels along at a relatively consistent pace until, near the end, another suspenseful situation (perhaps a car chase?) creates a dramatic peak followed by a release of tension.

Music uses the same idea of tension release to build anticipation, hold the listener's interest, and, eventually, create some sort of grand climax. In western European classical music, the tension-release factor is most often found in the melodic and harmonic elements that make up what we call music. In west African tribal music, the tension-release factor is primarily rhythmic. In jazz, the tension-release factor usually includes all three areas: rhythm, melody, and harmony.

Rhythm describes the speed and the repetition pattern of sounds in a musical piece. One basic element of rhythm is the *beat*, the pulse or repetition of sound, which may be heard or felt by clapping or tapping along with the music. Beats may be either *accented* (emphasized) or *unaccented*. Another basic element of rhythm is *tempo*, which refers to how fast or slow a piece is played—in other words, the speed of the beats. If the speed is regular, the tempo is said to be *constant*.

Meter describes the pattern of grouping accented and unaccented beats. For instance, a pattern of

LOUD *soft* LOUD *soft*

would be *duple meter*, a grouping of beats by twos. A pattern of

LOUD *soft* *soft* LOUD *soft* *soft*

is called *triple meter*, a grouping by threes. Most jazz is in duple meter, or is "in four"; some is in three, and occasionally, a jazz piece like Dave Brubeck's *Take Five*, is in *compound meter*, a combination of 3 and 2, such as

LOUD *soft* *soft* LOUD *soft*

In written music, a grouping of beats fits into a unit called a *measure*, or *bar*. A measure is the unit of music from one (vertical) bar line to the next—for example,

A symbol, called the *time signature*, appears in modern notation to describe the meter. Placed at the beginning of the music, it may consist of two numbers, such as $\frac{2}{4}$, $\frac{3}{4}$, or $\frac{4}{4}$, or a shorthand symbol, such as ¢ (which indicates $\frac{2}{2}$) or c (which indicates $\frac{4}{4}$). The top number indicates how many beats there are per measure, the bottom number tells what kind of note receives one beat. For example, in $\frac{3}{4}$ time, there are three beats per measure, and a quarter note, ♩, is assigned the length of one beat. Here, then, are some examples of duple, triple, and compound meter, with the appropriate time signatures.

Duple meter: *Yankee Doodle*

Triple meter: *America*

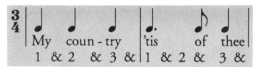

Compound meter: *Take Five* (Instrumental)

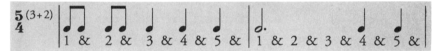

Some rhythmic devices important to jazz are *polyrhythms*, several different rhythmic patterns played simultaneously; *layered rhythms*, polyrhythms that are added one at a time; *cross-rhythms* (*polymeter*), several differently constructed meters played simultaneously; and *syncopation*, a displaced accent on the normally weak beat:

soft LOUD *soft* LOUD

These rhythmic devices were discussed in Chapter Two.

LISTENING ASSIGNMENT

"Take Five," Dave Brubeck Quartet (by Paul Desmond). *Time Out*, Columbia (CD) CK 40585 ▪ This recording is in $\frac{5}{4}$ time, a combination of $\frac{3}{4}$ and $\frac{2}{4}$. The only compound-meter tune to become a jazz standard, its attractive layered rhythms have made it one of the most important recordings to come out of the cool era. Why does this recording sound so different?

▪/▪ FORM

Form describes the internal structure of a musical composition. Form is to music as grammar is to language. By organizing music into sections and smaller units, form brings order out of chaos and introduces logic and development into the art of music.

In the development of western European music, form became increasingly important as music became more complex. The changes in musical form that occurred over the centuries in western Europe seem closely related to changes that occurred in the visual arts, particularly in architecture. The sweeping lines and complex support structures of the typical medieval cathedral are echoed in the complex counterpoint of the music that was being played in them a few years later. *Polyphonic music,* a musical style that integrates two or more melodies simultaneously, reached its zenith during the baroque period in music (1600–1750), bringing with it a high degree of development in the area of form. Much like the advanced architectural discoveries that allowed for the construction of the great cathedrals, advances in the development of form in music allowed for the development of the great polyphonic works of J. S. Bach, George F. Handel, and others.

The basic form of a musical performance is similar to the basic form of a speech. A speech is generally organized with the following goals in mind:

1. Tell the audience what you are going to talk about.
2. Talk about it.
3. Tell them what you said (summarize the important points).

In a jazz performance, this means:

1. Introduce the melody without a great deal of ornamentation or change.
2. Develop different aspects of that melody through improvised solos.
3. Return to the original melody (this time *with* some ornamentation or adjustment).

The smallest unit in musical form is called a *motif.* A motif expresses a distinctive idea or theme. Sometimes two or three notes can constitute a motif. This would be comparable to a phrase taken from a sentence or to a very short sentence. For example, the first six notes of our national anthem, *The Star-Spangled Banner,* is a motif.

A slightly larger unit is called a *phrase.* This would be comparable to a complete sentence. In a simple blues song, it would be the first line—

period: a musical passage within a composition, complete in itself—the musical equivalent of a paragraph

twelve-bar blues: a common musical form in blues and jazz made up of three four-bar phrases

for example: "I hate to see the evenin' sun go down."*

The next leap is to a *period*, a passage within a composition that is complete in itself. This is the musical equivalent of a paragraph. Thus, "I hate to see the evenin' sun go down [repeat] because my baby left town."

The longer the musical composition, the more important the organizational factor of form. If you were going to build your own wilderness cabin or beach hut, you could do it without knowing much about stress, balance, and weight. However, should you decide to erect a two-story building, you could not do it safely without knowing something about these concepts. The same principle holds in the area of music.

Most jazz songs are based on short and simple song forms. This is due partially to the early influence of 78-rpm records, which could not record more than four minutes of music per side. Later, when long-playing records allowed jazz musicians to take up to twenty-four minutes per side, the element of form became more interesting and important in jazz.

When describing form, individual musical phrases are represented by the letters **A**, **B**, **C**, and so on. Most of the common forms alternate repetitive phrases (**A–A**) with a contrasting phrase (**B**). This is typical of one of the basic principles of art: a balance of unity (repetition) and variety (alternation). The blues are a good example of the repetition of the first phrase followed by a contrasting phrase. The common twelve-bar blues form is represented by **AAB** and has three four-bar phrases, as in the following example:

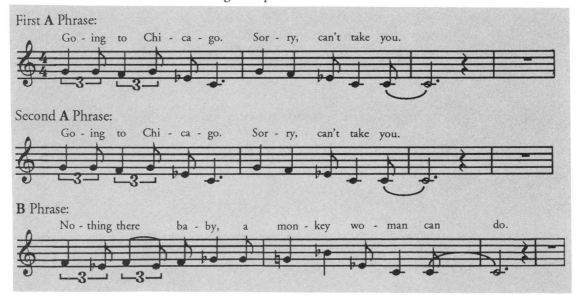

First **A** Phrase:
Go - ing to Chi - ca - go. Sor - ry, can't take you.

Second **A** Phrase:
Go - ing to Chi - ca - go. Sor - ry, can't take you.

B Phrase:
No - thing there ba - by, a mon - key wo - man can do.

*St. Louis Blues, W. C. Handy.

binary form: a musical form having two closely related sections, denoted by AB or by AABB

ternary form: a three-part musical form, denoted by ABA, AABA, or by ABC

A statement is made in the first four bars, repeated in the next four (sometimes with slight variation), and answered or commented on in the last four. The two-part song forms (**ABAB** and **AABB**) are also popular in jazz. Ragtime and fusion use forms that are more complex.

Here are some recognizable songs and their forms:

Happy Birthday – (**AABA**)   *Yankee Doodle* – (**AB**)
Silent Night – (**ABC**)   *God Save the Queen* – (**AB**)
Star Spangled Banner – (**AABC**)   *Mickey Mouse March* – (**ABA**)

Binary Form.   A *binary* form is a basic musical form having two closely related sections.

A Phrase:

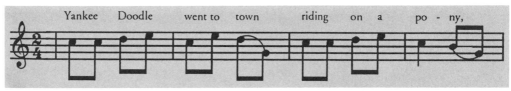

B Phrase:

The first widely popular blues in America, the Civil War era tune *Frankie and Johnny*, was in binary form **AB**.

Ternary Form.   The *ternary*, or three-part, song form, was the most common song form for jazz until the 1970s, when rock music began to influence jazz styles. There are several variations of this form, but the most common is an **AABA** form. Listeners like this form. You play (or sing) the **A** phrase, repeat it for emphasis, change the subject for contrast at the **B** section, and then summarize by returning to the original **A** section. Lyrics change for each phrase, even though the melody remains the same. A familiar example of this form is the Happy Birthday song.

Happy birthday to you.	(First **A** phrase)
Happy birthday to you.	(Second **A** phrase)
Happy birthday dear (name).	(**B** phrase)
Happy birthday to you.	(Third **A** phrase)

Very characteristic of African music and also American folk and pop

verse: the part of a song following an introduction and preceding a chorus, often sung as a solo

chorus: the refrain, which recurs after the verses

tone: a musical sound of definite pitch and quality

pitch: the degree to which an instrument, voice, or sound is high or low

timbre: tone color

interval: the difference in pitch between two tones

note: a symbol used to represent a tone, indicating its pitch and duration

half step: the smallest defined interval in music

whole step: an interval of two half-steps

scale: a succession of tones, ascending or descending according to fixed intervals

major scale: a scale with the sequence of intervals: whole step, whole, half, whole, whole, whole, half

music is the larger form of *verse* and *chorus*. Usually, the verse tells the story, whereas the chorus reflects on the story and has the more interesting melodic line. Often the chorus is repeated twice at the end. Many of the verses of the pop songs used in jazz in the 1940 and '50s were dropped altogether. Interestingly enough, rock music revived the verse-chorus form.

■/■ MELODY

Eduard Hanslick, in *The Beautiful in Music,* called melody "inexhaustible" and "preeminently the source of musical beauty."

In the eleventh century in western Europe, premeditated composition slowly replaced spontaneous improvisation as a way of expressing new musical ideas. The technique of improvisation is a common one in musical cultures around the world and was a common practice in western European music until about the ninth century, when the need to preserve the music used in celebrating the mass and other religious rites demanded some sort of preservation through the act of writing music.

Eventually, the art of composing replaced the art of improvising, as tradition and predictability became more important than spontaneity. Consequently, a system was developed for accurately preserving a piece of music by writing it down.

Because western Europeans treasured the written word, all important ideas, historical records, and concepts were written down and stored in libraries and universities. Music received the same treatment, except that musical ideas could not be written down until after the development of musical notation. Since the process of writing anything down in permanent form was expensive, only the most important melodies were preserved.

A *melody* is a succession of musical sounds, or tones, producing a distinct musical idea. Tones can differ with regard to their *pitch*, that is, how high or low they sound, and their *timbre*, or tone color, which is often based on the nature of their source (type of instrument or voice). Melodies are constructed from tones and *intervals*, that is, the differences in pitch between two successive tones. The interval between the *notes* F and F♯, for example, is called a *half step*, whereas the interval between F and G is a *whole step*. Regular arrangements of intervals form *scales*. In the *major scale*, the specified arrangement of intervals is

whole step   whole   half   whole   whole   whole   half

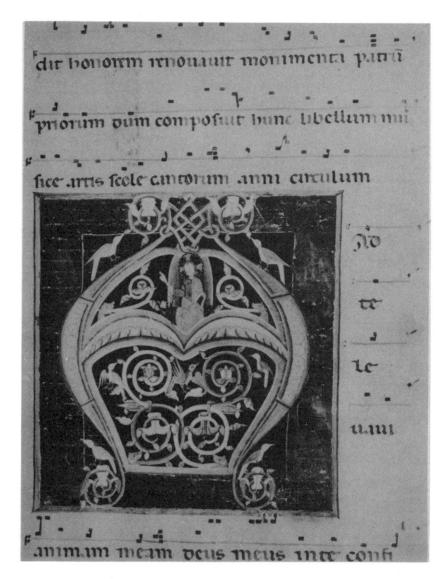

Music notation from a manuscript, 1256. [Picture Collection, The Branch Libraries, The New York Public Library.]

blue note: a flatted note common in blues and jazz, created by lowering the third, fifth, or seventh note of the major scale one half step

Most melodies are built around the notes of a particular scale, and the relationship of intervals in that scale will consequently affect the sound of the melody.

Blues and jazz melodies frequently use *blue notes*, the lowered third, fifth, or seventh notes of the major scale, to alter the sound of the scale.

melodic curve: an upward or downward movement in pitch in a melody

The tension between the lowered pitches in the blues melody and the regular unadjusted pitches in the chords of the harmony creates the "blues" effect so commonly used in jazz.

Emotional effects are also created by the *melodic curve*, the rise and fall of the melody. Generally speaking, upward-moving melodic lines build tension and anticipation, while melody lines moving downward release tension. For example, the melody of *Somewhere over the Rainbow*, leaps upward on the syllable "where" for a dramatic effect, and climbs again in smaller intervals on the words, "the rainbow" for a more flowing anticipatory effect.

A descending melodic curve occurs in the following illustration. Notice that this downward moving melody has none of the tension of the upward curve.

■/■ COUNTERMELODY

A *countermelody*, which is a melody played (or sung) simultaneously with the main melody, enhances the main melody, but does not challenge or interfere with it. Countermelody is like a good dance partner, one who follows the leader in a complimentary style, sometimes imitating or commenting on the ideas introduced by the leader. For example, note the use of simultaneous complimentary melodies in the familiar jazz tune, *Take the A Train*, written by pianist/composer/arranger Billy Strayhorn in collaboration with Duke Ellington.

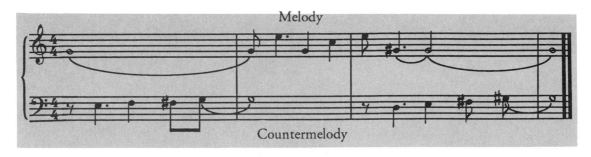

Melody

Countermelody

treble clef: the upper part of the musical staff, labeled with the symbol 𝄞, and containing the notes above middle C

bass clef: the lower part of the musical staff, labeled with the musical symbol 𝄢, and containing the notes below middle C

polyphony: the use of multiple countermelodies

counterpoint: the combining of two or more simultaneous melodies

diatonic scale: major scale

chord: a combination of two or more notes sounded simultaneously

chord progression: a series of chords that relate to each other

One melody occurs in the *treble clef*, 𝄞, the upper part of the musical staff, while the other occurs in the lower-pitched *bass clef*, 𝄢.

The interest and excitement created by countermelody is an important part of jazz. In jazz, the bass player usually plays a countermelody against the main melody of the soloist. Some types of jazz use more than one countermelody. The use of multiple countermelodies, or *polyphony*, is one of the main characteristics of New Orleans and Chicago Dixieland. Sometimes *counterpoint*, the combining of two or more simultaneous melodies, occurs between the vocalist and one or more of the instrumentalists accompanying the singer.

Dixieland, Latin jazz, and jazz rock frequently use countermelodies. In addition, many big-band arrangements, like Count Basie's classic *One o'Clock Jump* gradually add melodies on top of one another, building toward a grand final shout chorus.

■/■ HARMONY

"With its countless ways of transforming, inverting, and intensifying," said Eduard Hanslick in *The Beautiful in Music*, harmony "offers the material for constantly new developments."

Now and then, the *diatonic scale* (major scale) is found elsewhere in the musics of the world, but the concept of *harmony*, one group of simultaneously produced notes moving to another group of simultaneously produced notes, seems to be particularly European in nature. The result has been a strong emphasis on melody and harmony in western European music, with a contrasting strong emphasis on rhythm and layered rhythms in African music. These two concepts came together in jazz, with its African, American, and European roots.

Harmony is built on *chords*, which are two or more tones sounded simultaneously, and on chord progressions. Chords come in many different forms and connect with each other in various ways. Chords are usually constructed by taking alternate notes of the scale and combining them. For example:

seventh chord: a chord made up of four notes, so called because the fourth note of the chord is actually the seventh note of the scale pattern

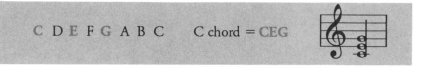

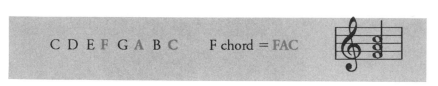

Four-note chords are called "seventh" chords because the fourth note of the chord is usually the seventh note in the scale pattern. Thus,

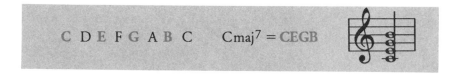

Blues songs use the same three primary chords found in hymns, folk songs, Country-and-Western music, and some pop songs.

Chord progressions, the sequential arrangement of chords enhancing a melody, are the foundation on which solo jazz choruses are built. Jazz improvisers often create spontaneous, original melodies over chord progressions from familiar songs. To do this, the soloist listens to the chord, and then spontaneously constructs a melody that will fit that chord and relate to the next chord.

Chord progressions can be used to create specific effects. In blues songs, for instance, the chords change in specific places. Until the 1950s, jazz musicians favored the sophisticated chord progressions of earlier Broadway show songs, like George Gershwin's *I Got Rhythm*. After the 1950s, rock, and later fusion, introduced other types of chords and chord progressions.

A good rhythm section "feeds" chords to the soloist by *comping* them (playing them in a syncopated rhythmic pattern, which adds rhythmic as well as harmonic interest to the solo). The soloist then "takes off" on an original melody that compliments the chords behind the solo.

Jazz players must be familiar with the chord progressions of hundreds of standard jazz tunes. They must be able to anticipate each chord before it is played by the rhythm section so that they can instantly prepare a melodic idea that works.

■/■ TEXTURE

articulation: the length
of time individual notes
are held

The tribal music of western Africa must have sounded like musical chaos
to the western European explorer in the eighteenth and nineteenth centuries. Africans had no written music; they played and sang everything
by ear, didn't follow regular bar lines, and never played or sang anything
the same way twice. Each performance was an improvisation, leaving just
enough of the original melody to make it recognizable.

Moreover, the emotional African vocal style, with its buzz tones,
moans, wails, shrieks, falsettos, and shouts, must have sounded to the
western-trained ear like a choir from hell. You can see why most early
explorers found the African vocal style to be too high, too loud, and too
harsh.

A lot of the sounds heard in jazz today are still not found in any
other style of western music. There may be some African influences in
gypsy and flamenco folk music, but, generally speaking, Europeans had
already sacrificed raw emotion for style by the eighteenth century.

Texture refers to the way in which rhythm, chords, range, register,
and tone color combine to produce a total effect.

There are four basic vocal tone colors: bright, clear, dark, and raspy.
There are hundreds of instrumental tone colors, all a blend of different
overtones, like shades of colors in paintings. Musical instruments can
often change their tone color by the use of mutes or special electronic
adjustments. Different combinations of instruments produce different
textures. A large ensemble has more textures available than does a small
one. A single instrument, like a piano, has a limited number of textures
available.

■/■ STYLE

Style consists of three important and different aspects:

1. *Tempo* (how slow or fast a piece of music is played).
2. *Dynamics* (how soft or how loud it is played).
3. *Articulation* (how long individual notes are held.)

Because jazz imitates the nuances of language and dialect more closely
than does classical music, the elements of tempo, dynamics, and articulation are very important in determining jazz style. The subtle nuances in
these three areas are not always capable of being notated or written
down. That's why written musical examples of jazz or blues can only

legato: smooth and connected

staccato: short and abruptly disconnected

approximate the authentic style. It's up to the singer, conductor, or performer to authenticate the performance by providing the appropriate means of expression for that particular jazz style. Lack of familiarity with the historical style will produce unauthentic performances. This often happens today when European-trained concert pianists try to play ragtime compositions or European-trained singers try to sing spirituals or the blues.

Tempos have varied throughout the history of jazz. The extreme tempos in jazz range from 40 beats per minute (a very slow ballad) to over 320 beats per minute (a very fast bop tune). Jazz has a much wider tempo range than do pop and rock music, which usually run from 65 to 176 beats per minute.

Dynamically, jazz varies from very loud to very soft. Dynamics are used to shade the sounds and to add contrast and balance. Jazz is much more sophisticated dynamically than is pop music, which tends to be loud, for the most part.

The way in which the notes are articulated can make a major difference in the style of a song, much like an accent can add to or detract from an actor's performance. Phrasing that is connected and smooth creates a flowing effect. Articulation that is short and separated creates a hammering, interrupted effect. Most of the time, a jazz melody is smooth, with connected notes. The traditional musical term for this is *legato*. The opposite effect, where notes are short and separated, is called *staccato*. Generally speaking, legato has a lyrical effect, whereas staccato has a drum-like effect. Jazz uses a wider range of articulation than does pop music, giving jazz more contrast, variety, and balance.

LISTENING ASSIGNMENT

"West End Blues," Louis Armstrong, and "East St. Louis Toodle-oo," Duke Ellington. *Smithsonian Collection of Classic Jazz*, side B, #4, and side D, #11 ▪ Listen to each of these songs seven times, each time focusing on one of the seven elements of music discussed in this chapter. Note how the songs contrast with each other.

SUMMARY

Many cultures have attributed to music a powerful influence over nature and human emotion. Our own society consciously makes use of music to modify environments and to affect listeners positively.

Music consists of seven basic elements: rhythm, form, melody, countermelody, harmony, texture, and style. *Rhythm*, used to create interest and excitement in music, depends on the effective use of *beats*—the repetition of sound, *meter*—the grouping of beats (indicated by the *time signature*), and *tempo*—the speed of the beats.

Form organizes music into sections and smaller units, bringing order to the whole. A *motif* is the smallest unit—just a few notes long. The next largest unit is called a *phrase*, and the musical equivalent of a paragraph is called a *period*. The most common forms in jazz are the twelve-bar blues form and the two-part song form. The basic *binary form* has two related sections, whereas the *ternary form*, popular in jazz until the 1970s, has three parts.

Melody is a succession of *tones*, which have their own *pitch* (that is, how high or low they sound) and *timbre* (tone quality). Melodies are constructed from tones and the *intervals*, or differences in pitch, between two tones. Regular arrangements of intervals form *scales*. Most melodies are built around the notes of a particular scale. *Melodic curves* (variations in pitch) are used to create emotion, and *blue notes*, notes that are slightly lowered in pitch, are used in jazz to create tension and dissonance. *Countermelody* complements and enhances the main melody. *Counterpoint*, the combining of melodies with countermelodies, is frequently used in jazz, as is *polyphony*, the use of multiple countermelodies. *Harmony* involves the use of *chords*, which are two or more notes sounded simultaneously, and *chord progressions* for special effects and for supporting the melody.

Texture refers to the overall effect of rhythm, chords, range, and tone color. *Style* refers to the often subtle nuances created by variations in tempo, dynamics, and articulation of notes.

Together, with varying emphasis, these elements are the building blocks of all musical compositions.

■ Questions on Chapter 11

A. *In your own words* write one or two sentences describing each of the terms listed in Questions 1–25.

1. rhythm _____

    _____

2. form _____

    _____

3. melody _____

    _____

4. countermelody _____

_____

5. harmony _____

_____

6. texture _____

_____

7. style _____

_____

8. beat _____

_____

9. meter _____

_____

10. measure _____

_____

11. time signature _____

_____

12. polyphonic music _____

_____

13. motif _____

_____

14. phrase _____

_____

15. period _____

_____

16. verse _____

_____

17. chorus _____

_____

18. tone _____

_____

19. interval _____

_____

20. tonal center _____

_____

21. melodic curves _____

_____

22. chord _____

_____

23. articulation _____

_____

24. legato _____

_____

25. staccato _____

_____

In Questions 26–35 fill in the blanks.

26. _____ is a grouping of beats by twos.

27. _____ is a grouping of beats by threes.

28. _____ is a grouping of beats in a combination of twos and threes.

29. _____ is a common musical form in blues and jazz consisting of three four-bar phrases.

30. A musical form having two closely related sections is called _____ form.

31. A musical form having three closely related sections is called _____ form.

32. A _____ is the smallest interval in music.

33. A _____ is a flatted note created by lowering the third, fifth, or seventh note of the major scale one half step.

34. _____ consists of two or more simultaneous combined melodies.

35. A line marking the division between measures in written music is known as a _____.

B. For Questions 36–42 choose a jazz song and consider its musical parts.

36. Tap along with the *beat*. Describe the *tempo* and *meter*.

37. Describe the song's *form*, using terms discussed in this chapter.

38. Describe the *melody*. How does it make use of *melodic curves*? Does it use *blue notes*?

39. Are there any *countermelodies*? Describe them. How do they offset the melody?

40. How does the *harmony* interact with the melody?

41. Can you describe the overall *texture* of the song? (Useful terms include *open*, *airy*, *smooth*, *light*, *full*, *dense*, and *harsh*.)

42. How do the musicians make use of tempo, dynamics, and articulation to define the group's *style*?

■ Topics for Further Research

A. What were the origins of written music? What did early written music look like? How did this early notation develop into modern musical notation?

B. What effect has electronics had on jazz texture and style? Give some specific examples of artists or recordings whose use of electronics has had an impact on jazz texture and/or style.

■ Further Reading

Bernstein, Leonard. *Joy of Music*. New York: Simon & Schuster, 1959.

Coker, Jerry. *The Elements of Jazz* (with instructional tape). New Albany, Ind.: Aebersold, 1993.

White, Gary. *Music First!* (with instructional tape). Dubuque, IA: Wm C Brown Group, 1989.

■ Further Listening

Jazz: How to Play and Improvise (CD and book). Aebersold (vol. 1).

Nothin' But the Blues (CD and Book). Aebersold (vol. 2).

■ Films and Videos

Chick Corea: Electric Workshop (video).

Modes: No More A Mystery (instructional video). Frank Gambale.

Sound? (video).

Universal Mind of Bill Evans, The (video).

PART III

Social
and
Technological
Changes

12

ELECTRONICS, THE COMPUTER, AND JAZZ

/■/

Here comes Robby Robot
with a smile on his face.
Sits down at the piano
and destroys the place!
He can play fast,
He can play slow—
Boy can that computer really go!
But wait a minute, folks,
something ain't right.
This cat's jerky
and very uptight.
He sounds awfully stiff
and he ain't got no soul.
Poor Robby Robot
can't rock 'n' roll.
He makes a lot of noise
and he plays his part,
but poor Robby Robot
ain't got no heart.
Give me a smoky nightclub
and the smell of gin—
and then watch a real
jazz player begin.

—JW

vocoder: an electronic device that synthesizes speech sounds

splicing: the uniting or joining of two pieces or sections of magnetic tape or film

THREE areas of technological development that have revolutionized our way of life since the end of World War II include

1. nuclear fission,
2. rocketry (space), and
3. electronics.

Of the three, electronics (including the development of the computer) seems to have had the greatest impact on contemporary American society.

Electromagnetic tape was first used during World War II when the British devised radar systems. At about the same time, other developments in computer technology led to new types of musical instruments and new ways of recording and reproducing sound.

In Germany after World War II, the Bell Telephone Laboratory demonstrated the *vocoder*, a synthesizer of speech sounds. By 1951, experiments in the synthesizing of music were well underway, and in 1961, an electronic studio opened in Moscow.

Electronic music consists of sounds, natural and electronic, that are recorded on magnetic tape and then transformed electronically into "new" sounds. This can be done by splicing the tape, speeding it up or slowing it down, or by reversing its direction. Some of the sounds thus produced may provide background accompaniment; some are meant to function as solo "instruments." The completed work is an assembly of tapes spliced together into a final composition. Music produced in this way gives the composer unlimited resources of pitch, dynamics, texture, and rhythm.

Electronic music began to attract composers in the 1950s. In 1968, the first International Electronic Music Competition was held at Dartmouth College in New Hampshire. Over one hundred entries were received and judged at this competition.

By 1968, several electronically driven rock groups had emerged. The Mothers of Invention were described as "a ten-man electronic chamber orchestra that specializes in satirical rock and jazz."*

By the 1970s, electronic concepts and techniques were gradually being introduced into the pop and jazz worlds. Some of the successful early experiments in electronic music were made by Tangerine Dream (Christopher Franke, Edgar Froese, and Peter Baumann) and by Mike Oldfield, Don Ellis, Frank Zappa, Chick Corea, and Stevie Wonder.

---

*Watt, Douglass, "Popular Records," *The New Yorker*, June 14, 1969, p. 92.

■/■ NEW RECORDING TECHNIQUES

Electronic music would not have been possible without advances in the area of sound recording and reproduction. Increasingly realistic sound-reproduction techniques and longer playback capacities brought the *feeling* of jazz into the living room.

The development of new ways of recording music allowed the sound engineer, formerly outside of the loop of creativity, to enter the loop and become part of the creative process. Today, recording engineers are important not only for their technical know-how, but also for their creative imagination and their ability to apply their ideas through use of the new technology.

Powered mixer. [Yamaha Corporation of America.]

Herbie Hancock and Chick Corea. [Photofest.]

The recording process had become extremely sophisticated by the late 1960s. More advanced equipment enabled engineers to record more volume, particularly in the lower frequencies of bass drum and bass guitar. Producers could delay decisions about balancing the instruments against each other. Recording machines jumped from two tracks to four, to eight, to sixteen, and eventually, to twenty-four tracks.

Since several tracks could now be dedicated to capturing the essence of each instrument, the process improved the recording of certain instruments like the drums and the bass. A new "presence," not available prior to this new technique, was now available. Electronic sounds, sounds of nature, earlier musical styles, and ethnic musical styles—all could be added and mixed into the final recording.

Multitrack recording opened up new ways of creating as well as recording music. In the not-too-distant future, this new technology, including the DAT process, which allows a musical signal to be transformed into computer language and stored on a computer disk, will allow jazz fans to access their musical choice through their home computers, which will be patched into a network system that will feed the desired program back through their computers into their DAT FM digital playback system via an earth-orbiting communications satellite. The cost of this service will be added to their monthly communications bill.

The computer and related technology allows modern society to customize life styles and individual tastes in art and entertainment.

Jazz musicians took advantage of these new recording techniques, but avoided electronic gimmicks. The jazz artists most successful at adapting to the new multitrack recording techniques were Herbie Hancock, Chick Corea, the Brecker Brothers, and Miles Davis. Rock was the arena in which most of the experimentation occurred. Some rock musicians visited Africa, where they recorded native music and mixed it with rock. Guitarist John McLaughlin successfully mixed rock, jazz, and the music of India with his Mahavishnu Orchestra.

One of the increasingly popular concepts developed through multitrack recording is the mix of music representing the past, the present, and the future. All three time periods are simultaneously presented to the listener—creating an aural time-traveling effect. The Beatles' *Magical Mystery Tour, Sergeant Pepper's Lonely Hearts Club Band*, and *Abbey Road*, as well as Mike Oldfield's *Tubular Bells* are all typical examples of this mixing of musical eras.

LISTENING ASSIGNMENT

"Tubular Bells," Mike Oldfield. *Tubular Bells*, Virgin Records (CD) 90589-2 ▪ This song uses multitrack recording techniques to create the impression of different time periods: The use of primitive sounds suggests the past, contemporary rock rhythms suggest the present, and advanced electronic sounds suggest the future.

▪/▪ ELECTRONIC INSTRUMENTS

The first instrument to go electric in jazz was the guitar, in 1935. The second was the bass, in the 1940s. Next came the electric piano, in the '50s. The synthesizer replaced the electric piano in the fusion-jazz rhythm section in the '70s.

Eventually, the violin, flute, vibes, trumpet, and sax all became amplified. Today, every instrument in a jazz combo may be electrified. Most can be patched into synthesizers, as well, creating thousands of new and

The album cover for *Sergeant Pepper's Lonely Hearts Club Band.* [Picture Collection, The Branch Libraries, The New York Public Library.]

unusual sounds. In today's world of music, it's hard to separate the electronically generated musical sound from the naturally produced sound.

If string instruments (violins, violas, cellos, and bass viols) were the most important instruments to come out of the Renaissance and pianos were the most important ones to come out of the industrial revolution, then synthesizers are the most important instruments to come out of the electronic-cybernetic age.

Synthesizers, music computers that create sounds electronically, continued to develop throughout the 1980s. Live performances by contemporary groups increasingly relied on prerecorded sounds integrated with live musical sounds for their final product. The awesome potential unleashed by the synthesizer created a musical revolution. Composers could create sounds on a synthesizer that only a few years before could be created only by a symphony orchestra, a rock band, and a few jazz combos combined.

Gil Malle, an innovative West Coast jazz composer/arranger, was one of the first to combine jazz and electronics in a film score (*The Fantastic Journey*, 1961).

New technological breakthroughs made superstars out of some rock-pop keyboardists. The synthesizer equivalent of an Art Tatum or Bud Powell is yet to come, but the door to a new type of keyboard creativity has been opened, and sooner or later a definitive player will step through that door. At the present time, the pianist/arranger/composer Chick Corea and the award-winning composer and musician Herbie Hancock are probably the most creative, artistic, and exciting electronic funk-jazz-fusion players on the the jazz scene.

Electric guitar.   **Synthesizer.**   [Yamaha Corporation of America.]

Electronic music today encompasses such diverse musical styles as the eclecticism of Philip Glass (a minimalist who blends jazz, rock, Western classical music, and ideas from India), the powerful electronically driven Elektric Band of Chick Corea, and even the trancelike music of Tangerine Dream and fellow Germans Kraftwerk and Klaus Schulze.

Tangerine Dream was founded in Berlin twenty years ago; it has remained one of the world's most unusual and adventurous electronic groups. Its post-psychedelic, high-tech brew has been called *technopop*, a term that would also apply to Kraftwerk and Klaus Schulze as well as to Tokyo's Ryuichi Sakamoto.

Philip Glass. [Photofest.]

Tangerine Dream. [Photofest.]

LISTENING ASSIGNMENT

"Spain," Chick Corea. *Light as a Feather*, Polygram 827148 ▪ In this early example of fusion, Chick Corea combines Spanish music with the jazz samba. Note how Flora Purim uses her voice as an instrument on this recording. The solo instruments are flute and synthesizer. Which other instruments are used?

■/■ JAZZ COMPOSITION

Electronics has revolutionized every aspect of music—from its creation to its performance to its publication and preservation. It has changed not only the musical instruments and the recording methods used but also the way in which musicians create and think about music. All musical styles—from folk to bop have been revolutionized by the new technology. The electronically trained musician can assume the roles of creator, composer, improviser, arranger, orchestrator, conductor, and recording engineer—all at the same time.

Today, hundreds of the young musicians composing, recording, and mixing pop tunes, jazz tunes, soundtracks, jingles, and special effects in

Rhythm synthesizer—an advanced drum machine. [Yamaha Corporation of America.]

drum machine: a type of sequencer that allows drum sounds and other percussive effects to be stored on a digital disk and later to be re-created

MIDI: Musical Instrument Digital Interface, a computer language used to carry musical ideas between a synthesizer and a computer

sampling: the process of recording and storing natural sounds electronically

sitar: a stringed instrument of India with a small body and long fretted neck

their home studios, using relatively inexpensive home equipment, have yet to learn to read music. Technology has made it possible for them to create music without any formal musical training. Computers, synthesizers, sequencers, drum machines, and multitrack digital-recording techniques have allowed these musicians to develop—musicians who, while musically illiterate, are still capable of creating and performing quality music. Paul McCartney, the famous ex-Beatle, admits to being unable to read music.

With the aid of these same devices, it is now possible to write and hear music without using a musical instrument. The computer does it all, even to the point of communicating and interacting directly with synthesizers and other equipment by means of a computer language called MIDI. Through the electronic process called *sampling*, synthesizers and computers can record and store almost any sound or tone, traditional or nontraditional, including the sounds of third-world instruments, such as the East Indian sitar. The African process of combining syncopated layered rhythms can now be done by the computer, as well.

▪ MIDI ▪

MIDI (**M**usical **I**nstrument **D**igital **I**nterface) is a computer language that enables the computer to talk to or interact with a synthesizer, drum machine, or sequencer. MIDI allows the modern composer to

1. write music on a computer,
2. have it performed instantly by channeling it (via MIDI) to a synthesizer from the computer,
3. record the music electronically, again with computer language, and

4. add to or overlap a series of phrases by using a sequencer.

For instance, Jan Hammer composed and recorded most of the musical score for the television series "Miami Vice" on his computer using the language, MIDI. This was then put on a floppy disc and sent via modem (computer telephone hook-up) to the television studio, where the music was mixed down into the dialogue-and-effects soundtrack.

The ability to transfer sound to a mathematical formula has revolutionized the concept, use, making, and storing of musical sounds. The only thing left for the live musician is the creating, processing, and evaluating of the musical sounds.

Recently developed computer programs can allow any instrument to improvise through a synthesizer. The initial sound is modified by a preselected electronic filter. The computer then analyzes the performance and stores it in its memory banks. Each performance can be replayed at a later time or printed for further study or analysis.

Musicians, particularly composers, have always envied painters and writers because they can create when they want to and can control the presentation of their product to an audience. Any performing musician must be part of a rigid pattern of muscle and tonal memory—exerted at each performance. The control of these muscle movements is incredibly complex and is subject to error.

Until the present time, composers could control their creative efforts only up to the point where they reached the performer or conductor. Many a composer has gone home after a performance of his or her music wondering how the performer or conductor could have deviated so far from the original idea.

Composers have always yearned for the day when they could exert complete control over their efforts. Today that's possible. Composers can bypass the live-performance trap and have their music re-created in front of listeners with a mathematical consistency of performance. No more wrong notes or sloppy intonation! All this is a result of research into computer chips and the invention of the *tonal sequencer*, a computerized recording device that can preserve and reproduce a perfect musical performance every time.

Tonal sequencers have gone from being a curiosity to being a key element in the music-making process for untold thousands of players and composers. The programmable musical sequencer may prove to be the most important advance in music since the invention of notation.

Today, pop-rock groups in concert often reproduce over half of their performance through the use of sequencers, freeing up the "live" part of the performance and allowing the musicians to be more creative and spontaneous. For instance, the drum machine can keep the beat of a tune, freeing the drummer to improvise. Fusion-jazz artists are moving in a similar direction.

On a recent tour, the New York City jazz vocal group, The Manhattan Transfer, featured a computer-controlled light show as well as many complicated prerecorded arrangements as a part of their act. Computers and sequencers can control and integrate staging, lighting,

The Manhattan Transfer. [Photofest.]

LISTENING ASSIGNMENT

"Take Me Out to the Ball Game," Matt Catingub. *Hi-Tech Big Band*, Seabreeze SBC 2025 ▪ In this startling example of electronic technology applied to big-band jazz, all the sounds are synthesized except the bass, drums, and lead alto. Catingub played all three "live" tracks and created the others on a synthesizer. Listen closely. Can you distinguish this band from a regular big band? Which instruments sound the most synthetic? Which sound "real"?

prerecorded music—everything but the spontaneous improvisations of the artists and the audience's reaction to them.

Jazz artists are not predictable. They have good nights and bad nights. This fact disturbs producers, managers, and public-relations people, who like everything to be constant, particularly when a lot of money is involved. That's why rock groups are relying more and more on lip-syncing to prerecorded tapes. This means losing some spontaneity but gaining consistency. Besides, if it *looks* spontaneous, most audiences will think it *is* spontaneous.

Live performances today go far beyond anything that could be executed technically by an individual or ensemble. Hence the increasing tendency not only to lip-sync lyrics, but to suggest a level of artistic virtuosity on the part of the group or the player that isn't really there.

SUMMARY

Developments in electronic technology have had a profound impact on the development of jazz and popular music. Advances in the recording process in the 1960s led to new techniques such as *multitrack recording*, which enabled complex mixing of different sounds into a recording. Electronic sounds and sounds from nature were used as well as musical styles from different cultures and time periods.

The electric guitar was invented in 1935, and the electric bass and piano soon followed. Eventually, all instruments in a jazz combo would be electrified.

Synthesizers revolutionized the music industry in the 1970s and '80s by allowing composers to create sounds electronically. A single musician could now compose, record, and mix all the parts of a song with the right equipment. Through *electronic sampling*, any sound could be recorded and stored, making it possible to produce music without even the use of a musical instrument. The *tonal sequencer*, a computerized recording device, enabled composers to recreate their compositions perfectly and consistently, without the influence of a separate performer or conductor.

No one knows what long-term effects the new technology will have on jazz, where so much emphasis is on individualized sound, spontaneity, and personalized phrasing concepts.

Jazz composition involves carefully balancing an improvisation (the spontaneous) atop the foundation of a composed piece (the preconceived). The new technology threatens this balance. If jazz performances are reduced to scattering a few spontaneous notes on top of a rich bed of overproduced prerecorded electronic sounds, jazz will lose its excitement, trading it in for the predictable sounds of the sequencer and computer.

■ Questions on Chapter 12

A. *In your own words* write one or two sentences describing each of the terms listed in Questions 1–5.

1. vocoder _____

_____

2. splicing _____

_____

3. MIDI _____

_____

4. drum machine _____

_____

5. sampling _____

_____

B.

6. How has the development of computer technology affected jazz?

7. What innovations were made possible by the development of multitrack recording techniques?

8. What is a synthesizer? How is it used in modern music today?

9. What is a tonal sequencer? How does it differ from a synthesizer?

10. What dangers are there to jazz in relying too heavily on technology?

■ Topics for Further Research

A. Compare the vinyl record, the cassette tape, and the compact disk. How do each of these store and play back music? What are the advantages and disadvantages of each?

B. What is a *DAT processing recorder*? How does it work? How will it affect our listening habits? What other technologies are being developed that will affect the music industry?

Further Reading

Keyboard Magazine editors. *The History of Analog and Digital Synthesis*. Cupertino, Calif.: GPI Publications, 1988.

Naisbitt, Alan and Patricia Auburdene. *Mega-Trends Two Thousand*. New York: William Morrow & Co., 1990.

Toffler, Alvin. *Power Shift*. New York: Bantam Books, 1990.

Further Listening

Akoustic Band, Chick Corea. GRP Records GRD 9582.

Birds of Fire, The Mahavishnu Orchestra. Columbia CK-31996.

Hi-Tech Big Band, Matt Catingub. Seabreeze SBC 2025.

I Sing the Body Electric, Weather Report. Columbia CK 46107.

Miami Vice, Jan Hammer. MCA MCAD 6150 (vol. 1–2).

Films and Videos

Blade Runner (1982). Soundtrack by Vangelis.

Chariots of Fire (1981). Soundtrack by Vangelis.

Chick Corea: Electric Workshop (video).

Dune (1984). Soundtrack by Toto and others.

Keep, The (1983). Soundtrack by Tangerine Dream.

Koyaanisqatsi (1983). Soundtrack by Philip Glass.

13
THE PRESENT AND
FUTURE STATUS OF JAZZ

/ ■/

Everything's plastic,
everything's fast.
Instant satisfaction—
just one big blast!
Electronic this,
digital that.
Meantime,
where's jazz at?

—JW

———

NEVER in the history of jazz were there so many options for the jazz musician as there were in the 1980s and '90s. The cornucopia of available musical sounds combined with a continuing breakdown of the barriers between the various jazz styles opened up vast new realms for exploration. The only limitations on experimentation were conceptual, technical, and financial ones.

■/■ INFLUENCES

tabla: a small Indian
hand drum

The most important influences on jazz as the twentieth century draws to a close have been advances in technology, third-world culture, commercialism, and government support. Technological advances were covered in Chapter 12.

Third-World Culture. The classical music of northern India is supposedly the oldest music in the world. It is largely improvised and includes complex syncopated and layered rhythms. Small hand drums called *tablas* are the primary source of the rhythmic vitality of this music.

In the 1960s and '70s, many top rock groups and stars were drawn to the philosophy, religion, and cultural traditions of India. Many of them, like John McLaughlin, leader of the Mahavishnu Orchestra, began

Paul Horn.

pop: a commercialized style of rock

assimilating the music of India into contemporary rock. Jazz players like flutist Paul Horn were also fascinated by these musical sounds and brought them into jazz.

The pop-music craze, rap, can be traced back to Africa, where the *griots*, or musical poets, of the tribe were appreciated for their ability to create interesting lyrics to syncopated layered rhythms spontaneously and rapidly.

Unfortunately, the growing black awareness that began in the 1960s and extended through the '80s had a *negative* effect on jazz. In fact, jazz almost disappeared in most of the black communities in this country. Many black-awareness leaders argued that it was a bastardized art form: a mishmash of African and American music played on white musical instruments using European harmony and form. Many young black musicians consequently turned away from jazz and toward the music of Africa (including gospel and soul music) and Jamaica. This disappearance of jazz from black communities meant a decrease in the number of new black jazz musicians.

On the other hand, some of the more creative rock artists became interested in third-world sources of jazz. Paul Simon's *Graceland* and *The Rhythm of the Saints* are just two of many albums in the rock and pop community that were inspired by the third world.

Commercialism. The desire for instant gratification in America in the 1980s made it increasingly difficult for any serious art form to find an audience. The national attention span seemed to be shrinking, and audiences seemed increasingly impatient with any form of complexity in art or entertainment. One of the results was the de-Africanization of rock. The removal of layered rhythms, sophisticated melodic, rhythmic, and harmonic patterns, blue notes, and improvised solos left rock, particularly heavy-metal, with jerky, distorted, and blaring sounds.

Pop, a commercialized form of rock, relied on a limited number of simple and overused, yet usually singable or danceable, forms—a technique that was financially successful, but artistically stagnant.

Then, in the late 1980s, the pitched battles fought between pure jazz musicians and rock musicians seemed to cease and an uneasy alliance developed. Jazz musicians became less uncomfortable in a rock format, and rock musicians seemed less intimidated by jazz writers and players. It became fashionable for rock artists, particularly those with a few million dollars in the bank, bravely to challenge their record companies to allow them to produce albums containing real jazz. Rock artists were increasingly integrating jazz styles and soloists into their recordings and live performances. Rock singer and actor Sting's successful films and albums are heavily jazz-influenced. The Rolling Stones also support jazz by taking well-known jazz soloists on their rare tours. It seems that rock had decided to take another look at jazz, particularly bop. Other successful attempts to integrate rock, pop, and jazz include Linda Ronstadt's collaboration with jazz arranger Nelson Riddle in recapturing the glamour of the big-band singer of the 1930s. These are just a few examples of pop stars dabbling in jazz and jazz stars mixing with the celebrities of the time.

Some critics claim this cross-fertilization is a desperate attempt to buy credibility for a style of music that has run out of new ideas. These critics claim that if rock becomes too "artsy," too intellectual, it will lose its large audience and huge profits, but the presence of a jazz musician or two on stage lends credibility to a rock concert.

An ad for *The Jazz Singer*. [Picture Collection, The Branch Libraries, The New York Public Library.]

short-subject film: also
called a *short*, a short
film, such as a documentary, often shown in conjunction with a feature-length film

bio pic: a biographical
movie

Government Support. By the 1980s, jazz had reached a point
where its practitioners were receiving public awards and honors at the
Kennedy Center in Washington, D.C., and there were increasing local,
state, and federal grants available for jazz education.

Many cities and communities in America today put on jazz festivals.
In fact, jazz festivals may be the fastest-growing form of live entertainment in America. Rock festivals, on the other hand, are on the decline—
due to their high cost, insurance problems, and the increase in fan violence.

Violence and drug or alcohol abuse is seldom a problem at jazz
festivals. Jazz fans seem to be more mature and better able to control
extremes of behavior. The music is friendlier, mellower, and less threatening than rock, and it is certainly easier on the ears.

Many cities have also set up resident jazz orchestras, supported by
boards of directors. New York, Los Angeles, and Dallas now have such
orchestras.

The danger in this trend is that committees on local, state, and national grant and funding boards now control who will receive government
support. When the government subsidizes the arts, artists are able to pay
their bills, it's true, but audiences no longer determine what will survive.

■/■ JAZZ ON FILM

One of the primary modes of entertainment in the past decade was the
movies. The availability of films—new and old—was nearly unlimited as
more and more Americans had access to cable television and VCRs as
well as to movie theaters and network television.

Jazz has been a recurrent theme in motion pictures. The first "talking"
film, although not really about jazz, was titled, *The Jazz Singer*. One of
the earliest jazz films was shot in 1930 and was called *The King of Jazz*. It
featured Paul Whiteman and his orchestra and a group called The
Rhythm Boys, which included the young Bing Crosby. Many *short-subject
films* featuring jazz singers and soloists were made during this period.

In the 1940s, it became part of the standard Hollywood formula to
include a well-known big band in musical comedies. Harry James and
his band, Count Basie, Benny Goodman, Fats Waller, Duke Ellington
and his orchestra, Louis Armstrong, Tommy Dorsey and his orchestra,
and Paul Whiteman all appeared in movies.

"Bio pics" based on the lives of jazz musicians were also popular in
the 1940s and '50s. The Dorsey brothers, Bix Beiderbecke, Glenn Miller,
W. C. Handy, Benny Goodman, and Gene Krupa all received some kind
of biographical treatment.

A scene from *Round Midnight.* [Photofest.]

Two good biographical types of films were produced in the 1980s. *Round Midnight*, a 1986 American-French film is about a burned-out, boozy American expatriate jazzman, working in 1950s Paris, who embraces a friendship with a fan who virtually adopts him. The movie was inspired by the relationship between jazz musician Bud Powell and Francis Paudras. And *Bird*, a 1988 film, is about the brilliant, but troubled, jazz legend Charlie "Bird" Parker.

The 1980s and early '90s were more important, however, for the number of concerts that were recorded on film than they were for the jazz-related movies produced. These concerts included live jazz performances from the Village Vanguard and other jazz clubs, film footage of several jazz festivals and concerts, and documentaries of contemporary and early jazz artists. The films feature such top contemporary jazz artists as Wynton Marsalis, Chick Corea, Herbie Hancock, Ornette Coleman, and others, and have exposed television and movie audiences to music that they might not otherwise have encountered.

A partial list of jazz-related movies and jazz concert films produced from 1930 to 1992 follows.

1930 ***The King of Jazz*** (93 min.) – Paul Whiteman and his orchestra, The Rhythm Boys (including the young Bing Crosby) ▪ Highlight: Performance of Gershwin's *Rhapsody in Blue*.

1941 ***Blues in the Night*** (88 min.) – Music by Harold Arlen ▪ Surprisingly, the title song is never played in its entirety.

1942 ***Springtime in the Rockies*** (90 min.) – Harry James and his band ▪ James band at its best, with Helen Forest, introducing *I Had the Craziest Dream*.

Private Buckaroo (68 min.) – Harry James, The Andrew Sisters ▪ Vehicle for the Andrews trio.

Orchestra Wives (97 min.) – Glenn Miller Orchestra ▪ Gives the Miller crew a chance to fill the screen with some wonderful arrangements. Vintage music includes *I've Got a Gal in Kalamazoo*, *At Last*, and *Serenade in Blue*.

1943 ***Stage Door Canteen*** (85 min.) – Count Basie, Benny Goodman ▪ Romance between soldier and hostess in fabled canteen. One of the many wartime all-star movies.

Stormy Weather (77 min.) – Lena Horne, Cab Calloway and his band ▪ Pianist and vocalist Fats Waller interprets his own *Ain't Misbehavin'*, which has become a classic.

Cabin in the Sky (100 min.) – Duke Ellington and his orchestra, Lena Horne, Louis Armstrong, Ethel Waters ▪ One of Hollywood's first general-release black films. Ethel Waters sings *Happiness Is a Thing Called Joe*.

DuBarry Was a Lady (100 min.) – Tommy Dorsey and his orchestra, including Buddy Rich ▪ Most of the original Cole Porter score was scrapped.

Presenting Lily Mars (104 min.) – Tommy Dorsey and his band, Bob Crosby and his band ▪ The bands help keep audiences awake.

1944 ***Two Girls and a Sailor*** (124 min.) – Harry James, Lena Horne ▪ Weak love-triangle plot, but good musical numbers.

1947 ***The Fabulous Dorseys*** (88 min.) – Tommy Dorsey, Jimmy Dorsey, Paul Whiteman ▪ Limp dual "biography" of the bandleading Dorsey brothers as they fight their way to the top while constantly arguing with each other, trombone and clarinet at the ready. Paul Whiteman is along for the ride. In between renditions of *Marie* and *Green Eyes*, there is a jam session with Art Tatum and Charlie Barnet.

1950 ***Young Man with a Horn*** (112 min.) ▪ Story of a dedicated trumpet player, inspired by Bix Beiderbecke's life. Harry James dubbed Kirk Douglas's trumpet solos.

1953 ***The Jazz Singer*** (107 min.) – Peggy Lee ▪ Remake of the ground-breaking 1927 version.

1954 ***The Glenn Miller Story*** (113 min.) – Gene Krupa, Louis Armstrong ▪ Highly romanticized story of the famous trombonist and popular bandleader, whose music is the highlight of the film. Guest appearances by Armstrong and Krupa. Lots of big-band sound.

Diana Ross as Billie Holiday in *Lady Sings the Blues.* [Photofest.]

1955   ***Pete Kelly's Blues*** (95 min.) — Peggy Lee, Ella Fitzgerald ▪ Dixieland jazz is done to a turn in this reenactment of the people and sounds of the jazz world of Kansas City in the 1920s.

The Man with the Golden Arm (119 min.) — Frank Sinatra ▪ Controversial film about drug addiction. All-jazz soundtrack by Elmer Bernstein. Directed by Otto Preminger.

1956   ***High Society*** (107 min.) — Bing Crosby, Frank Sinatra, Louis Armstrong ▪ Highlight: Bing and Satchmo's *Now You Have Jazz.*

1958   ***St. Louis Blues*** (93 min.) — Nat "King" Cole, Eartha Kitt, Pearl Bailey, Cab Calloway, Ella Fitzgerald, Mahalia Jackson ▪ Innumerable outstanding tunes superbly performed in this so-called life story of composer W. C. Handy, who wrote the title tune.

1958 TO 1961   ***Peter Gunn*** (TV series) ▪ Henry Mancini began a trend with his smooth, jazzy themes.

1959   *The Gene Krupa Story* (101 min.) ▪ This fictionalized biography of the late great drummer invents "facts" to make musical hokum. Hackneyed version of Krupa's rise to fame and addiction to dope.

1960   *Jazz on a Summer's Day* (85 min.) – Louis Armstrong, Mahalia Jackson, Chuck Berry, Dinah Washington, Thelonious Monk, Gerry Mulligan, George Shearing, Anita O'Day, Jack Teagarden, Sonny Stitt ▪ Superb jazz concert film catches the high points of the 1958 Newport Jazz Festival. Lots of 1950s jazz. A must for jazz afficionados. Roster reads like a who's who of pop jazz.

1961   *Paris Blues* (98 min.) ▪ Off-beat account of two jazz musicians living on the Left Bank in Paris. Great Duke Ellington jazz score enhances this boys-meet-girls drama. Musicians fall for lovely tourists. What the plot lacks in originality is amply made up for by the good music. An explosive "Battle Royal" number is thrown in as a bonus. A must for jazz fans.

1966   *A Man Called Adam* (103 min.) – Louis Armstrong, Mel Tormé, Frank Sinatra, Jr. ▪ Story about a world-class trumpet player.

1968   *Mingus* (63 min.) ▪ Portrait of Charles Mingus, the bassist, considered to be one of the most influential figures in jazz.

1972   *Lady Sings the Blues* (144 min.) ▪ Diana Ross re-creates the songs of the legendary jazz singer Billie Holiday, duplicating the style without reverting to mimicry. Cliché biography deals with Holiday's drug addiction.

1976   *Leadbelly* (126 min.) ▪ Poignant bio-pic about the famed blues and folk singer, who was also a master of the 12-string guitar. Colorful, brawling, and boozing, with stunning musical renditions of classical favorites, such as *Rock Island Line* and *Goodnight Irene*.

1977   *New York, New York* (163 min.) ▪ Egomaniacal jazz saxophonist and sweet-natured singer. Songs are great.

  Scott Joplin (119 min.) ▪ Colorful biography of the legendary ragtime composer. Made for television, then released for theater.

1978   *The Last Waltz* (117 min.) – Eric Clapton, Muddy Waters ▪ Documentary about The Band's 1976 farewell concert.

  Always for Pleasure (58 min.) ▪ A celebration of life through the rollicking, sensual ritual of music and dance. Great ethnic American music in the form of Dixieland jazz, blues, and rock 'n' roll.

1980   *One Trick Pony* (98 min.) – Paul Simon ▪ Aging rock star, played by Simon, finds his popularity slipping. Tries to weather changes in audience tastes. Scored by Simon.

  The Duke Ellington Story (86 min.) ▪ Film compilation of the jazz legend. Composer-pianist is seen in a 1962 TV special, *Goodyear Jazz*; a 1930 musical, *Tan and Black*, and in a concert at the Cote d'Azur in 1966.

An ad for *Stormy Weather.*
[Photofest.]

1982

Say Amen, Somebody (100 min.) – Willie Mae Ford Smith, Thomas A. Dorsey, Sallie Martin, The Barrett Sisters, The O'Neal Twins ▪ Wonderful gospel documentary about the lives and careers of "Mother" Willie Mae Ford Smith and "Professor" Thomas Dorsey.

Live from the Jazz Showcase (52 min.) – Art Ensemble of Chicago. ▪ Some of the most talented musicians to fill out the African-American avant-garde jazz scene since Sun Ra. Improvisational jazz.

Live at the Village Vanguard, Vol. 1 (59 min.) ▪ Jazz artists sizzle.

Live at the Village Vanguard, Vol. 2 (57 min.) ▪ Jazz pianist Michel Petrucciani gets a boost from guitarist Jim Hall.

Live at the Village Vanguard, Vol. 3 (59 min.) ▪ Jazz quartet includes Peter Erskine's crisp drumming.

Playboy Jazz Festival, Vol. 1 and 2 (181 min.) – McCoy Tyner, Grover Washington, Jr., Dave Brubeck, Ornette Coleman, Wild Bill Davidson, Sarah Vaughan, The Manhattan Transfer, Dexter Gordon. ▪ Two days of jazz squeezed into two approximately 90-minute tapes. Mainstream, to Latin, to funk.

1983

An Evening with Ray Charles (50 min.) ▪ Shot for British TV at the Jubilee Auditorium in Edmonton, Alberta (Canada). Charles proves why he is the definition of soul. Captures this musical genius at his best.

Jazzman (80 min.) ▪ Russia's first jazz quartet brims with rhythmic jazz and foot-tapping Dixieland music.

Jazz at the Smithsonian: Art Blakey (58 min.) – Art Blakey and the Jazz Messengers ▪ One of the great bop drumming masters brings hard-bopping jazz to the Smithsonian in Washington, D.C. He is joined by trumpeter Wynton and saxophonist Branford Marsalis. An evening of jazz.

Blues Alive (92 min.) ▪ Night of the blues.

1984

Herbie Hancock and the Rockit Band (73 min.) ▪ Composer-musician Hancock brings his mix of electronic funk-jazz-fusion together in this 1983 performance. Some lightning percussion by Anton Fier.

1985

The Gig (96 min.) ▪ Touching comedy-drama about a group of middle-aged, middle-class men whose jazz group is hired for its first professional "gig."

Chick Corea & Gary Burton: Live in Tokyo (60 min.) ▪ Jazz pianist Corea and vibraharpist Burton display their musical gifts. Arrangements shift from bop to Latin grooves.

One Night with Blue Note, Vol. 1 and 2 (120 min.) – Herbie Hancock, Art Blakey, McCoy Tyner ▪ Tribute to major jazz recording label. Solo performances by guitarist Stanley Jordan and pianists Cecil Taylor and McCoy Tyner.

Zoot Sims in a Sentimental Mood
(52 min.) – Zoot Sims, Red Mitchell
▪ This last live recorded performance by
the late jazz tenor saxophonist was filmed
in 1984. Sims and bassist Red Mitchell
chat between numbers.

1986 ***Round Midnight*** (131 min.) –
Dexter Gordon, Herbie Hancock
▪ The unusual friendship between an
American jazzman and a devoted fan in
1950s Paris causes both to thrive and
prosper. A touching tale that pays homage to jazz musicians and their world.
Inspired by the relationship between bop
pianist Bud Powell and graphic artist
Francis Paudras. In the film, the jazzman
is a saxophone player, and he is
portrayed by real-life tenor-sax great
Dexter Gordon. Music director Herbie
Hancock and his colleagues not only
create great jazz right on screen, but also
help establish a perfect ambiance. This
semi-fictionalized story is a bittersweet
mood piece and a must for jazz fans.

Dizzy Gillespie in Redondo Beach
(60 min.) ▪ Gillespie, trumpet master
of bop, sails through a hot set of music
that includes elements of Latin and bop.

Max Roach in Washington, D.C.
(60 min.) ▪ Fusion jazz by percussionist Roach, whose drumming has influenced many of today's musicians.

1987 ***Ornette—Made in America*** (80
min.) ▪ Portrait of jazz musician
Coleman, innovative force in contemporary music. He performs with a symphony orchestra. Documentary includes
rare early performances.

***Celebrating Bird: The Triumph of
Charlie Parker*** (58 min.) – Charlie
Parker, Dizzy Gillespie, Charles
Mingus, Thelonious Monk ▪ Chron-
icles jazz legend Parker's career. Parker,
nicknamed "Bird," created a new style of
jazz. Other jazz greats add to the pleasure.

***Paul Simon: Graceland, The Afri-
can Concert*** (90 min.) ▪ Miriam
Makeba sings about her South African
homeland in this rhythm-rich Paul Simon
concert, based on African music.

***B. B. King and Friends: A Night of
Red Hot Blues*** (56 min.) – B. B.
King, Eric Clapton ▪ Dedicated to
the memory of blues harmonica master
Paul Butterfield.

1988 ***Bird*** (161 min.) ▪ Clint Eastwood's
perceptive portrait of the brilliant, but
troubled, jazz legend Charlie "Bird"
Parker. Eastwood re-creates the smoky
nightclubs and seedy hotel rooms that
Parker and his weary wife inhabited.
This ultimate jazz movie features Parker's
inspired improvised solos.

Stormy Monday (Great Britain; 93
min.) – Sting ▪ Melanie Griffith and
Sean Bean try to stop a ruthless American
businessman from taking over a jazz
nightclub, owned by Sting.

Wynton Marsalis: Blues and Swing
(79 min.) ▪ Trumpeter Marsalis performs with his jazz guitarist.

***Thelonious Monk: Straight No
Chaser*** (90 min.) ▪ Comprehensive
documentary of the legendary jazz
pianist/composer, crammed with footage
of Monk performing.

Duke Ellington and orchestra in *Cabin in the Sky.* [Photofest.]

1989   ***The Ladies Sing the Blues*** (60 min.)
– Billie Holiday, Dinah Washington,
Bessie Smith, Lena Horne, Peggy
Lee, Sarah Vaughan ▪ Some of the
finest ladies of blues are beautifully
represented here in great archival foot-
age. Narration is weak, music is power-
ful. Billie Holiday is backed by sidemen
Coleman Hawkins, Lester Young, and
Ben Webster as they groove together on
Fine and Mellow.

1990   ***Mo' Better Blues*** (127 min.) ▪ Self-

absorbed horn player leads a jazz quintet
at a trendy New York club.

1992   ***Manhattan Transfer: Live*** (80 min.)
▪ Nineteen songs from the Grammy-
winning vocal group, including *Birdland*
and *How High the Moon.*

Malcolm X (201 min.) – Lionel
Hampton ▪ This turbulent saga of the
famed black activist contains a jazz score,
with Lionel Hampton playing himself.

■/■ ACOUSTIC JAZZ

acoustic jazz: jazz produced without electrically amplified or modified instruments

By the 1980s, jazz groups and artists were finding it harder and harder to attract sympathetic and supportive audiences. Music is a language, and modern jazz had lost its ability to communicate to its audience—or anyway, to most of it.

Acoustic jazz, jazz produced without electrically amplified or modified instruments, almost died in the 1980s as record companies turned to the electronically created and amplified fusion. Discouraged fans of traditional jazz began to patronize the clubs, festivals, and record labels that presented the kind of jazz they were used to.

Some of the young players emerging at this time had the courage to go back in time to explore the mine of older jazz styles, looking for gold. Some found the gold, leading to a rebirth of acoustic jazz. Today, a new generation of talented young jazz musicians is going back to acoustic instruments, recognizable tunes, and solo styles like those of Louis Armstrong, Duke Ellington, Charlie Parker, and John Coltrane.

Wynton Marsalis. [Photofest.]

Grammy awards: annual awards recognizing achievement in various categories of the recording industry

It is interesting to note that in this era of synthetically produced sounds and mathematically conceived projects, the true superstars of jazz are still mainly acoustic-instrument players. There is some crossover with keyboards, with Chick Corea and Herbie Hancock performing on both acoustic piano and synthesizer. Probably the most popular acoustic solo instrument in the 1990s is the soprano sax. There has also been a resurgence of interest in the acoustic guitar.

The increasingly sophisticated developments in playback systems have been encouraging to acoustic jazz instruments, since their tone quality can be truly reproduced for the first time. The subtle nuances of trumpet players, saxophonists, acoustic bass, and keyboard players can now be captured and reproduced without any loss of fidelity.

■/■ NEW ORLEANS

Besides giving us most of the early instrumental jazz styles, New Orleans today is furnishing jazz with a wave of dynamic new players.

Wynton and Branford Marsalis.   Classical trumpeter Wynton and jazz saxophonist Branford Marsalis are in the forefront of this wave. The phenomenal success of these two talented young brothers, who managed to escape the changeover from jazz to rhythm-and-blues, is a relief to jazz fans. Their father, Ellis Marsalis, a well-known jazz educator and pianist, trained many of the wave of neotraditionalists at the New Orleans Center for the Creative Arts.

Wynton Marsalis, the most popular jazz trumpet player to come along since Miles Davis, was the first of the group of young jazz artists from New Orleans to appear on the scene. His rise to fame and fortune began when Columbia Records took a chance on him at a time when it looked like fusion and jazz-rock were the only products selling on the market. Their gamble paid off. Since his first album with Columbia in the early 1980s, Marsalis has gone on to win eight Grammy awards.

LISTENING ASSIGNMENT

"Stardust," Wynton Marsalis. *Think of One*, Columbia FCT39530 ▪ Wynton Marsalis demonstrates his tone, technique, and virtuosity on an old classic. He plays superbly and the arrangement is excellent. Compare Marsalis' style to those of Louis Armstrong and Miles Davis. How do each of these styles differ?

Branford Marsalis. [Photofest.]

Active in films as well as on television, Wynton has established a higher profile with the general public than any other jazz artist who emerged in the 1980s. In 1988, a 79-minute video called *Wynton Marsalis Blues and Swing* captured him in performance with his jazz quartet at the Westwood Playhouse in Los Angeles and while conducting student workshops at the Duke Ellington School of the Arts in Washington, D.C. and at Harvard. In October 1989, *Time* magazine selected him for a cover story.

In January 1991, Wynton gave several lectures on the music and style of Duke Ellington at the International Association of Jazz Educators' convention in Washington, D.C. Wynton believes that Duke Ellington is the composer who best captured the "essence" of America in his music.

More recently, he was a surprise guest at a gathering to celebrate the life and legacy of Louis Armstrong and to mark the formal dedication of the Louis Armstrong Archives at Queens College in Flushing, NY. Here, Marsalis used one of the archive's most valued treasures—one of Armstrong's original trumpets—to fill the library rotunda with individual riffs and a rousing jam session of W. C. Handy's *St. Louis Blues*.

When Wynton is touring, he takes the time to visit local schools in order to preach the "jazz gospel." He stays in touch with many of the students he meets, offering them pointers over the phone, inviting them to sit in on his gigs, and sometimes even giving them musical instruments.

Wynton's success as the jazz trumpeter of the 1980s was closely followed by the success of his brother Branford, who emerged as the jazz tenor saxophonist of the decade. Branford Marsalis began his career as saxophonist with his brother's group, but broke off from this combo when offered the solo spot with successful rock star Sting. It was here that he found acclaim and a public musical identity. Most recently, he has succeeded Doc Severinsen as the bandleader on NBC's "Tonight Show," with host Jay Leno.

▪ Jazz Neotraditionalist Players ▪

A partial list of new jazz players with New Orleans roots include:

Saxophone	
Tenor	Christopher Hollyday, Branford Marsalis
Trumpet	Terence Blanchard, Roy Hargrove, Philip Harper, Marlon Jordan, Wynton Marsalis
Guitar	Harold Arlen, Mark Whitfield
Piano	Harry Connick, Jr., Benny Green, Geoff Keezer, Marcus Roberts
Organ	Joey DeFrancesco
Drums	Winard Harper

▪ Author's Choice: Best of the Decade ▪

1920s   **Jazz Singer:** Louis Armstrong
Blues Singer: Bessie Smith
Solo Pianist: Earl Hines
Combos: Louis Armstrong's
Hot Five and Hot Seven
Big Band: Fletcher Henderson
Third Stream: Paul Whiteman
Orchestra
Composer/Arranger: Fletcher
Henderson
Songwriter: Eubie Blake

1930s   **Jazz Singer:** Billie Holiday
Blues Singer: Jimmy Rushing
Gospel: Mahalia Jackson
Solo Pianist: Art Tatum
Combo: Benny Goodman combo
Big Bands: Duke Ellington,
Benny Goodman
Third Stream: Duke Ellington
Composer/Arrangers: Duke
Ellington, Sy Oliver
Songwriters: Duke Ellington,
Fats Waller

1940s   **Jazz Singer:** Ella Fitzgerald
Blues Singer: Jimmy Rushing
Gospel: Thomas A. Dorsey Choir
Vocal Group: Mills Brothers
Solo Pianist: Bud Powell
Combo: Gillespie–Parker–Roach–
Powell–Mingus (together on
Greatest Jazz Concert album)
Big Bands: Count Basie, Duke
Ellington, Woody Herman
Third Stream: Duke Ellington
Experimental: Sun Ra
Composer/Arrangers: Duke
Ellington, Charlie Parker, Billy
Strayhorn

Songwriter: Duke Ellington
Latin: Machito

1950s   **Jazz Singers:** Mel Torme, Sarah
Vaughan
Blues Singer: Muddy Waters
Vocal Group: Lambert, Hendricks,
and Ross trio
Pianists: Erroll Garner, George
Shearing
Combos: Dave Brubeck combo,
Miles Davis combo, Gerry
Mulligan combo
Big Bands: Count Basie, Duke
Ellington, Woody Herman, Stan
Kenton
Experimental: Moondog, Sun Ra
Third Stream: Stan Kenton
Composer/Arrangers: Dave
Brubeck, Stan Kenton
Songwriters: Joe Greene, Jimmy
Van Heusen
Latin: Eddy Cano, Perez Prado

1960s   **Jazz Singer:** Carmen McRae
Blues Singer: Joe Williams
Gospel: Reverend Jimmy
Cleveland, Clara Ward Singers
Vocal Groups: Four Freshman,
Hi Lo's, Swingle Singers
Solo Pianists: Erroll Garner, Oscar
Peterson
Combos: Art Blakey combo, John
Coltrane combo, Miles Davis
combo, Modern Jazz Quartet,
Thelonious Monk combo, Horace
Silver combo
Big Bands: Count Basie, Duke
Ellington, Woody Herman, Stan
Kenton, Buddy Rich

Third Stream: Duke Ellington, Stan Kenton
Experimental: Ornette Coleman
Composer/Arrangers: John Coltrane, Gil Evans, Benny Golson
Songwriters: Joe Greene, Antonio Carlos Jobim, Henry Mancini
Latin: Willie Bobo, Charlie Byrd, Stan Getz, Perez Prado

1970s

Jazz Singers: Betty Carter, Ray Charles, Eddie Jefferson
Blues Singer: B. B. King
Vocal Groups: The Manhattan Transfer, Singers Ltd.
Gospel: Andrae Crouch
Solo Pianist: Bill Evans
Combos: Cannonball Adderley combo, Miles Davis combo
Jazz-Rock Combos: Blood, Sweat, and Tears, Chicago
Big Bands: Don Ellis, Thad Jones/ Mel Lewis
Third Stream: Gil Evans, John Lewis
Experimental: Cecil Taylor
Composer/Arrangers: Bill Evans, Gil Evans, Bill Holman, Thelonious Monk
Songwriters: Mose Allison, Michel Legrand, Thelonious Monk
Latin: Willie Bobo, Tito Puente, Cal Tjader

1980s

Jazz Singers: Al Jarreau, Bobby McFerrin, Diane Schuur
Blues Singer: B. B. King
Gospel: Aretha Franklin
Vocal Groups: The Manhattan Transfer, The Pointer Sisters
Solo Pianists: Chick Corea, Keith Jarrett, McCoy Tyner
Combo: Wynton Marsalis combo

Fusion Combos: Chick Corea combo, Weather Report
Jazz-Rock Combo: Crusaders
Big Band: Maynard Ferguson, Rob McConnell, Doc Severinsen's Tonight Show Orchestra
Third Stream: Quincy Jones
Experimental: Chicago Art Ensemble, Paul Simon, World Saxophone Quartet
Composer/Arrangers: Chick Corea, Herbie Hancock, Wayne Shorter, Joe Zawinul
Songwriters: Chick Corea, Johnny Mandel
Latin: Gato Barbieri, Irakere, Antonio Carlos Jobim, Tania Maria

1990s

Jazz Singers: Harry Connick, Jr., Mel Torme
Blues Singer: Jeannie Cheatham, Dr. John
Vocal Groups: The New York Voices
Gospel: Carmen, The Wynans
Solo Pianists: Makoto Ozone, Michel Petrucciani, Marcus Roberts
Combos: Branford Marsalis combo, Wynton Marsalis combo
Fusion Combos: Steps Ahead, Yellow Jackets
Experimental: Anthony Braxton, Brian Eno, Paul Simon, World Saxophone Quartet
Big Bands: Harry Connick, Jr., Rob McConnell
Third Stream: Jack Elliot, Quincy Jones, New American Orchestra
Composer/Arrangers: Chick Corea, Pat Metheny
Songwriters: Harry Connick, Jr., Dave Frishberg

Harry Connick, Jr. [Drawing by David Zuckerman.]

Harry Connick, Jr. One of the most surprising young artists to come out of New Orleans in this new wave is singer/pianist/composer/actor Harry Connick, Jr., whose vocal style many compare to that of the early Frank Sinatra. Connick also learned his craft from Ellis Marsalis at the New Orleans Center for the Creative Arts. Touring the United States with a thirteen-piece band, Connick packs them in wherever he goes. His audiences cross all age, social, and ethnic barriers. His blues roots in New Orleans attract black audiences, his sophisticated crooning of Sinatra-type ballads attracts the thirty- to forty-year-old set, and his Thelonious Monk-style of piano playing attracts main-line jazz enthusiasts.

The most exciting thing about this new wave of jazz traditionalists is the public's receptivity. Their records are selling well, their concerts are well attended, and they are sought after for films and television commercials.

■/■ EDUCATION

Where did this wave of new talent come from? Very quietly, beginning just after World War II, jazz began to infiltrate the traditional music programs in universities, colleges, and high schools around the country. In 1968, a small group of determined and dedicated people formed the International Association of Jazz Educators, which has become one of the most influential art-education organizations in the world. As a result of the efforts of this association, which now has over 7,000 members all over the world, there are, today, jazz-studies programs and majors at more than one hundred colleges in the United States.

In addition, the Scripps Institute of Ethnic Music in Berkeley, California, the ethnic-music department at UCLA, and other, similar institutions around the world are devoting their time, money, and talent to capturing and preserving the performance practices of many third-world musical styles before they disappear.

■/■ SURVIVAL

In the meantime, however, the problem facing most jazz artists is one of personal and professional survival. This is particularly true if these jazz artists happen to favor innovative styles of jazz.

Clubs. Today, club performances by well-known jazz musicians are rare. Jazz nightclubs open and close with a regularity that makes even the

Former presidents of the International Association of Jazz Educators. Top row, from left to right: Herb Wong, Warrick Carter, Jack Wheaton, Thomas Ferguson; bottom row: Clem De Rosa, William F. Lee, John Roberts, M. E. Hall.

most enthusiastic jazz fan wary of investing in them. Somehow, a few of these clubs have managed to survive, sometimes at great financial sacrifice on the part of their owners. Often the musicians themselves subsidize these clubs by playing for very little money. One of the longest-running jazz clubs in America is the Village Vanguard in Greenwich Village.

Recording. The fabulous wealth developed from rock and pop music from the 1950s on squeezed the less commercially successful style of jazz into an economic corner. Jazz accounts for less than 9 percent of total record sales in the United States today. Although this is up from 4 percent just a few years ago, it is an indication of where the record companies' interest lies. The small but steady returns on a jazz album do not appeal to an entertainment business that is increasingly dominated by profit-oriented business executives.

Jazz has never been a heavy moneymaker. The average jazz album, if successful, sells around 50,000 units today. The average rock or pop album has to sell at least 500,000 units to be considered successful. In addition, the more difficult, different, challenging, and new the music, the lower the record sales. Most domestic record companies, therefore, will not record innovative jazz artists. Fortunately, overseas record sales

The Village
Vanguard.

The Blue Note in Greenwich
Village, which calls itself the
"Jazz Capital of the World."

and production have helped to ease the pain of the declining domestic jazz record industry. Also, many modern jazz players and composers have formed their own booking agencies and record companies.

Old jazz has had more success in recent years. Old tapes, records, and live concerts—often originally recorded under less than ideal conditions—can now be remixed and "boosted" in quality. Reprocessed old jazz records can sound like they were recorded yesterday. There are indications that some serious and important steps are being taken to preserve and protect this music. The Thelonious Monk Institute will soon construct a $12 million building on the campus of Duke University and has a foundation grant of many millions on which to operate.

The Smithsonian Institution in Washington, D.C. has released several collections of jazz and has sponsored jazz programs on public broadcasting stations. The Smithsonian has also reissued a remastered version of the lengthy conversations and performances of Leadbelly and Jelly Roll Morton that were recorded by Alan Lomax.

Jazz Festivals.   Today's jazz artists must rely more and more upon festivals, overseas gigs, and government support.

Numerous jazz festivals are held throughout the United States each year, featuring both local talent and international jazz artists. Some of the most important American jazz festivals include the Monterey Jazz

The author presenting an award at the Monterey Jazz Festival, 1987.

Festival, the world's oldest continuous jazz festival—begun in 1958; the New Orleans Jazz and Heritage Festival, a ten-day celebration featuring thousands of musicians; and the Sacramento Jazz Jubilee, the largest traditional jazz festival in the world.

These festivals, large or small, are important for the competition and idea-sharing they generate amongst jazz musicians, for the large-scale exposure of jazz to the public, and for the opportunities they provide to local groups who are invited to play.

While the number and attendance of American jazz festivals seems to be growing, the most successful jazz festivals are found overseas. European summer jazz festivals are blossoming. In the summer of 1988, the Montreux Jazz Festival in Switzerland, the North Sea Festival in the Netherlands, and the Umbria Festival in Italy all broke attendance records. There is no jazz festival in the United States that can present the number and quality of artists offered in the gigantic North Sea Festival in as short a period of time and remain financially successful.

As a result, more and more of the definitive jazz artists are coming from outside of the United States; and many American jazz musicians have gone to live in countries like France, Germany, the Netherlands, Sweden, Denmark, Norway, and Japan—where the response to their music is more rewarding. There is a possibility, as a matter of fact, that the Japanese, the western Europeans, and even the Russians may take jazz from its present state of funky instability in the United States and launch it into a new orbit of world respectability and enthusiasm.

■/■ WHAT'S NEEDED

American jazz artists in general—and the innovative ones in particular—are finding it harder and harder to make a living, at least in this country. They are often left with the choice of becoming pop artists (or playing Jacuzzi jazz), relying on the tried-and-true jazz styles of the past and forsaking all invention, or pursuing their careers overseas. Some have managed by doing a little of all three.

Colleges and universities have helped jazz innovators by offering artist-in-residence opportunities, workshops, and occasionally, subsidized concerts. Eventually, however, some sort of support in the form of grants from the government or private foundations must be found. Local symphony orchestras and ballet and opera companies are kept alive in America by local, state, regional, and national subsidies and grants. A similar base of support must be found for the most promising, the most talented, the most original, and the most dedicated jazz artists.

■ Jazz Festivals ■

INTERNATIONAL

Argentina	Italy
Aruba	Japan
Belgium	Mexico
Brazil	Netherlands
Canada	Norway
Denmark	Poland
France	Russia
Germany	South Africa
Great Britain	Sweden
India	Switzerland
Israel	Trinidad and Tobago

AMERICAN

January | Central Illinois Jazz Festival • Decatur, IL

February | Coconut Grove Arts Festival • Coconut Grove, FL

March | Kansas City Winter Jazz Festival • Kansas City, MO

April | Sarasota Jazz Festival • Sarasota, FL
University of Minnesota/Morris Jazz Festival • Morris, MN
Fullerton College Jazz Festival • Fullerton CA (*Oldest and largest festival on the west coast*)
Forth Worth Arts Festival • Fort Worth, TX (*Largest regional performing arts festival in the Southwest*)
New Orleans Jazz and Heritage Festival • New Orleans, LA (*Thousands of musicians!*)

May | Sunfest • Palm Beach, FL
Sacramento Jazz Jubilee • Sacramento, CA (*Largest traditional jazz festival in the world*)

	US Air Jambalaya Jam • Philadelphia, PA Main Street Jazz • Columbia, SC Mobile Jazz Festival • Mobile, AL
Summer	JVC Jazz at the Bowl • Los Angeles, CA Infiniti Jazz at the Bowl • Los Angeles, CA
June	Playboy Jazz Festival • Location varies
July	Texas Jazz Festival • Corpus Christi, TX Jazz Wednesday • New York, NY Bright Moments Festival • Amherst, MA The Big Gig • Richmond, VA American Music Festival • Englewood, CO
August	Mt. Hood Festival of Jazz • Gresham, OR Fujitsu Concord Jazz Festival • Concord, CA Classical Jazz • New York, NY Annual 18th and Vine Heritage Festival • Kansas City, MO Utah Jazz and Blues Festival • Salt Lake City, UT JVC Jazz Festival • Newport, RI Long Beach Jazz Festival • Long Beach, CA Telluride Jazz Festival • Telluride, CO Aspen Jazz Festival • Aspen, CO
September	Seattle Arts Festival • Seattle, WA Monterey Jazz Festival • Monterey, CA (*The world's oldest continuous jazz festival*) Bull Durham Blues Festival • Durham, NC Hidden Valley Jazz Festival • Pittsburgh, PA Jazz on the Rocks • Sedora, AZ Chicago Jazz Festival • Chicago, IL San Diego Street Scene • San Diego, CA Long Beach Blues Festival • Long Beach, CA
October	Santa Barbara International Jazz Festival • Santa Barbara, CA Clearwater Jazz Holiday • Clearwater, FL Jacksonville Jazz Festival • Jacksonville, FL Gateway Jazz Festival • St. Louis, MO
November	Scottsdale Dixieland Jazz Festival • Scottsdale, AZ

SUMMARY

The 1980s and early '90s saw a number of important influences on jazz. There was a growing interest in third-world cultures, particularly in the music of Africa. This both infused new ideas into jazz and led to a decline in interest in jazz by emphasizing African (rather than African/European/American) music. Rap music, for example, has its roots in the African traditions of adding improvised lyrics to syncopated rhythms.

Commercial pressures threatened to drain any real creativity out of popular music and to alienate pure jazz artists. The late '80s saw some degree of alliance between rock and jazz, as musicians in the two genres cautiously integrated both styles into their compositions and performances.

Government support of jazz in the form of grants, awards, and honors helped sustain innovative artists, but introduced issues of control. Many communities supported jazz through resident jazz orchestras and through an increasing number of jazz festivals.

The closing years of the twentieth century have also been important for the number of jazz films and jazz concerts on film or video—clear-cut evidence of the reemerging national interest in this music.

In reaction to the preponderance of electronic music in the 1980s, a number of talented young musicians emerged with renewed interest in older jazz styles and acoustic instruments. Wynton and Branford Marsalis are in the forefront of a wave of new talent coming out of New Orleans. Wynton has been enormously popular as a trumpet player, has won many awards and honors, and is active in film and in music education. His brother Branford distinguished himself as the most outstanding jazz tenor saxophonist of the '80s. Harry Connick, Jr., also from New Orleans, draws large audiences from all social, ethnic, and age groups with his multiple talents as singer, pianist, composer, and actor.

Various educational organizations, including the *International Association of Jazz Educators*, were founded to promote jazz around the world. Survival is a problem facing jazz today. Jazz nightclubs have difficulty staying in business, and most domestic record companies will not produce jazz albums, which are less commercially successful than rock albums.

Interest in jazz has sparked in Europe and Japan, where many of the best-attended jazz festivals are presently held. Many of the leading jazz artists have gone to live abroad, where there is more enthusiasm for their music.

Jazz artists in the United States, however, must rely more and more on smaller jazz festivals and on government support. Such support must be forthcoming for the professional survival of innovative and talented jazz artists and their potential contributions to jazz as it matures through the '90s and into the next century.

■ Questions on Chapter 13

A. *In your own words* write one or two sentences describing each of the terms listed in Questions 1–3.

1. pop _____
_____

2. short-subject film _____
_____

3. acoustic jazz _____
_____

In Questions 4–8 write a sentence or two identifying each of the following artists.

4. Wynton Marsalis _____
_____

5. Branford Marsalis _____
_____

6. Harry Connick, Jr. _____
_____

7. Chick Corea _____
_____

8. Herbie Hancock _____
_____

B.
9. What were the important influences on jazz in the 1980s and '90s? In what ways were these influences positive or negative?

10. In what new directions is jazz currently headed?

11. List some of the many social, technological, and historical influences that have affected jazz throughout its development.

12. In an age of electronic music, why do some jazz enthusiasts prefer acoustic jazz?

13. What problems face jazz today?

14. What can we do to ensure jazz's survival?

■ Topics for Further Research

A. In what ways does government support the arts? Is censorship a problem? What are the conflicts and how would you resolve them?

B. How has the use of music changed in our society?

■ Further Reading

Giddins, Gary. *In the Moment: Jazz in the '80s*. New York: Oxford University Press, 1986.

——————. *Riding on a Blue Note*. New York: Oxford University Press, 1981.

McLuhan, Marshall. *The Medium Is the Massage*. New York: Simon & Schuster, 1989

Toffler, Alvin. *Future Shock*. New York: Bantam Books, 1971.

■ Further Listening

Alone with Three Giants, Marcus Roberts. Novus 3109.

And I'll Sing Once More, Chistopher Hollyday. Novus 63133.

Back on the Block, Quincy Jones. Warner Brothers 26020.

Blue Light, Red Light, Harry Connick, Jr. Columbia 48685.

Don't Try This at Home, Michael Brecker. MCA/Impulse MCAD-42229.

Heart of Gold, Ellis Marsalis Trio. Columbia CK 47509.

Portrait of Wynton Marsalis, A. CBS Records 44726.

Samurai Samba, Yellowjackets. Warner Brothers 2-25204.

■ Films and Videos

Airto and Flora Purim: The Latin Jazz All-Stars (video). Brazilian jazz.

Bob James Live (video). From the Queen Mary Jazz Festival.

Mo' Better Blues (1990). Soundtrack by Branford Marsalis and Terence Blanchard.

Playboy Jazz Festival (video).

When Harry Met Sally (1989). Soundtrack by Harry Connick, Jr.

■/■/■/■/■/■/■/■/■/■/■/■/■/■/■/■/■/■

GLOSSARY

/■/

A **a cappella:** without instrumental accompaniment

acoustic guitar: a guitar that is not electrically amplified or modified

acoustic jazz: jazz produced without electrically amplified or modified instruments

afouche: a Brazilian instrument consisting of strands of metal beads wrapped around a wooden handle

alto: the lowest pitched female voice; also called *contralto*

alto flute: a large flute that is lower in pitch than an ordinary flute

arpeggio: a chord in which the notes are played up or down in rapid succession, rather than simultaneously

arranger: the person who adapts a composition to the voices and instruments in the band

articulation: the length of time individual notes are held

art song: a song having interdependent vocal and piano parts, meant to be sung in recital

avant-garde: unorthodox and experimental music

B **ballad:** a slow and sentimental narrative folk song

ballet: a choreographed story, without dialogue, accompanied by an orchestra

ballroom dance: any of a variety of social dances performed by couples in a ballroom, usually

banjo: a plucked string instrument

bar: *see* measure

baritone: a male voice that falls between the tenor and bass

barn dance: a social gathering, originally held in a barn, featuring square dancees and other forms of country music

baroque: the style in music, art, and architecture, characterized by ornament and dramatic effect, that was at its height in Europe from approximately 1600 to 1750

bass: the lowest pitched voice

bass clef: the lower part of the musical staff, labeled with the musical symbol ♯, and containing the notes below middle C

bass drum: the largest and lowest pitched drum of a drum set

bass guitar: an electric guitar with bass strings, also called *electric bass*

basso: a bass voice

bassoon: a low-pitched woodwind instrument with a long double tube and double-reed mouthpiece

basso profundo: a bass voice of the lowest range

bass viol: *see* string bass

baton: a rod or staff used to conduct an orchestra

beat: the pulse or repetition of sound

bebop: *see* bop

big band: a jazz ensemble of ten or more pieces, usually made up of saxophones, trumpets, trombones, and a rhythm section (piano, bass, drums, and guitar)

big-band shouters: Kansas City-style urban blues singers with strong voices

binary form: a musical form having two closely related sections, denoted by AB or by AABB

bio pic: a biographical movie

blackamoor: a black person

black bottom: a dance characterized by emphatic, sinuous hip movements

block chord: four or more chord tones all within an octave

bluegrass: an instrumental country-music style

blue note: a flatted note common in blues and jazz, created by lowering the third, fifth, or seventh note of the major scale one half step

blues: a secular vocal style, characterized by the frequent use of flatted (blue) notes, originated by blacks in the late 19th century

board fade: the gradual fading out of a musical piece by the recording engineer

bolero: a lively Spanish dance in triple meter; the Cuban form is in a slow duple meter

bongos: a pair of small tuned drums played with the fingers

boogie-woogie: a popular jazz piano style before World War II which evolved from the blues; also called "barrel house" after the New Orleans saloons in which it was born.

bop: a post-World War II jazz style that features highly complex solos, dissonant chords, and extreme tempos; also called *bebop*

bordello: a house of prostitution

bossa nova: a jazz-influenced music and dance style of Brazil

brass band: a marching band made up primarily of percussion, brass, and wind instruments

brass instruments: a family of wind instruments usually made of brass, and played by the buzzing of lips through a brass mouthpiece

broadside: an early form of sheet music

bugle: a brass instrument resembling a cornet, but without valves

buzz tone: a distorted or raspy vocal or instrumental tone

C   **cabaret:** a restaurant or nightclub providing food, drink, and live entertainment

cadence: a sequence of notes that indicates the end of a verse or chorus

Cajun music: the folk music of the Cajuns of Louisiana

cakewalk: a dance with a strutting or marching step

call-and-response form: group repetition of, or response to, a soloist's (or another group's) verse or refrain

calliope: a harsh-sounding musical instrument consisting of a set of steam whistles that are activated by a keyboard

calypso: a musical style of West Indian origin characterized by the steel drum and improvised lyrics

campana: *see* cowbell

candomble: a cult of African origin found in the Bahia state of Brazil

cantor: the chief singer and leader of prayer in a synagogue

carol: a joyful song, often a Christmas song

cello: the tenor instrument of the string family

cencerro: *see* cowbell

cha cha: a fast ballroom dance, similar to the mambo, with a quick three-step movement

channeler: a person through whom spirits of the dead are supposedly able to contact the living

Charleston: a vigorous rhythmic ballroom dance, popular in America in the 1920s, with origins in Africa

Chinese rivet "sizzle" cymbal: a large suspended cymbal on a drum set that creates a buzz tone

chord: a combination of two or more notes sounded simultaneously

chord progression: a series of chords that relate to each other

chord voicing: the position of chord-tones within each chord

chorus: the refrain, which recurs after the verses

clarinet: a single-reed wind instrument with finger holes and keys

claves: cherry-wood sticks struck together for rhythmic accompaniment in Afro-Latin music

clavichord: a keyboard instrument in which depressing a key causes a metal blade (a *tangent*) to strike a string

climax note: the highest note in the melody, usually occurring toward the end

coloratura: a high-pitched lyric soprano who specializes in runs and trills

comic sallies: sketches that poke fun at society or specific individuals

commercial art: art created for the marketplace

compact disk (CD): a disk on which music and other sounds are stored digitally and decoded for playback by laser

comping: accompanying a soloist with a syncopated rhythmic pattern

compound meter: a grouping of beats in a combination of twos and threes, indicated by the time signature $\frac{5}{4}$

concerto: an instrumental solo accompanied by a symphony orchestra

conga: 1. a Cuban dance performed in a single line, consisting of three steps forward, followed by a kick; **2.** a tall conical drum played with the hands

contrabass: *see* string bass

contrabassoon: an instrument that is an octave lower in pitch than the ordinary bassoon; also called *double bassoon*

contralto: *see* alto

contrapuntal line: the secondary of two or more combined melodies

cool jazz: a jazz style of the 1950s, laid back and with subtle rhythm, unusual harmonies, and simple solo styles

coon songs: late 19th- and early 20th-century songs by white minstrels about blacks that reinforced racial stereotypes; also called *Ethiopian songs*

cornet: a soprano brass instrument

countermelody: an additional melody that complements the main melody

counterpoint: the combining of two or more simultaneous melodies

countertenor: a rare voice that is pitched higher than a tenor; also called *male alto*

Country-and-Western: a popular-music style with roots in American folk, hillbilly, and cowboy music

cowbell: an Afro-Cuban percussion instrument, sometimes called *cencerro* or *campana*

cowboy song: a work song of cowboys

crash cymbal: a suspended cymbal on a drum set used for special effects

Creole: a Louisiana native of French and black ancestry

cross-rhythm: the combination of contrasting time signatures, for example, $\frac{4}{4}$ simultaneously with $\frac{3}{4}$; also called *polymeter*

cross-section voicing: the combining of one or two instruments from each section of a big band

cutting contest: a competition between players of like instruments during a jam session

cymbals: brass or bronze disks played by striking with a mallet or against one another to produce a sharp, ringing sound

D **Dahomey:** former name of the African country, Benin

danzón: a Puerto Rican dance of African origin

definitive practitioner: an artist who takes the art to new levels of excellence and expressiveness

developmental approach: an improvisational technique that emphasizes the development of a solo from the melodic and rhythmic ideas of a specific musical phrase

diatonic scale: major scale

digital audio tape (DAT): a cassette tape on which music and other sounds are stored in computer language

disc jockey: the person who conducts a radio broadcast of recorded music

dissonance: a combination of tones that together produce a harsh or discordant sound

Dixieland: an instrumental jazz style born out of New Orleans marching bands

double bass: *see* string bass

double bassoon: *see* contrabassoon

double entendre: a double meaning

double-time pattern: a sudden increase in tempo to twice as fast as the original

downbeat: the first beat of a measure, normally accented

dramatic baritone: a powerful baritone voice with a wide range

dramatic soprano: a mezzo soprano with a powerful voice

dramatic tenor: a powerful tenor voice with a wide range; also called *Wagnerian tenor*

dramatizing the lyrics: distorting the lyrics by means such as repetition, pitch change, or dynamic changes

drum: a percussion instrument consisting of a hollow body, covered by a tightly stretched membrane which is struck with hands or sticks

drum machine: a type of sequencer that allows drum sounds and other percussive effects to be stored on a digital disk and later to be re-created

duple meter: a grouping of beats by twos

dynamic range: the range of sounds, from the softest to the loudest

dynamics: variations in volume

E **electric bass:** *see* bass guitar

electric guitar: a guitar that can be electrically amplified

electric piano: a keyboard instrument that produces its sound electronically

elevator music: unimaginative, nondemanding background music

Ethiopian songs: *see* coon songs

F **falsetto:** an unnaturally or artificially high male voice

fiddle: a violin

field holler: a solo work song of post-Civil War rural black sharecroppers

fine art: art created for aesthetic purposes

flügelhorn: a mellow-sounding alto brass instrument

flute: a wind instrument that produces sound as air is blown across a hole

flutter-tongue: the rapid repetition of tongue movements on a wind instrument producing a buzz tone

folk art: functional art, passed down informally within its cultural context

folk music: music handed down within a culture, often by oral tradition

foot-pedal: a drum-set device that allows a drummer to operate the bass drum with his foot

form: the internal structure of a musical composition

four-to-the-bar: four notes to the measure—characteristic of swing music

fox-trot: a couples dance with various combinations of slow and quick steps

free jazz: a free-form jazz style that disregards traditional structures

French horn: an alto instrument of the brass family

fret: a raised bar placed at regular intervals along the neck of some string instruments

fugue: a polyphonic type of composition used in baroque music

funk: a musical style that combines rhythm-and-blues and gospel

funky: having an earthy "blues-based" quality

fusion: a blend of blues, rock, bop, ethnic music, along with electronics and other musical influences; heavily dependent on synthesizer use

fuzz pedal: a footswitch for distorting the tone of an electric guitar

G   **GI Bill:** a congressional bill enacted after World War II to provide educational and housing benefits for veterans

glissando: the technique of sliding up or down to the next melodic note, creating a continuous sound; also called *portamento*

gospel: a religious vocal style that developed after the Civil War, emphasizing the New Testament and personal salvation. It evolved into modern gospel in the 1930s.

Grammy awards: annual awards recognizing achievement in various categories of the recording industry

Great Depression: the period of economic crisis and stagnation following the stock-market crash in 1929

griot: a storyteller/poet/musician who entertains and keeps an oral history of a west African tribe or village

guarcha: a Cuban dance rhythm of African origin

guiro: a Brazilian instrument consisting of a hollow gourd scraped with a stick

guitar: a stringed instrument with a long fretted neck, a flat body, and typically, six strings which are plucked or strummed

H   **half step:** the smallest defined interval in music

hard bop: an aggressive "hot" jazz style popular in the 1960s and early '70s, characterized by driving rhythm sections and tenor-sax soloists

Harlem Renaissance: a period of great artistic productivity in the 1920s and '30s in the black community of Harlem, New York City

harmonica: a small wind instrument containing a set of metal reeds over which a player exhales or inhales to produce the tones

harmony: the combination of tones into chords and chord progressions

harp: an instrument consisting of strings stretched across a frame which are plucked with the fingers

harpsichord: the precursor to the piano; a keyboard instrument in which strings are plucked by leather or quill parts attached to keys

head: the original melody of an improvised tune

heavy metal: a heavily amplified, aggressively played rock style

high-hat cymbals: a pair of cymbals mounted on a rod so that the push of a pedal can drop the upper onto the lower

high life: a musical style involving African rhythms and American blues, pop, and rock

hillbilly music: the folk music of the mountains of the South

hora: a traditional Roumanian circle dance, now popular in Israel

hymn: a religious or patriotic song of praise

I **Ibo:** a member of an African tribal group in Nigeria renowned for trade and art

impressionist: a composer who uses unusual tone colors, rich harmonies, and subtle rhythms to evoke a mood or impression

improvisation: spontaneous composition

innovator: an artist who experiments with new forms and ideas

inside solo style: traditional solo style

interlocutor: in a minstrel show, the man in the middle who banters with the end men and also acts as an announcer

interval: the difference in pitch between two tones

intonation: something played or sung with a centered pitch

J **jacuzzi jazz:** watered-down, unimaginative jazz used as background music

jam session: an informal or impromptu gathering and performance of jazz musicians which encourages experimentation with new sounds and new styles

jazz: a 20th-century improvisatory style combining African, American, and western European influences

jazz ballet: jazz music for dancers, in which both the players and dancers can improvise

jazz-rock: a style that combines essential elements of jazz and rock

jazz samba: a modified Brazilian dance rhythm, favored by fusion groups

jazz violin: a violin used as a jazz instrument for an improvised solo

Jew's harp: a small instrument whose frame is held in the teeth while a metal piece is plucked, producing a twanging tone

jig: a lively, springy, irregular dance in triple meter

Jim Crow: a caricature of the male plantation slave

jitterbug: a strenuously acrobatic dance performed to boogie-woogie and swing music

jubilee: an all-black pre-Civil War plantation show

jujuism: a system of west African tribal beliefs that attributes magical powers to an object or to a ritual

juke joint: a black rural dance hall

K   **kalimba:** an instrument consisting of metal blades (*tangents*) plucked with the fingers, sometimes called an *African hand piano* or *mbira*

kettledrum: a drum shaped like a large pot or kettle; also called *timpani*

key: *see* tonal center

keyboard instrument: an instrument, such as the synthesizer, piano, or organ, operated by pressing the keys on a keyboard

key-hammers: the hammers of a piano, operated by a keyboard, which strike strings to create sound

L   **Latin music:** the music of Latin America, particularly Cuba and Brazil

layered rhythm: polyrhythms that are often added one at a time

lead line: the main melody

legato: smooth and connected (referring to notes)

light opera: an operetta; a light, amusing opera with some spoken dialogue

lindy: an energetic jitterbug dance, with African influences

litany: a solo line, often followed by a group response, resembling a form of prayer

logo: a widely recognized symbol or image for easy identification

lowered note: a note that has been moved down one half step

lyrical approach: an improvisational technique utilizing a singable solo line and the dramatic use of rests

lyric baritone: a baritone voice having low volume and modest range

lyric soprano: a soprano voice having a relatively low volume and modest range

lyric tenor: a tenor voice having low volume and modest range

M   **macumba:** a cult of African origin prevalent in southern and central Brazil

major scale: a scale with the sequence of intervals: whole step, whole, half, whole, whole, whole, half

makin' juba: a lively dance, accompanied by rhythmic hand-clapping and body-slapping, developed by plantation slaves

mambo: a fast ballroom dance of Caribbean origin

maracas: a pair of gourd-shaped rattles filled with seeds or pebbles and used as a rhythm instrument

march: a musical piece with a measured, regular rhythm in duple time

mariachi band: a small band dressed in native costumes, playing traditional Mexican dance music

marimba: an instrument made of strips of wood that are amplified underneath with tubes and that are struck with sticks

measure: the unit of music contained between two bar lines; also called *bar*

melodic curve: an upward or downward movement in pitch in a melody

melody: a succession of single notes producing a distinct musical idea

meter: the grouping of accented and unaccented beats

mezzo soprano: a voice that falls between a soprano and alto in pitch

middle passage: the trip across the Atlantic by slave ships from the west coast of Africa to the Caribbean

MIDI: Musical Instrument Digital Interface, a computer language used to carry musical ideas between a synthesizer and a computer

minstrel show: a popular 19th-century entertainment originally involving white singers, dancers, and comedians performing in blackface. After the Civil War, black minstrelsy flourished.

minstrelsy: *see* minstrel show

minuet: a slow dance piece in triple meter

modern gospel: a popularized form of emotional spiritual music rooted in early gospel, often accompanied by Hammond organ, bass, drums, and saxophone

MOR: record-company slang for *Middle Of the Road*, referring to bands that played for both the jazz fan and the pop-music fan

motif: a short, distinctive idea or theme in an artistic work

Motown: 1. an upbeat popular style of rhythm-and-blues which originated with black vocalists and groups in Detroit in the 1950s; **2.** the record company that defined this style

multitrack recording: a technique in which different sounds are electronically recorded on separate tracks and later mixed by the sound engineer

musicologist: a scientist or scholar who studies music history, theory, and/or the physical nature of sounds

mute: a device used to soften the sounds of brass instruments

Muzak: a corporation that introduced recorded background music for commercial purposes in the 1950s

N **New Age music:** mood music whose primary purpose is to modify the acoustical environment

nonharmonic music: music that lacks functional harmony

nonimitative scat singing: using the voice in place of an instrument for the vocal sound quality

Norteño music: the folk music of northern Mexico

note: a symbol used to represent a tone, indicating its pitch and duration

novelty song: a humorous song involving surprise lyrics

O   **obbligato:** a high-pitched decorative part above the melody—usually played by the clarinet in a Dixieland ensemble

oboe: a wind instrument with a double-reed mouthpiece

octave: in western European music, an interval of twelve half steps

opera: a play set to music, in which the dialogue is sung to the accompaniment of an orchestra

ostinato: a short, repeated musical idea, usually in the bass range

outside solo style: free solo style, unrestricted by traditional notions of tempo, meter, tonal center, and chord progression

overdubbing: adding other recorded sounds or another musical track to a recording

P   **percussion instruments:** a family of instruments played by striking with the hands or a stick or other object

period: a musical passage within a composition, complete in itself—the musical equivalent of a paragraph

personalization: the use of recognizable elements of style that identify a performer

phrase: a short unit of song—the musical equivalent of a sentence

piano: a musical instrument in which felt-covered hammers, operated from a keyboard, strike metal strings

piccolo: the highest pitched instrument of the flute family

pipe organ: a keyboard instrument in which compressed air entering pipes creates sound

pitch: the degree to which an instrument, voice, or sound is high or low

player piano: a piano with prerecorded piano rolls and pump pedals

plunger: a device used by jazz brass players to distort sounds

polka: a lively couples dance in duple meter

polychord: simultaneous sounding of two different chords

polymeter: *see* cross-rhythm

polyphonic music: music incorporating two or more melodies at once

polyphony: the use of multiple countermelodies

polyrhythm: the combination of two or more simultaneous rhythmic patterns

pop: 1. a commercialized style of rock; **2.** any popular music written for the mainstream public before the rock 'n' roll era

portamento: *see* glissando

prelude: a piece of music used as an introduction to a fugue

preserver: an artist who keeps older styles alive and refines them

product identification: the association of an image with a product

progressive jazz: an experimental modern-jazz style characterized by often highly dissonant and rhythmically complex arrangements and solos

Pulitzer Prize: one of several annual prizes in journalism, literature, music, and other arts, established by Joseph Pulitzer

R **race records:** subsidiary record labels specializing in music by and for black Americans

rag: a ragtime composition, syncopated and lively

ragtime: a syncopated, late 19th-century piano style based on the musical forms of the rondo, the minuet, and the march

range: the scope of musical pitches possible for an instrument or voice

rap: a popular music style characterized by spontaneous, rhyming lyrics, strong rhythms, and the virtual absence of melody or harmony

reed instrument: an instrument that has a cane reed attached to a mouthpiece, which passes the vibration caused by a stream of air into the tube of the instrument

reel: a fast dance in which partners face each other in two lines

reggae: a Jamaican popular-music style blending calypso, blues, and rock 'n' roll

register: the tonal range of an instrument or voice from its lowest note to its highest

Renaissance: the period of the revival of art and learning in Europe, from the 14th through the 17th centuries

reversed-lead voicing: melody written for the lowest pitched instrument

revue: a form of theatrical entertainment including parodies of current events and fads

rhapsodic approach: a virtuoso improvisational technique involving double-time patterns, wide skips in register, and extreme dynamic and tonal variations

rhythm: the pattern of long and short notes and accented and unaccented beats, encompassing both tempo and meter

rhythm-and-blues: a popular-music style with strong repetitive rhythms and simple melodies, often using blue notes

ride cymbal: a large suspended cymbal on a drum set

riff: a short, repeated phrase used as an accompaniment for a soloist

ring spiritual: a shout spiritual repeated over and over, often for as long as six hours, while singers are moving rhythmically in a circle

Roaring Twenties: the 1920s, regarded as a boisterous era of prosperity and social change

rock: a popular music-style that developed from rock 'n' roll in the 1960s

rock 'n' roll: a popular-music style, derived from rhythm-and-blues and Country-and-Western, characterized by a heavily accented beat and repetitive phrase structure

rondo: a musical form with a short, catchy theme that alternates with contrasting material

rumba: a Cuban dance with complex rhythms

running spiritual: a spiritual sung in conjunction with the rhythmic African glide step, danced in a group around the church

rural blues: early blues of the rural South, specifically, the Texas Panhandle and the Mississippi Delta regions

S   **samba:** a rhythmic Brazilian march of African origin that became a stylized ballroom dance

samba whistle: a whistle used to signal dance-step changes in a samba march

sampling: the process of recording and storing natural sounds electronically

saxophone: a wind instrument consisting of a conical brass tube, keys, and a single-reed mouthpiece

scale: a succession of tones, ascending or descending according to fixed intervals

scat: *v.* to imitate a jazz instrument vocally

scat singing: 1. singing without a text or imitating a jazz instrument; 2. vocal improvisation

sea chantey: a sailor's work song

Second Awakening: a Protestant religious-revival movement in the United States from 1780 to 1830 which introduced white worshippers to the black spiritual and ring shout

semicadence: a sequence of notes occurring midway through a verse or chorus

seventh chord: a chord made up of four notes, so called because the fourth note of the chord is actually the seventh note of the scale pattern

short-subject film: a short film, such as a documentary, often shown in conjunction with a feature-length film; also called a *short*

shout: before the Civil War, a syncopated circle dance that revived the African custom of worshiping by singing and dancing

shout spiritual: a spiritual sung in conjunction with the "shout" dance

sitar: a stringed instrument of India with a small body and long fretted neck

slide: the U-shaped section of a trombone that can be pushed in or out to change the length of the air column and alter the pitch

snare drum: a drum with strings (snares) stretched across the bottom to add a reverberating effect and create a buzz tone

sock-cymbals: a pair of cymbals controlled by a foot pedal

solo break: a technique in which rhythmic accompaniment stops suddenly and briefly in order to draw attention to the soloist

sonata: a solo form common to western European classical music, usually three or four movements (sections) in length

soncubano: a song-and-dance form of African origin—prevalent in Panama and on the Caribbean coast of Columbia

soprano: the highest pitched female voice—also a young male voice

sotto voce: a very soft voice

soul: an emotional, personalized form of rhythm-and-blues

sousaphone: a type of brass tuba

speakeasy: a nightclub where alcohol was served illegally during Prohibition

spinet: a small harpsichord or a small upright piano

spiritual: a religious song emphasizing Old Testament bondage themes

splicing: the uniting or joining of two pieces or sections of magnetic tape or film

square dance: a dance involving four couples arranged in a square

staccato: short and abruptly disconnected (referring to notes)

Storyville: a black entertainment district in New Orleans, in whose streets, bordellos, and cabarets early jazz and blues developed in the late 19th and early 20th centuries

street music: marches and religious music played in brass-band fashion

stride piano: a jazz piano style that evolved in Harlem from ragtime, characterized by a smooth left hand and a trumpet-like right hand

string bass: the largest and lowest pitched instrument of the string family; also called *double bass, bass viol, contrabass*

string instruments: a family of instruments having strings stretched across a frame that are bowed or plucked

style: the effect of subtle nuances in tempo, dynamics, and articulation that distinguishes and identifies the music of a particular musician, region, cultural group, or time period

swing: *n. or adj.* a four-beat jazz style popular in the 1930s and early '40s, often performed by big bands, having a smoother beat and more flowing phrasing than Dixieland; *v.* to produce the rhythmic element that encourages dancing, clapping, etc.

swing era: a period of American music in the 1930s and '40s dominated by big-band swing music

symphony: a classical music work for orchestra in three or four movements

syncopation: a displaced accent on the normally weak beat or upbeat

synth drums: small drum pads hooked up to a synthesizer that can be programmed to re-create a wide range of percussion effects

synthesist: an artist who works with and perfects existing ideas, styles, and works

synthesizer: a computerized device that enables a composer to create and combine an unlimited variety of musical sounds electronically

T **tabla:** a small Indian hand drum

tambos: the large, hollow bamboo sticks used in place of drums in the ceremonies of Trinidad blacks

tambourim: a variant of the tambourine, without metal jingles

tambourine: a small open drum with metal jingles

tap dancing: a dance in which rhythm is audibly tapped out by the dancer's feet

tempo: speed

tenor: a male voice intermediate in pitch between the baritone and countertenor

tension note: a note added between chord tones to create harmonic tension

ternary form: a three-part musical form, denoted by ABA, AABA, or by ABC

texture: the total effect produced by rhythm, chords, range, register, and tone color

Third Stream jazz: a style that combines elements of classical music and jazz

timbales: two conjoined open metal drums, similar to bongos, but wider in diameter and played with drumsticks

timbre: *see* tone color

time signature: a symbol, such as $\frac{4}{4}$ or $\frac{3}{4}$, used in written music to describe the grouping of beats per measure

timpani: *see* kettledrum

Tin Pan Alley: the early center of music publishing in America, 28th Street in New York City

TOBA circuit: a vaudeville booking agency for black talent in the South and East in the 1920s and '30s

toms: *see* tom toms

tom toms: low-pitched drums of various sizes attached to a drum set; also called *toms*

tonal center: the pitch or tone on which a piece of music centers

tonal quality: *see* tone color

tonal sequencer: a computerized device for recording and reproducing musical phrases exactly

tone: a musical sound of definite pitch and quality

tone color: the quality of sound of a particular instrument or voice; sometimes called *timbre* or *tone quality*

transactional analysis: a school of psychology emphasizing personal relationships

traps: *see* trap set

trap set: a drum set, a conglomeration of drums and cymbals played by a single drummer; also called *traps*

treble clef: the upper part of the musical staff, labeled with the symbol 𝄞, and containing the notes above middle C

triangle trade: a pattern of colonial trade between New England, the West Indies, and west Africa, involving the importation of slaves to the New World

triple meter: a grouping of beats by threes

trombone: a tenor brass instrument with a slide

trumpet: a powerful soprano brass instrument consisting of a cup-shaped mouthpiece, a curved tube, and a flaring open end

tuba: the bass instrument of the brass family

twelve-bar blues: a common musical form in blues and jazz made up of three four-bar phrases

twist: a couples dance with African influences, composed of strong rhythmic turns and twists of the body

U   **underground railroad:** a pre-Civil War network for helping slaves escape

     upbeat: a normally unaccented beat following the downbeat

V   **variety show:** a vaudeville show consisting of individual performances of songs, dances, and skits

vaudeville: one of the most popular entertainment forms in America from about 1900 to 1930—consisting of animal acts, jugglers, singers, mimes, and other individual and group performances

verse: the part of a song following an introduction and preceding a chorus, often sung as a solo

verse-chorus form: the alternation of a familiar, fixed chorus with an original verse

vibes: *see* vibraharp

vibraharp: a melodic percussion instrument played by striking small metal bars with hammers; also called *vibraphone, vibes*

vibraphone: *see* vibraharp

vibrato: a rapid alternation between two very close pitches

violin: the soprano instrument of the string family, held horizontally against the shoulder or collarbone and bowed

virginal: a rectangular harpsichord popular in the 16th and 17th centuries

visceral rhythms: earthy, emotion-based rhythms

vocalise: a technique in which clever lyrics are written and sung to a previously recorded well-known instrumental jazz solo or arrangement

vocoder: an electronic device that synthesizes speech sounds

voodoo: a West Indian religion involving supernatural ceremonies, derived from African cult worship and elements of Catholicism

W **Wagnerian tenor:** *see* dramatic tenor

wah-wah brass: a tone-distortion technique used by jazz brass players

wah-wah pedal: a footswitch for distorting the tone of an electric guitar

walking tenths: the left-hand style often used in stride piano, involving a ten-step interval in which the upper and lower notes move simultaneously upward or downward in a scalelike fashion

West Coast cool: *see* West Coast jazz

West Coast jazz: cool jazz with some Latin influences, played predominantly by white studio musicians in the 1950s; also called *West Coast cool*

whiskey voice: a raspy singing voice

whole step: an interval of two half steps

wood block: a simple percussion instrument consisting of a hollow block of hard wood struck with a stick or mallet

woodwind instruments: a family of instruments in which sound is produced by a current of air passing over a reed or an open aperture

work song: a folk song sung by workers or prisoners, often with a rhythm to match that of their work

X   **xylophone:** a high-pitched, bright-sounding instrument made of graduated wooden bars which are struck with mallets

Z   **Zip Coon:** a late-nineteenth century caricature of the urban black male

BIBLIOGRAPHY

/■/

ALBERTSON, CHRIS. *Bessie*. Briarcliff Manor, N.Y.: Stein & Day Publishers, 1972.

ALLEN, WILLIAM F., CHARLES WARE, and LUCY GARRISON. *Slave Songs of the United States*. New York: Peter Smith Publishing, 1960.

ARMSTRONG, LOUIS. *Satchmo: My Life in New Orleans*. Englewood Cliffs, N.J.: Prentice-Hall, 1954.

BAKER, DAVID, ed. *New Perspectives on Jazz*. Washington, D.C.: Smithsonian Institution Press, 1990.

BALLIETT, WHITNEY. *Sound of Surprise*. New York: E. P. Dutton, 1959.

————. *Dinosaurs in the Morning: Forty-one Pieces on Jazz*. Philadelphia: J. B. Lippincott Co., 1962.

————. *American Musicians: Fifty-six Portraits in Jazz*. New York: Oxford University Press, 1986.

BARLOW, WILLIAM. *Looking Up at Down: The Emergence of Blues Culture*. Philadelphia: Temple University Press, 1989.

BARON, STANLEY. *Benny: King of Swing*. New York: Da Capo Press, 1987.

BARZUN, JACQUES. *Music in American Life*. New York: Doubleday & Co., 1956.

BECHET, SIDNEY. *Treat It Gentle: An Autobiography*. New York: Hill & Wang, 1960.

BENNETT, LERONE. *Before the Mayflower*, 6th ed. Chicago: Johnson Publishing, 1988.

BERNSTEIN, LEONARD. *Joy of Music*. New York: Simon & Schuster, 1959.

BERTON, RALPH. *Remembering Bix: A Memoir of the Jazz Age*. New York: Harper & Row, Publishers, 1974.

BLANCO, CHARLES. *Sonny Rollins: The Journey of a Jazzman*. Boston: G. K. Hall & Co., 1983.

BLESH, RUDI, and HARRIET JANIS. *They All Played Ragtime*. New York: Oak Publications, 1971.

BORROFF, EDITH. *Music in Europe and the United States: A History*, 2nd ed. New York: Ardsley House, Publishers, 1990.

BRASK, OLE, and DAN MORGENSTERN. *Jazz People*. New York: Harry N. Abrams, 1976.

BUDDS, MICHAEL J. *Jazz in the Sixties*. Iowa City, Iowa: University of Iowa Press, 1978.

BUERKLE, JACK V., and DANNY BARKER. *Bourbon Street Black*. Oxford: Oxford University Press, 1973.

CARR, IAN. *Miles Davis: A Biography*. New York: William Morrow & Co., 1982.

CASE, BRIAN, and STAN BRITT. *The Illustrated Encyclopedia of Jazz*. New York: Harmony Books, 1978.

CHARTERS, SAMUEL B. *Jazz: New Orleans 1885–1963*. New York: Da Capo Press, 1983.

———, and LEONARD KUNSTADT. *Jazz: A History of the New York Scene*. New York: Da Capo Press, 1981.

CHILTON, JOHN. *Who's Who of Jazz*. London: Chilton Book Co., 1972.

———. *Billie's Blues*. Briarcliff Manor, N.Y.: Stein & Day Publishers, 1975.

CLAGHORN, CHARLES E. *Biographical Dictionary of Jazz*. Englewood Cliffs, N.J.: Prentice-Hall, 1983.

COLE, BILL. *Miles Davis*. New York: William Morrow & Co., 1976.

COLLIER, JAMES LINCOLN. *The Making of Jazz: A Comprehensive History*. Boston: Houghton Mifflin Co., 1978.

———. *Louis Armstrong: An American Genius*. New York: Oxford University Press, 1983.

CORYELL, JULIE, and LAURA FRIEDMAN. *Jazz-Rock Fusion*. New York: Delta Books, 1979.

DANCE, HELEN OAKLEY. *Stormy Monday (The T-Bone Walker Story)*. New York: Da Capo Press, 1991.

DANCE, STANLEY. *The World of Duke Ellington*. New York: Charles Scribner's Sons, 1970.

———. *The World of Earl Hines*. New York: Charles Scribner's Sons, 1977.

———. *The World of Count Basie*. New York: Charles Scribner's Sons, 1981.

DANKWORTH, AVRIL. *Jazz: An Introduction to Its Musical Basis*. Oxford: Oxford University Press, 1968.

DAVIS, FRANCIS. *In the Moment: Jazz in the 1980s.* New York: Oxford University Press, 1986.

DAVIS, MILES, and QUINCY TROUPE. *Miles: The Autobiography.* New York: Simon & Schuster, 1990.

DEVEAUX, SCOTT, and WILLIAM H. KENNEY, ed. *The Music of James Scott.* Washington, D.C.: Smithsonian Institution Press, 1992.

DEXTER, DAVE. *The Jazz Story.* Englewood Cliffs, N.J.: Prentice-Hall, 1964.

DIXON, WILLIE, with DON SNOWDEN. *I Am the Blues.* New York: Da Capo Press, 1991.

DOROUGH, PRINCE. *Popular-Music Culture in America.* New York: Ardsley House, Publishers, 1992.

ELLINGTON, DUKE. *Music Is My Mistress.* New York: Doubleday & Co., 1973.

ELLINGTON, MERCER, and STANLEY DANCE. *Duke Ellington: An Intimate Memoir.* Boston: Houghton Mifflin Co., 1975.

FEATHER, LEONARD. *The Book of Jazz.* New York: Horizon Press, 1961.

————. *The Encyclopedia of Jazz in the Sixties.* New York: Horizon Press, 1966.

————. *From Satchmo to Miles.* Briarcliff Manor, N.Y.: Stein & Day Publishers, 1972.

————. *Inside Jazz.* New York: Da Capo Press, 1977.

————. *The Jazz Years: Eyewitness to an Era.* New York: Da Capo Press, 1987.

————, with IRA GITLER. *The Encylopedia of Jazz in the Seventies.* New York: Da Capo Press, 1987.

FELSTEIN, SIDNEY. *Jazz: A People's Music.* New York: Da Capo Press, 1975.

FERRIS, WILLIAM. *Blues from the Delta: An Illustrated Documentary on the Music and Musicians of the Mississippi Delta.* New York: Doubleday & Co., 1978.

FIRESTONE, ROSS. *Swing, Swing, Swing: The Life and Times of Benny Goodman.* New York: W. W. Norton & Co., 1993.

FOSTER, GEORGE MURPHY. *Pops Foster: The Autobiography of a New Orleans Jazzman.* Berkeley: University of California Press, 1971.

GAMMOND, PETER. *Scott Joplin and the Ragtime Era.* New York: St. Martin's Press, 1975.

GIDDINS, GARY. *Riding on a Blue Note.* New York: Oxford University Press, 1981.

————. *Rhythm-a-thing: Jazz Tradition in the '80s.* New York: Oxford University Press, 1985.

GILLESPIE, DIZZY, with AL FRASER. *To Be or Not To Bop.* New York: Doubleday & Co., 1979.

GIOIA, TED. *The Imperfect Art: Reflections on Jazz and Modern Culture.* New York: Oxford University Press, 1988.

GITLER, IRA. *Jazz Masters of the Forties.* New York: Collier Books, 1970.

————. *Swing to Bop: Jazz in the 1940s.* New York: Oxford University Press, 1985.

GLEASON, RALPH. *Celebrating the Duke.* New York: Dell Publishing Co., 1975.

GOLDBERG, JOE. *Jazz Masters of the Fifties.* New York: Macmillan Publishing Co., 1965.

GROUT, DONALD J., and CLAUDE PALISCA. *A History of Western Music,* 4th ed. New York: W. W. Norton & Co., 1988.

HADLOCK, RICHARD B. *Jazz Masters of the Twenties.* New York: Collier Books, 1974.

HAMEL, PETER. *Through Music to the Self.* Boston: Shambhala Publications, 1979.

HANDY, W. C. *Father of the Blues: An Autobiography.* New York: Da Capo Press, 1991.

HARRISON, MAX. *Charlie Parker.* San Diego: A. S. Barnes & Co., 1960.

HAZEN, MARGARET, and ROBERT HAZEN. *The Music Men: An Illustrated History of Brass Bands in America, 1800–1922.* Washington, D.C.: Smithsonian Institution Press, 1987.

HENTOFF, NAT. *The Jazz Life.* New York: Da Capo Press, 1975.

————. *Jazz Is.* New York: Random House, 1976.

————. *Boston Boy.* New York: Alfred A. Knopf, 1986.

————, and ALBERT MCCARTHY. *Jazz: New Perspectives on the History of Jazz.* New York: Da Capo Press, 1975.

HITCHCOCK, H. WILEY. *The New Grove Dictionary of Modern Music.* London: Macmillan, 1986.

HODIER, ANDRÉ. *Jazz: Its Evolution and Essence.* New York: Grove Press, 1956.

————. *Toward Jazz.* New York: Grove Press, 1962.

HOLIDAY, BILLIE, with WILLIAM DUFTY. *Lady Sings the Blues.* New York: Doubleday & Co., 1956.

HUGHES, LANGSTON, and MILTON MELTZER. *Black Magic: A Pictorial History of the African-American in the Performing Arts.* New York: Da Capo Press, 1991.

JAMES, MICHAEL. *Dizzy Gillespie.* San Diego: A. S. Barnes & Co., 1959.

JEWELL, DEREK. *Duke: A Portrait of Duke Ellington.* New York: W. W. Norton & Co., 1977.

JONES, LEROI. *Black Music.* New York: William Morrow & Co., 1971.

————. *Blues People: Negro Music in White America.* New York: William Morrow & Co., 1971.

JONES, MAX, and JOHN CHILTON. *Louis: The Louis Armstrong Story.* Boston: Little, Brown & Co., 1971.

KAUFMAN, FREDERICK, and JOHN P. GUCKIN. *The African Roots of Jazz.* Sherman Oaks, Calif.: Alfred Publishing Co., 1979.

KEEPNEWS, ORRIN. *Pictorial History of Jazz.* New York: Crown Publishers, 1966.

KEIL, CHARLES. *Urban Blues.* Chicago: University of Chicago Press, 1966.

KERNFELD, BARRY. *The New Grove Dictionary of Jazz,* 2 vols. New York: Macmillan Publishing Co., 1988.

KINKLE, ROGER D. *The Complete Encyclopedia of Popular Music and Jazz (1900–1950),* 4 vols. New Rochelle, N.Y.: Arlington House Publishers, 1974.

KRISS, ERIC. *Barrelhouse and Boogie Piano.* New York: Oak Publications, 1974.

LEE, WILLIAM F. *People in Jazz: Jazz Keyboard Improvisors of the 19th and 20th Centuries.* Hialeah, Fla.: Columbia Pictures Publications, 1984.

LEONARD, NEIL. *Jazz and the White Americans.* Chicago: University of Chicago Press, 1962.

LIFSCHITZ, EDWARD, ed. *The Art of West African Kingdoms.* Washington, D.C.: Smithsonian Institution Press, 1987.

LOMAX, ALAN. *Mister Jelly Roll.* Berkeley: University of California Press, 1950.

———. *The Folk Songs of North America.* New York: Doubleday & Co., 1975.

LONGSTREET, STEPHEN. *Sportin' House: New Orleans and the Jazz Story.* Los Angeles: Sherbourne Press, 1965.

McCARTHY, ALBERT. *Big Band Jazz.* New York: G. P. Putnam's Sons, 1974.

MEEKER, DAVID. *Jazz in the Movies: A Guide to Jazz Musicians, 1917–1977.* New York: Da Capo Press, 1982.

MELLERS, WILFRED. *Music in a New Found Land: Themes and Developments in the History of American Music.* New York: Oxford University Press, 1987.

MURO, DON. *An Introduction to Electronic Music Synthesizers.* Melville, N.Y.: Belwin-Mills Publishing, 1975.

NANR, CHARLES. *The Jazz Text.* New York: Van Nostrand Reinhold Co., 1979.

OLIVER, PAUL. *Bessie Smith.* San Diego: A. S. Barnes & Co., 1961.

———. *Savannah Syncopators: African Retentions in the Blues.* Briarcliff Manor, N.Y.: Stein & Day Publishers, 1970.

———. *The Meaning of the Blues.* New York: Collier Books, 1972.

————, MAX HARRISON, and WILLIAM BOLCOM. *The New Grove Gospel, Blues and Jazz.* New York: W. W. Norton & Co., 1986.

PANASSIE, HUGHES. *The Real Jazz.* Translated by Anne Sorrelle Williams. San Diego: A. S. Barnes & Co., 1960.

PLEASANTS, HENRY. *The Great American Popular Singers.* New York: Oxford University Press, 1959.

————. *Serious Music and All That Jazz.* New York: Simon & Schuster, 1968.

————. *The Agony of Modern Music.* New York: Touchstone Books, 1977.

PORTER, LEWIS. *Lester Young.* Boston: G. K. Hall & Co., 1985.

————. *A Lester Young Reader.* Washington, D.C.: Smithsonian Institution Press, 1992.

RAYMOND, JACK. *Show Music on Record: The First 100 Years.* Washington, D.C.: Smithsonian Institution Press, 1992.

REISNER, ROBERT. *The Jazz Titan.* New York: Doubleday & Co., 1960.

————. *Bird: The Legend of Charlie Parker.* New York: Charterhouse Press, 1973.

RIIS, THOMAS L. *Just before Jazz: Black Musical Theater in New York, 1890–1915.* Washington, D.C.: Smithsonian Institution Press, 1989.

ROACH, HILDRED. *Black American Music: Past and Present.* Boston: Crescendo, 1973.

ROBERTS, JOHN STORM. *Black Music of Two Worlds.* New York: William Morrow & Co., 1974.

ROSENTHAL, DAVID H. *Hard Bop: Jazz and Black Music, 1955–1965.* New York: Oxford University Press, 1992.

RUSSELL, ROSS. *Bird Lives! The High Life and Hard Times of Charlie "Yardbird" Parker.* New York: Charterhouse Press, 1973.

RUSSELL, TONY. *Blacks, Whites, and Blues.* Briarcliff Manor, N.Y.: Stein & Day Publishers, 1970.

SALES, GROVER. *Jazz, America's Classical Music.* Englewood Cliffs, N.J.: Prentice-Hall, 1984.

SAUNDERS, STEVEN, and DEANE L. ROOT. *The Music of Stephen C. Foster.* Washington, D.C.: Smithsonian Institution Press, 1990.

SCHULLER, GUNTHER. *Early Jazz: Its Roots and Musical Development.* New York: Oxford University Press, 1986.

————. *The Swing Era: The Development of Jazz, 1930–1945.* New York: Oxford University Press, 1989.

SEITZ, WILLIAM C., and MARLA PRICE, ed. *Art in the Age of Aquarius, 1955–1970.* Washington, D.C.: Smithsonian Institution Press, 1992.

SHAPIRO, NAT, and NAT HENTOFF, eds. *Hear Me Talkin' to Ya*. New York: Dover Publications, 1955.

————. *Jazz Makers*. New York: Rinehart, 1957.

SHAW, ARNOLD. *The Jazz Age: Popular Music in the 1920s*. New York: Oxford University Press, 1987.

SIDRAN, BEN. *Talking Jazz: An Illustrated Oral History*. Petaluma, Calif.: Pomegranate Art Books, 1992.

SIMON, GEORGE. *The Big Bands*, rev. ed. New York: Macmillan Publishing Co., 1971.

————. *Glenn Miller*. New York: Thomas Y. Crowell, 1974.

SIMPKINS, C. O. *Coltrane: A Biography*. New York: Schocken Books, 1966.

SMITH, EDWARD D. *Climbing Jacob's Ladder: The Rise of Black Churches in Eastern American Cities, 1740–1877*. Washington, D.C.: Smithsonian Institution Press, 1988.

SOUTHERN, EILEEN. *The Music of Black Americans: A History*, 2nd ed. New York: W. W. Norton & Co., 1983.

STANDIFER, JAMES, and BARBARA REEDER. *Source Book of African and Afro-American Materials for Music Educators*. Washington, D.C.: Contemporary Music Project, 1972.

STEARNS, MARSHALL. *The Story of Jazz*. New York: Oxford University Press, 1956.

————, and JEAN STEARNS. *Jazz Dance. The Story of American Vernacular Dance*. New York: Macmillan Publishing Co., 1968.

STEWART, REX. *Jazz Masters of the Thirties*. New York: Macmillan Publishing Co., 1972.

SUDHALTER, RICHARD, PHILIP EVANS, and WILLIAM DEAN-MYATT. *Bix: Man & Legend*. New Rochelle, N.Y.: Arlington House, 1974.

TALMADGE, WILLIAM. *Afro-American Music*. Washington, D.C.: Music Educators National Conference, 1957.

THOMAS, J. C. *Chasin' the Trane: The Music and Mystique of John Coltrane*. New York: Doubleday & Co., 1975.

TOFFLER, ALVIN. *Future Shock*. New York: Bantam Books, 1971.

————. *The Third Wave*. New York: Bantam Books, 1981.

————. *Power Shift*. New York: Bantam Books, 1990.

ULANOV, BARRY. *Duke Ellington*. New York: Farrar, Strauss & Young, 1946.

VACHÉ, WARREN W., SR. *Crazy Finger: Claude Hopkins' Life in Jazz*. Washington, D.C.: Smithsonian Institution Press, 1992.

WALKER, LEO. *The Wonderful Era of the Great Dance Bands*. New York: Doubleday & Co., 1972.

WELLS, DICKY, and STANLEY DANCE, ed. *The Night People: The Jazz Life of Dicky Wells.* Washington, D.C.: Smithsonian Institution Press, 1991.

WHEATON, JACK. *The Technological and Sociological Influences on Jazz as an Art Form in America.* Ann Arbor, Mich.: University of Michigan Press, 1976.

WILDER, ALEC. *American Popular Song: The Great Innovators (1900–1950).* New York: Oxford University Press, 1972.

WILLIAMS, MARTIN, ed. *The Art of Jazz.* New York: Grove Press, 1960.

————. *King Oliver.* San Diego: A. S. Barnes & Co., 1960.

————. *Jazz Masters of New Orleans.* New York: Macmillan Publishing Co., 1970.

————. *The Jazz Tradition.* New York: Oxford University Press, 1983.

WILSON, JOHN S. *The Collector's Jazz: Traditional and Swing.* Philadelphia: J. B. Lippincott Co., 1959.

————. *The Collector's Jazz: Modern.* Philadelphia: J. B. Lippincott Co., 1959.

WONDER, JACQUELYN, and DONOVAN WONDER. *Whole-Brain Thinking.* New York: Ballantine Books, 1984.

DISCOGRAPHY

/■/

African-American Folk Songs and Rhythms, Ella Jenkins. Smithsonian/ Folkways SF 45003.

African Drums. Smithsonian/Folkways FE 4502.

Africa South of the Sahara. Smithsonian/Folkways 4503.

Afro-American Music: A Demonstration Recording. Smithsonian/Folkways 2692.

American Popular Song: Six Decades of Songwriters and Singers. Smithsonian.

Anatomy of Improvisation. Verve 8230.

Anthology of Music of Black America. Everest 3254.

Any Woman's Blues, Bessie Smith. Columbia G-30126.

Are You Ready for Christmas?: Black Church Service, Rev. Audrey F. Bronson and Becky Carlton. Smithsonian/Folkways 32425.

Art of Jazz Piano. Epic Records 3295.

Asch Recordings 1939–47, Vol. 1: Blues, Gospel and Jazz. Smithsonian/ Folkways AA 1/2.

Basic Miles, Miles Davis. Columbia C-32025.

Bass, The. Impulse ASY-9284-3.

Bebop Era, The. RCA Victor LPV-519.

Beginning, The, Vol. 1: 1926–28, Duke Ellington. Decca 9224.

Bessie Smith Story, The. Columbia C-3L27.

Best of Bird, The, Charlie Parker. Warner 2WB-3198.

Best of Count Basie, The. MCA 2-4050.

Best of Dixieland, The. RCA Victor LSP-2982.

Best of Stan Getz, The. Roulette 119.

Better Git It in Your Soul, Charles Mingus. Columbia CG-30628.

Big Band Era. RCA PK-5099.

Big Band Jazz. Smithsonian 2200, 2202.

Big Bands' Greatest Hits. Columbia CG-31212.

Big Bill Broonzy Sings Country Blues. Smithsonian/Folkways 31005.

Biggest Little Band (1937–41), The, John Kirby. Smithsonian 2013.

Billie Holiday Story, The. MCA-2-4006E.

Birth of Big Band Jazz, The. Riverside RLP 12-129.

Birth of the Cool, Miles Davis. Capitol N-16168.

Bix Beiderbecke and the Wolverines. Riverside RLP-12-123.

Bix Beiderbecke Story, The. Columbia CL-845.

Blanton Webster Band, The, Duke Ellington. RCA 5691-1-RB.

Blind Willie Johnson. Smithsonian/Folkways FG-3585.

Blues, The, W. C. Handy. Smithsonian/Folkways FG-3540.

Blues and the Abstract Truth, Oliver Nelson. Impulse 5.

Blues Groove, Coleman Hawkins. Prestige 7753.

Blues in Modern Jazz, The. Atlantic 1337.

Blues Roll On, The. Atlantic 1352.

Blues Roots: Chicago—the 1930s. Smithsonian/Folkways RF 16.

Blues Roots: Mississippi. Smithsonian/Folkways RF 14.

Blues Tradition, The, Big Bill Broonzy and Eddie Jefferson. Milestone 2016.

Body and Soul, Coleman Hawkins. Quintessence OJ-25131.

Boogie-Woogie Piano Rarities. Milestone 2009.

Capitol Records Jazz Classics. Capitol.

Carnegie Hall Concerts, Duke Ellington. Prestige 34004.

Carnegie Hall Jazz Concert, The, Benny Goodman. Columbia OSL-160.

Charlie Christian, Benny Goodman. Columbia CL-652.

Chicago Dixieland in the Forties. Smithsonian/Folkways 2817.

Chicago Jazz Album. Decca 8029.

Classic Jazz Piano Styles. RCA Victor LPV-543.

Clifford Brown and Max Roach. Emarcy 814645-2.

Collector's History of Classic Jazz. Murray Hill 92794.

Complete Blue Note Recordings, The, Thelonious Monk. Mosaic MR4-101.

Complete Capitol Recordings, The, Art Tatum. Capitol C2-92866/7.

Complete Pablo Group Masterpieces, The, Art Tatum. Pablo 6PACD 4401-2.

Complete Pablo Solo Masterpieces, The, Art Tatum. Pablo 7PACD 4404-2.

Complete Pacific Jazz and Capitol Recordings, The, Gerry Mulligan. Mosaic MR5-102.

Complete Works for Piano, The, Scott Joplin. RCA CRL-5-1106.

Composer's Concepts, Dizzy Gillespie. Mercury EMS-2-410.

Concert by the Sea, Erroll Garner. Columbia CS-9821.

Concert of Sacred Music, Duke Ellington. RCA LPM-3582.

Concertos: For Piano and Orchestra (the "Jazz Concerto"), Aaron Copland. CHS 1238.

Conversations with Myself, Bill Evans. Verve V-8526.

Count Basie and His Orchestra, 1938–40. Decca DEC-8049.

Count Basie in Kansas City: Benny Moten's Band. RCA LPV-514.

Country Blues. Smithsonian/Folkways RF1, RF9.

Definitive Jazz Scene, The. Impulse A-99-101.

Development of an American Artist, 1940–46, The, Dizzy Gillespie. Smithsonian 2004.

Dixieland Jazz in the Forties. Smithsonian/Folkways 2853.

Drums, The. Impulse 9272.

Duke Ellington and Coleman Hawkins. Impulse A-26.

Duke Ellington, 1938. Smithsonian 2003.

Ella Fitzgerald and Chick Webb. Smithsonian/Folkways 2818.

Ellington Era (1927–40), The. Columbia CL 855-8.

El Salon Mexico, Aaron Copland. Columbia CL-920.

Empress, The, Bessie Smith. CGT 30818.

Encyclopedia of Jazz on Records. Decca DXSF-7140.

Essential Billie Holiday, The. Verve V-8410.

Experiment in Modern Music: Paul Whiteman at Aeolian Hall, An. Smithsonian 2028.

Fantasy Years, The, Dave Brubeck. Atlantic SD2-317.

Father of the Stride Piano, James P. Johnson. Columbia CL-1780.

Fifty Years of Jazz Guitar. Columbia C6-33566.

Fisk Jubilee Singers. Smithsonian/Folkways FA 2372.

Folk Song America: A Twentieth Century Revival. Smithsonian 2702.

Folkways Jazz Series. Smithsonian/Folkways FJ 2801-2811.

Fractious Fingering, Fats Waller. RCA Victor LPV-537.

Free Jazz, Ornette Coleman. Atlantic 1311.

From Spirituals to Swing. Vanguard VRS-8523/4.

Genius of Bud Powell, The. Verve 2506.

Giants of Jazz. Time-Life Records.

Giant Steps, John Coltrane. Atlantic SD-1311-2.

Golden Age of Ragtime, The. Riverside 12-110.

Golden Years, The, Billie Holiday. Columbia 32121-4, 32127.

Great Band Era, The. RCA Victor RD4-25 (RRIS-5473).

Great Blues Singers. Riverside 121.

Greatest Jazz Concert Ever, The, Dizzy Gillespie, Charles Mingus, Charlie Parker, Bud Powell, Max Roach. Prestige 24024.

Greatest Jazz Concert in the World, The. Pablo 2625704.

Greatest Names in Jazz, The. Verve PR 2-3.

Guide to Jazz. RCA Victor LPM-1393.

Heavy Weather, Weather Report. Columbia PC 34418.

Her Greatest Years, Ethel Waters. Columbia KG 31571.

History of an Artist, The, Oscar Peterson. Pablo 2625702.

History of Classic Jazz. Riverside RB-005.

Hollers, Work and Church Songs, Vol. 1. Smithsonian/Folkways FJ 2801.

Hollywood Stampede, Coleman Hawkins. Capitol 11030.

Hot Fives, Louis Armstrong. Columbia CK 44049.

Hot Fives and Hot Sevens, Louis Armstrong. Columbia CK 44253, 44422.

Hot Sonatas, Joe Venuti with Earl Hines. Chiaroscuro 145.

How Long Has This Been Goin' on?, Sarah Vaughan. Pablo 2310-821.

Incomparable, The, Jelly Roll Morton. Riverside RLP-12-128.

In the Beginning, Dizzy Gillespie, Charlie Parker. Prestige 24030.

Introduction to American Negro Folk Music, An. Smithsonian/Folkways FA 2691.

I Remember Clifford, Clifford Brown. Mercury 60827.

I Sing Because I'm Happy, Mahalia Jackson. Smithsonian/Folkways 31101-2.

Jambo and Other Call-and-Response Songs and Chants, Ella Jenkins. Smithsonian/Folkways SF 45017.

Jazz, Vol. 1: The South. Smithsonian/Folkways 2801.

Jazz, Vol. 2: The Blues. Smithsonian/Folkways 2802.

Jazz, Vol. 3: New Orleans. Smithsonian/Folkways 2803.

Jazz, Vol. 4: Jazz Singers. Smithsonian/Folkways 2804.

Jazz, Vol. 5: Chicago, No. 1. Smithsonian/Folkways 2805.

Jazz, Vol. 6: Chicago, No. 2. Smithsonian/Folkways 2806.

Jazz, Vol. 7: New York 1922–34. Smithsonian/Folkways 2807.

Jazz, Vol. 8: Big Bands Pre-1935. Smithsonian/Folkways 2808.

Jazz, Vol. 9: Piano. Smithsonian/Folkways 2809.

Jazz, Vol. 10: Boogie-Woogie, Jump, and Kansas City. Smithsonian/Folkways 2810.

Jazz at Preservation Hall. Atlantic S-1409, 1410.

Jazz at the Philharmonic. Verve 2-2504.

Jazz at the Santa Monica Civic Center, 1972. Pablo 2625-701-2.

Jazz Holiday, A, Benny Goodman. MCA2-4018.

Jazz Makers, The. Columbia CL 1036.

Jazz Odyssey. Columbia C30-33.

Jazz Piano. Smithsonian 7002.

Jazz Piano Anthology. Columbia PG 32355.

Jazz Scene, The. Verve 8060.

Jazz: Some Beginnings 1913-16. Smithsonian/Folkways RF 31.

Jazz Story, The. Capitol W2137-41.

Jazz Trumpet, The. Prestige P-24112.

Jelly Roll Morton and His Red Hot Peppers. EMI DLP-1071.

Juke Blues. Kent KC 2030.

Jump for Joy, Duke Ellington. Smithsonian 1008.

Kansas City Jazz. Decca 8044.

Kenton Showcase, Stan Kenton. Creative World 1026.

Kind of Blue, Miles Davis. Columbia PC-8163.

King of the Blues Trombone, Jack Teagarden. Epic JSN 6044.

King of the Delta Blues Singers, Robert P. Johnson. Columbia PCT 1654.

King Oliver. Epic LN 3208.

Kings of the Blues. RCA RCX 202-204.

Leadbelly's Last Sessions. Smithsonian/Folkways FA 2941.

Legendary Singers. Time-Life Series.

Lester Young Story, The. Columbia JG-3483-7.

Library of Congress Recordings, The, Jelly Roll Morton. Riverside RLP 1001-1012.

Lightin' Hopkins. Smithsonian/Folkways 40019.

Live at Birdland, John Coltrane. Impulse MCA 29015.

Live at Montreux, Les McCann. Atlantic 2-3/2.

Livery Stable Blues, Original Dixieland Jazz Band. RCA RCX-1028.

Live with George Barnes at Concord, Joe Venuti. Concord CJ-30.

Living Legend, A, Art Pepper. Contemporary S76323.

Louis Armstrong and Earl Hines (1928). Smithsonian 2100.

Louis Armstrong Plays W. C. Handy. Columbia CK 40242.

Louis Armstrong Story, The. Columbia CL 851-4.

Maestro and Friend, The, Joe Venuti and Marian McPartland. Halcyon 112.

Maiden Voyage, Herbie Hancock. Blue Note 84195.

Mainstream Jazz. Atlantic 1301/S.

Many Moods of Duke Ellington. Quintescence 25101.

Master Musician, Sidney Bechet. RCA AXM2-5516.

Memorial Album, The, Sidney Bechet. Fontana 682-055TL.

Message for the People, A, Ray Charles. ABC Records X755.

Modern Jazz Quartet Plays Jazz Classics, The. Prestige 7425.

Monday Date, A, Earl Hines. Milestone MLP-2012.

Music from the South, Vol. 1: Country Brass Bands. Smithsonian/Folkways 2650.

Music of Equatorial Africa. Smithsonian/Folkways 4402.

Music of Jelly Roll Morton, The. Smithsonian.

Music of New Orleans, The, Vol. 1–3. Smithsonian/Folkways FA 2461-3.

Negro Church Music. Atlantic 1351.

Negro Prison Worksongs. Smithsonian/Folkways FE 4475.

Negro Spirituals. Smithsonian/Folkways FA 2038.

Negro Worksongs and Calls. Library of Congress AAFS 18.

New Orleans, Vol. IV, Preservation Hall Jazz Band. Columbia MK-44856.

New Orleans Jazz. Decca 8283.

New Orleans Piano, Professor Longhair. Atlantic SD 7225.

New Orleans: The Living Legends. Riverside 356-57.

New Wave in Jazz, The. Impulse A-90.

Night at Birdland, A, Art Blakey. Blue Note 81522.

Orchestra, The, Jimmie Lunceford. Columbia CL-634.

Piano Giants. Prestige 2402.

Piano Starts Here, Art Tatum. Columbia 9655.

Pieces of Eight (1939–55), Art Tatum. Smithsonian 2029.

Preachin' the Blues, Sonny Terry and Brownie McGhee. Smithsonian/Folkways 31024.

Quintessential, Earl Hines. Chiaroscuro 101.

Rare Solos, James P. Johnson. Riverside RLP 12-105.

Real Boogie-Woogie of Memphis Slim, The. Smithsonian/Folkways FG 3524.

Return to Forever, Chick Corea. ECM-Warner 1026.

Roots of Black Music in America. Smithsonian/Folkways 2694.

Roots: Rhythm and Blues. Smithsonian/Folkways RBF 20.

Round Midnight, Thelonious Monk piano solo. Riverside 235.

Round Midnight, Thelonious Monk quartet. Riverside 247.

Round Midnight (soundtrack), Herbie Hancock. Columbia CK-40464.

Satch Plays Fats, Louis Armstrong. Columbia CK 40378.

Saxophone, The. Impulse ASH 9253-3.

Saxophone Colossus. Sonny Rollins. Fantasy-Prestige P-24050.

Second Sacred Concert, Duke Ellington. Fantasy 8407/8.

Shape of Jazz to Come, The, Ornette Coleman. Atlantic SC-1317.

Singers and Soloists of the Swing Bands. Smithsonian 2601.

Skies of America, Ornette Coleman. Columbia KC-31562.

Sleepy John Estes, 1929–40. Smithsonian/Folkways RF8.

Smithsonian Collection of Classic Jazz. Smithsonian.

Solo Concerts, Keith Jarrett. ECM-Warner 1035-37.

Solo Flight, Charlie Christian. Columbia CG-30779.

Son House and J. D. Short: Blues from the Mississippi Delta. Smithsonian/Folkways 2467.

Soul of Jazz, The. Riverside S-5.

Story of the Blues, The. Columbia CGT-30008.

Stringing the Blues, Joe Venuti with Eddie Lang. CBS 88142.

Such Sweet Thunder, Duke Ellington. Columbia JCL 1033.

Swingin' Big Band and Jazz from the '30s and '40s. Smithsonian/Folkways 2861.

Symphony in Black, Duke Ellington. Smithsonian 1024.

Talking and Drum Solos: Footnotes to Jazz, Vol. 1, Baby Dodds. Smithsonian/Folkways 2290.

Thesaurus of Classical Jazz. Columbia C4L 18.

Third Sacred Concert, Duke Ellington. RCA APLI-0785.

This Is Benny Goodman. RCA VPM-6040.

This Is Duke Ellington. RCA VPM-6042.

Three Decades of Jazz, 1930s–60s. Blue Note LA-158-60.

Tommy Dorsey and His Orchestra. RCA RD-27069.

Town Hall Concert Plus, Louis Armstrong. RCA LPM-1443.

Verve Years, The, Dizzy Gillespie, Charlie Parker. Verve VE 2501.

Village Vanguard Sessions, The, Bill Evans. Milestone M-47002.

Voices of the Civil Rights Movement: Black American Freedom Songs, 1960–66. Smithsonian 2023.

What a Little Moonlight Can Do, Betty Carter. ABC Impulse ASD-9321.

World of Cecil Taylor, The. Candid 8006.

World of Swing, The. Columbia KG 32943.

Young Louis Armstrong. Riverside RLP-12-101.

JAZZ VIDEOS

/■/

The letters appearing at the end of each entry refer to the distribution company in the list following the videos on page 366.

After Hours (27 min). Cozy Cole, Roy Eldridge, Coleman Hawkins. JA.

Airto and Flora Purim: The Latin Jazz All Stars (60 min). Brazilian jazz. JA, VIEW.

All-Star Swing Festival (52 min). Count Basie, Dave Brubeck, Duke Ellington, Ella Fitzgerald, Dizzy Gillespie, Benny Goodman, Bobby Hackett, Joe Williams. VF.

Always for Pleasure (58 min). New Orleans Dixieland parades, jazz funeral, and Mardi Gras celebrations, 1977. VF.

Anything for Jazz (25 min). Jazz pianist Jaki Byard. RF.

Archie Shepp: "I Am Jazz . . . It's My Life" (52 min). JA.

Art Blakey: The Jazz Messenger (78 min). Documentary. JA.

Art Ensemble of Chicago: Live from the Jazz Showcase (50 min). IRL.

Barry Harris: Passing It On (25 min). Bop piano, instructional. JA, RF.

B. B. King: Live at Nick's (60 min). Urban blues style, live in concert. JA.

Ben Webster in Europe (31 min). JA.

Best of the Big Bands (75 min). Count Basie, Les Brown, Jimmy Dorsey, Tommy Dorsey, Benny Goodman, Lionel Hampton, Harry James, Gene Krupa, Buddy Rich, Teddy Wilson. AE.

Big Bands, vol. 101 (50 min). Count Basie, Duke Ellington, Lionel Hampton. VF.

Big Bands at Disneyland, 3 vols (57 min each). Cab Calloway, Lionel Hampton, Woody Herman. AE.

Big, Black, and Beautiful (60 min). Count Basie, Cab Calloway, Nat King Cole, Duke Ellington, Lionel Hampton, George Shearing. AE.

Bill Evans on the Creative Process (20 min). RF.

Bill Watrous (24 min). Jazz trombonist. SVS.

Bird (161 min). Documentary on the life of Charlie Parker. SVS.

Blues Alive (92 min). Buddy Guy, Albert King, John McVie, Mick Taylor, Junior Wells, and others. AE.

Blues for Central Avenue (60 min). Documentary of jazz in Los Angeles, with Ernie Andrews. JA.

Blues 1 (58 min). Ernie Andrews, Pee Wee Crayton, Leatta Galloway, Linda Hopkins, B. B. King, Eddie "Cleanhead" Vinson. AE.

Bobby Hutcherson and Dexter Gordon (60 min). 1986. VF.

Bobby McFerrin: Spontaneous Inventions (48 min). JA.

Bob James Live (63 min). From the Queen Mary Jazz Festival. JA.

Bob Wilber and the Smithsonian Repertory Company (59 min). 1983. SVS, VF.

Born To Swing: The Count Basie Alumni (50 min). RF.

Buddy Rich Memorial Concert (65 min). JA.

Cab Calloway and His Orchestra (30 min). AM.

Celebrating Bird: The Triumph of Charlie Parker (58 min). Documentary. JA.

Chick Corea: A Very Special Concert (60 min). Stanley Clarke, Joe Henderson, Lenny White. SVS, VF.

Chick Corea: Electric Workshop (60 min). JA.

Chick Corea & Gary Burton: Live in Tokyo (60 min). AE, VF.

Chick Corea: Keyboard Workshop (60 min). JA.

Chico Hamilton: The Jazz Life (53 min). SVS, VF.

Claude Bolling: Concerto for Classical Guitar and Jazz Piano (50 min). Angel Romero, George Shearing. PA.

Cobham Meets Bellson (36 min). Two top jazz drummers. JA, VIEW.

Coltrane Legacy, The (60 min). Documentary with Eric Dolphy, McCoy Tyner, and others. JA.

Complete Guide to Saxophone Sound Production, The (150 min). Demonstration by David Liebman. JA.

Count Basie Live at the Hollywood Palladium (60 min). AE.

Crusaders Live: Midnight Triangle (60 min). MCA.

Different Drummer: Elvin Jones (30 min). RF.

Dizzy Gillespie (19 min). 1981. AE, VF.

Dizzy Gillespie: A Night in Tunisia (28 min). JA, VIEW.

Dizzy Gillespie's Dream Band (16 min). AE, VF.

Duke Ellington Story, The (86 min). AE.

EAV History of Jazz. EAV.

Eddie Jefferson (50 min). Live from the Jazz Showcase. IRL, JA.

Egberto Gismonte (55 min). Brazilian rhythms in a live concert. JA.

Evening with Ray Charles, An (50 min). At Jubilee Auditorium in Edmonton, Canada, 1981. VF.

Fats Waller and Friends (29 min). AM.

Freddie Hubbard: Studio Live (59 min). SVS, VF.

George Duke: Keyboard Improvisation (60 min). Modern keyboard improvisation styles: funk, jazz-rock, rhythm-and-blues, fusion. JA.

George Duke: Keyboard/Vocal Accompaniment (60 min). One of the top keyboard players demonstrates contemporary styles. JA.

George Shearing: Lullaby of Birdland (55 min.) VIEW.

Gerry Mulligan (18 min). 1981. AE.

Gil Evans and His Orchestra (57 min). Live concert. JA, VIEW.

Grover Washington Jr. in Concert (60 min). AE, VIEW.

Guide to Modern Jazz Piano (90 min). Andy LaVerne. JA.

Herb Ellis: Swing to Jazz (60 min). Jazz guitar styles. JA.

Herbie Hancock and the Rockit Band (73 min). AE.

Herbie Hancock Trio: Hurricane (60 min). Ron Carter, Billy Cobham. JA, VIEW.

Jackie McLean on Mars (31 min). Modern-jazz documentary. JA.

Jaco Pastorius: Modern Electric Bass (90 min). Instructional. JA.

Jazz at the Smithsonian: Alberta Hunter (58 min). Blues and jazz singer. SVS, VF.

Jazz at the Smithsonian: Art Blakey (58 min). With Wynton Marsalis. SVS, VF.

Jazz at the Smithsonian: Art Farmer (57 min). SVS, VF.

Jazz at the Smithsonian: Benny Carter (57 min). SVS, VF.

Jazz at the Smithsonian: Joe Williams (58 min). SVS, VF.

Jazz at the Smithsonian: Mel Lewis (55 min). SVS, VF.

Jazz at the Smithsonian: Red Norvo (58 min). SVS.

Jazzball (60 min). Louis Armstrong, Cab Calloway, Duke Ellington, Gene Krupa, Peggy Lee, Red Nichols, Buddy Rich, Artie Shaw, and others. AE.

Jazz in Exile (50 min). Dexter Gordon, Steve Lacy, Phil Woods. RF.

Jazz is My Native Language (60 min). Toshiko Akiyoshi. JA.

Jazz on a Summer's Day (85 min). Louis Armstrong, Chuck Berry, Mahalia Jackson, Thelonious Monk, Anita O'Day, Dinah Washington. JA.

Jivin' in Bebop (59 min). Dizzy Gillespie. AM.

Joe Allard: The Master Speaks (50 min). Saxophone and clarinet demonstration. JA.

Joe Pass: Jazz Lines (40 min). Instructional. JA.

John Carter and Bobby Bradford: The New Music (28 min). RF.

John Patitiucci—Electric Bass (85 min). Instructional. JA.

John Scofield: On Improvisation (60 min). Instructional. JA.

Konitz: Portrait of an Artist as Saxophonist (83 min). JA.

L. A. All Stars: Big Joe Turner and Hampton Hawes (28 min). JA.

Ladies Sing the Blues, The (60 min). Billie Holiday, Lena Horne, Bessie Smith, Sarah Vaughan, Dinah Washington, and others. JA, VIEW.

Lady Day: The Many Faces of Billie Holiday (60 min). JA.

Last of the Blue Devils, The (90 min). Kansas City jazz, with Count Basie, Jay McShann, Joe Turner. RF.

Latin American Percussion (60 min). Demonstration. JA.

Lena Horne: The Lady and Her Music (134 min). AE.

Les McCann Trio (28 min). Live concert. JA.

Lionel Hampton's One Night Stand (50 min). B. B. King, Gene Krupa, Gerry Mulligan, Buddy Rich, Zoot Sims, Dusty Springfield, Mel Torme. AE.

Live at the Village Vanguard, vol 1 (59 min). Ron Carter, Freddie Hubbard, Cedar Walton, Lenny White. JA.

Live at the Village Vanguard, vol 2 (57 min). Michel Petrucciani Trio. JA.

Live at the Village Vanguard, vol 3 (59 min). John Abercrombie, Michael Brecker, Peter Erskine, Marc Johnson. JA.

Live at the Village Vanguard, vol 4 (63 min). Max Waldron Quartet with Woody Shaw. JA.

Live at the Village Vanguard, vol 5 (62 min). Roland Hanna, Lee Konitz, Mel Lewis, George Mraz. JA.

Live at the Village Vanguard, vol 6 (56 min). Dave Murray Quartet. JA.

Louis Armstrong and His Orchestra (33 min). 1942–1965. JA.

Louis Bellson and His Big Band (55 min). Michael and Randy Brecker. JA.

Mabel Mercer: A Singer's Singer (42 min). Live in concert. JA, VIEW.

Mabel Mercer: Cabaret Artist "Forever and Always" (58 min). Her last concert. JA, VIEW.

McCoy Tyner (53 min). 1986. SVS, VF.

Mahalia Jackson (34 min). AE.

Manhattan Transfer: Vocalese Live 1986, The (28 min). ATL.

Manu Dibango: King Makossa (60 min). Contemporary African music with jazz-rock roots. JA.

Max Roach Quartet (19 min). AE, VF.

Mel Lewis and His Big Band (38 min). Recorded in Jerusalem. JA, VIEW.

Mel Torme Special, The (53 min). SVS, VF.

Miles in Paris (60 min). JA.

Mingus (63 min). Documentary. JA.

Moscow Jazz Quintet: The "Jazznost" Tour. JA.

Music in Monk Time (60 min). SVA.

Nancy Wilson (60 min). Stanley Clark, Chick Corea, Joe Henderson, Lenny White, 1982. SVS.

Nancy Wilson at Carnegie Hall (52 min). JA.

New Orleans: 'Til the Butcher Cuts Him Down (53 min). New Orleans Dixieland and marching bands. JA.

Olantunji and His Drums of Passion (60 min). Master drummer from Nigeria and his Harlem School of African Music and Dance Ensemble. JA.

One Night with Blue Note, vol 1 (60 min). Herbie Hancock, Freddie Hubbard, Bobby Hutcherson, Stanley Jordan. SVS, VF.

One Night with Blue Note, vol. 2 (60 min). Art Blakey, Cecil Taylor, McCoy Tyner. SVS, VF.

Oregon (59 min). An unusual band that combines jazz-rock and folk music. JA.

Ornette Coleman Trio (26 min). With David Izenson and Charles Moffett. JA.

Paris Reunion Band, The (60 min). Nat Adderley, Walter Bishop Jr., Nathan Davis, Curtis Fuller, Joe Henderson, Woody Shaw, and others. JA.

Phil Woods in Concert (63 min). JA, VIEW.

Piano Legends (60 min). Documentary of pianists from Fats Waller to Cecil Taylor, hosted by Chick Corea. JA.

Playboy Jazz Festival, vol. 1 (91 min). Willie Bobo, Maynard Ferguson, Lionel Hampton, Grover Washington, Jr., Nancy Wilson. RCA.

Playboy Jazz Festival, vol 2 (90 min). Dave Brubeck, Ornette Coleman, Dexter Gordon, The Manhattan Transfer, Sarah Vaughan, Weather Report. RCA.

Prime Cuts: Jazz and Beyond (35 min). Clarke/Duke Project, Miles Davis, Al DiMeola, Herbie Hancock, Hiroshima, Chuck Mangione, Weather Report, Andreas Wollenweider. AE.

Rob McConnell (25 min). SVS.

Round Midnight (131 min). Drama. JA.

San Francisco Blues Festival (60 min). Clarence "Gatemouth" Brown and Clifton Chenier. SVS.

Sarah Vaughan and Friends (60 min). JA.

Scott Henderson: Jazz Fusion (60 min). Instructional. JA.

Shelly Manne Quartet (53 min). Ray Brown, Bob Cooper, Hampton Hawes. JA.

Sonny Rollins: Live (36 min). JA.

Sound? (27 min). John Cage and Rahsaan Roland Kirk. JA.

Spyrogyra (56 min). AE.

Stan Getz: Vintage Getz (108 min). JA.

Stephane Grapelli: Live in San Francisco—1985 (60 min). Jazz violin. JA.

Steve Gadd II: In Session (90 min). Bop to reggae. JA.

Sun Ra: A Joyful Noise (60 min). RF.

Talmage Farlow (60 min). Documentary of jazz guitarist. JA.

Thelonious Monk: Straight No Chaser (90 min). Documentary. JA.

Time Groove (70 min). Alex Acuna, Louis Bellson, Vic Firth, Steve Gadd, Harvey Mason, and Dave Samuels demonstrate percussion techniques. JA.

Time Keeping II (67 min). Peter Erskine. Drum instruction. JA.

Tony Williams: New York Live. JA.

Tribute to Billie Holiday, A (60 min). Morganna King, Carmen McRae, Ester Phillips, Nina Simone. AE, VF.

Trumpet Kings (60 min). Documentary, hosted by Wynton Marsalis. JA.

Universal Mind of Bill Evans, The (45 min). JA.

Zoot Sims Quartet (40 min). Chuck Berghofer, Larry Bunker, Roger Kellaway. JA.

DISTRIBUTION COMPANIES:

AE   American Express Special Offer Center
P. O. Box 520, Great Neck, NY 10022

AM   Amvest Video
937 East Hazelwood Ave., Rahway, NJ 07065

ATL   Atlantic Video
75 Rockefeller Plaza, New York, NY 10019

EAV   Education Audio Visual, Inc.
17 Marble Ave., Pleasantville, NY 10570

IRL   Instructional Research Lab
University of Illinois
Box 4348, Chicago, IL 60608

JA   Jamey Aebersold Jazz Aids
P. O. Box 1244C
New Albany, IN 47151

MCA   MCA Home Video, Inc.
70 Universal City Plaza,
Universal City, CA 91608

PA   Pioneer Artists
200 West Grand Ave., Montvale, NJ 07645

PHV   Paramount Home Video
5555 Melrose Ave., Los Angeles, CA 90038

RCA   RCA/Columbia Pictures Home Video
2901 Alameda Ave., Burbank, CA 91505

RF   Rhapsody Films
30 Charlton Street, New York, NY 10014

SP   Stevenson Productions
3227 Banks Street, New Orleans, LA 70119

SVA   Send Video Arts
650 Missouri Street, San Francisco, CA 94107

SVS   Sony Video Software
9 West 57th Street, New York, NY 10019

VF   Viewfinders, Inc.
P. O. Box 1665, Evanston, IL 60204

VIEW   Video International Entertainment World
34 East 23rd Street, New York, NY 10010

VNP   Video Now Productions
7435 Bolanger Drive, Cupertino, CA 95014

INDEX

/■/

AMERICAN HISTORY AND CULTURE	JAZZ AND RELATED MUSIC & DANCE
1940	
Migration of blacks and Puerto Ricans to northern cities	Development of rhythm-and-blues
Native Son, Richard Wright novel, 1940	Bop popular
Citizen Kane, Orson Welles film, 1941	Samba introduced
U.S. involvement in World War II, 1941–45	Modern drum set ("traps") devised
Atom bomb, 1945	Stan Kenton band debut, 1941
United Nations founded, 1945	Duke Ellington presents his suite, *Black, Brown and Beige* at Carnegie Hall, 1943
ENIAC, first electronic computer, 1946	*Oklahoma!*, Rodgers and Hammerstein musical, 1943
Popularity of television soars, late 1940s	*Ornithology*, Charlie "Bird" Parker, 1946
Jackie Robinson, first black in major league baseball, 1947	Chano Pozo introduces Afro-Cuban jazz in New York concert, 1947
Sound barrier broken by U.S. plane, 1947	Mambo introduced from Latin America, 1947
Long-playing record, 1948	Revival of the Charleston, 1949
A Streetcar Named Desire, Tennessee Williams play, 1948	Cool jazz develops, late 1940s
First color telecasts, 1949	
1950	
Beatnik era	Jazz center shifts to Los Angeles and San Francisco
McCarthy hearings begin in Senate, 1950	Third Stream jazz introduced
Brinks armored-car robbery, 1950	Avante garde jazz in vogue
Korean War, 1950–52	Cool jazz/West Coast jazz develops as a reaction to bop
First transcontinental telecast, 1951	Hard bop, centered in Philadelphia, develops as a reaction to cool jazz
Kefauver Senate investigation of organized crime, 1951	Rhythm-and-blues attracts large audiences
Catcher in the Rye, J. D. Salinger novel, 1951	Muzak introduces "elevator" music
H-bomb, 1952	Radio-Free Europe begins jazz broadcasting
Three-dimensional movies, 1952	College jazz concerts popular
Polio vaccine discovered by Jonas Salk, 1952	10,000 jazz clubs in U.S., early 1950s
Execution of Julius and Ethel Rosenberg, 1953	*Thelonious Monk: Straight No Chaser*, 1951
Brown vs. Board of Education, 1954	Newport Jazz Festival begins, 1954
Montgomery bus boycott, 1955	Rock 'n' roll develops, mid-1950s
RNA discovered, 1955	*Jazz at the Philharmonic* concerts, mid-1950s
First transatlantic telephone cable, 1956	Cannonball Adderley record debut, 1955
First civil rights bill approved since Reconstruction, 1957	*Rock around the Clock*, Bill Haley and the Comets, 1955
On the Road, Jack Kerouac novel, 1957	First electronic music synthesizer constructed, 1955
Frisbee introduced, 1957	Elvis Presley's national T.V. debut, 1956
First U.S. satellite in orbit, 1958	First U.S. government-sponsored international jazz tour, Dizzy Gillespie, 1956
Stereo discs marketed, 1958	*West Side Story*, Leonard Bernstein musical, 1957
National Aeronautics and Space Administration established, 1958	*A Drum Is a Woman*, Duke Ellington TV musical, 1957
Lolita, Vladimir Nabakov novel, 1958	*Miles Ahead*, recorded by Miles Davis and Gil Evans, 1957
Alaska and Hawaii admitted as 49th and 50th states, 1959	Motown Record Company founded, 1959
	Free jazz develops, late 1950s
	Vocalise popular, late 1950s
1960	
Hippie movement	Era of Bob Dylan and "protest" songs
First sit-in, 1960	Folk-song revival